The Hidden Hand

The Hidden Hand

Gorbachev and the Collapse of East Germany

Jeffrey Gedmin

The AEI Press

Publisher for the American Enterprise Institute
WASHINGTON, D.C.

1992

Distributed by arrangement with

National Book Network
4720 Boston Way
Lanham, Md. 20706

3 Henrietta Street
London WC2E 8LU England

Library of Congress Cataloging-in-Publication Data
Gedmin, Jeffrey.
   The hidden hand: Gorbachev and the collapse of East Germany /
Jeffrey Gedmin.
    p. cm.
  ISBN 0-8447-3794-1
  1. Germany (East)—Politics and government. 2. Germany
(East)—Foreign relations—Soviet Union. 3. Soviet Union—Foreign
relations—Germany (East). 4. Gorbachev, Mikhail Sergeyevich, 1931–
. 5. Perestroika—Germany (East). I. Title. II. Series.
DD289.G44 1992
327.470431—dc20

                                          92-2764
                                             CIP

1 3 5 7 9 10 8 6 4 2

ISBN 0-8447-3794-1 (alk. paper)

The AEI Press
Publisher for the American Enterprise Institute
1150 17th Street, N.W., Washington, D.C. 20036

Printed in the United States of America

*To my parents, Dorothy and Victor, and
to my friends Stefan, Brigitte, and Ingo*

Contents

Acknowledgments

Many people offered me indispensable advice in writing this book. I am much in debt to Joshua Muravchik for his experience and support as a mentor, friend, discussion partner, and editor. I am equally indebted to the American Enterprise Institute's president, Christopher C. DeMuth, and vice-president, David Gerson, for their interest and generous support. I am also grateful to Karlyn Keene, editor of the *American Enterprise*, and Evelyn Caldwell, AEI's librarian.

Numerous friends and colleagues took time from busy schedules to read and comment on parts or all of the manuscript: Stephen Burant, Paul Burke, Nicholas Eberstadt, Ernest Plock, Joshua Muravchik, and Jeana Williams. My friends Tim Goodman, Tom Buckley, Lisa Nipkow, and Peter Skerry offered encouragement and ideas, especially in the initial stage of work. I also owe thanks to many friends in East Germany, above all to Christel, George, Klaus, and Gabi. I thank Sandra Mulligan, Jennifer McCabe, Susan Alderfer, and a host of enthusiastic interns who helped at different times: Michael Stone, William Tell, Stephen Krause, Joseph Goodman, Wendy Wessman, Tanya Osensky, Richard Dion, Keith McNulty, Patrick O'Hagan, Leslie Talmadge, Joseph Matelis, and Candida Torzala. Thanks also go to my friend and colleague Gabriele Hills.

I am indebted to my AEI colleagues and the numerous acquaintances at the State Department and other government agencies who were kind enough to discuss with me parts of my work. Likewise I owe thanks to the German and the Soviet embassies in Washington, D.C., and the German Information Center in New York, especially to Hannelore Koehler and Inge Godenschweger.

1

Perestroika, Eastern Europe, and the German Question

In the autumn of 1989 tens of thousands of prodemocracy demonstrators in East Germany brought down the Berlin Wall and forced an end to forty years of Communist rule. One of East Germany's leading Communist theorists, Otto Rheinhold, had ominously warned that the "alliance between the Soviet Union and the GDR [German Democratic Republic] [was] the crucial axis" in the entire Soviet bloc.[1] Indeed, the political demise of Erich Honecker and his German Communist state proved to be central to one of the most important events of this century—the collapse of communism and the Soviet withdrawal from its Eastern European empire.

Emboldened by Gorbachev's "new thinking," the citizens of East Germany and Eastern Europe seized center stage in 1989 and delivered the final blow to the remnants of totalitarian control in their societies. "Freedom for Eastern Europe," as Jim Hoagland has written, "was not a gift from Moscow"[2] but the direct result of the "massive . . . peaceful protests that stunned the world in 1989."[3] Yet equally clear is the fact that it was Mikhail Gorbachev's Soviet Union—hitherto source and protector of Communist dictatorship in the bloc—which had set in motion the forces of change that eventually toppled regimes from Berlin to Prague, from Bucharest to Sofia.

As early as February 1987, Adam Michnik, the Solidarity activist, had pointed to the importance of the Gorbachev effect in his own country. "General Jaruzelski is being forced toward real reform by pressure from two sides," Michnik observed at the time. "On one hand there are the activities of the opposition and the yearnings of

1

Polish society, and on the other, there are the words and deeds of Mr. Gorbachev."[4] "Gorbachev is translated into Czech by the word hope," said actor Milos Kopecky that same year.[5] Indeed Alexander Dubcek, the Czechoslovak leader ousted by Soviet-led troops in 1968, recognized a "profound connection" between the Soviet leaders' reforms and the changes he had tried to initiate twenty years earlier.[6]

Although Gorbachev often emphasized that even in his own country reform was the result of "the people's wish" for changes,[7] his Foreign Minister Eduard A. Shevardnadze conceded that in the case of Eastern Europe the Soviet architects of *perestroika* had themselves begun "this peaceful revolution."[8] "One need only remember," once reminisced Shevardnadze, "how the people of Prague and Berlin received Gorbachev. People greeted him like a knight, asked him for help, to exert influence."[9]

Through its policies of *glasnost* and *perestroika*, the Communist party of the Soviet Union (CPSU) under Gorbachev created an atmosphere in the East bloc that unnerved rigid, orthodox Communist leaders and encouraged bold political and economic experimentation by their reform-minded counterparts. At the same time, Gorbachev's break from dogma offered prodemocracy activists fresh hope and opportunity to pursue their own agenda for change.

Perhaps in the end decisive, the Soviet Union gradually yet deliberately disengaged from its empire, renouncing the Brezhnev Doctrine, the cornerstone of the East bloc's stability. As the Kremlin made clear that the USSR would no longer be prepared to intervene militarily in the bloc's internal affairs, proponents of *perestroika* and democracy lost their fear to take initiative, and the despots of Eastern Europe, their nerve to rule.

The Soviet Union never intended to abandon the cause of socialism either in East Germany or elsewhere. In early 1986 Gorbachev told an interviewer from the French Communist newspaper *L'Humanité* that the Communist party in the Soviet Union was still "the leading and guiding force in our society. . . . It is up to the party to elaborate the strategy and tactics for the building of the new society, to implement cadres policy, and to educate the people ideologically." For Gorbachev, the party remained "one of the effective tools to expand democracy and involve millions of people in the solution of production, social, and political affairs."[10]

Likewise in Eastern Europe, Gorbachev seemed to believe that Communist leaders, once forced to create a domestic consensus with their citizenry, would be able to transform their societies into new, more efficient and productive Communist polities. In an April 1987 address to the Czechoslovak Communist Party Congress, Gorbachev had called for socialism's restructuring but observed that there were indeed boundaries to the scope of reform. All of society should be engaged in the process of reform, declared the Soviet leader, but the "party of the Communists . . . the unshakable foundation of socialism," should remain the initiator.[11] Although in retrospect Foreign Minister Shevardnadze insisted that Moscow was not merely "put[ting] a good face on things," by embracing the bloc's democratic transformation in 1989, he, too, had argued before Eastern Europe's upheaval that the Soviet "national interest" was to demonstrate that socialism "provides man more than any other socio-political system."[12] Thus, Gorbachev's policy on Eastern Europe was predicated on the assumption that reform Communists could play a leading role in establishing a revolutionary new "third way" between Western democratic capitalism and Soviet-style communism—something akin to Dubcek's "socialism with a human face." A number of Gorbachev's key associates—including Ivan Frolov, editor of *Pravda;* Gennadiy Gerasimov, Foreign Ministry spokesman; and East European adviser Georgi Shakhnazarov, all of whom had once worked in Czechoslovakia—had been deeply influenced by the aborted Prague Spring of 1968. According to Frolov, Gorbachev's circle of advisers firmly believed that the entire bloc could be liberalized, along the lines Dubcek had once proposed for Czechoslovakia.[13] In Gorbachev's view, then, reform in Eastern Europe would endow socialism with popular legitimacy, making it viable.

His profound miscalculation was, in Charles Gati's words, a complete failure "to come to terms with the depth of popular East European disillusionment with and opposition to any form of communism, reformed or otherwise. He did not seem to understand, concede that what he sought—a more efficient and more humane socialism—was anathema to most of the peoples of Eastern Europe."[14] What was intended to be a carefully calibrated campaign to reform socialism from above was soon derailed by mass popular movements, pressing for elections and demanding an end to Communist rule. In the case of East Germany, after the GDR's revolution Shevardnadze predictably rejected a merger with the Federal Republic as a dangerous path and threat to Soviet interest. But as the Soviet foreign minister would later write, the drive toward national unity had "its own internal dynamics."[15]

There was something beyond the simple desire for a more efficient, humane socialism that shaped the thinking of Soviet reformers. Reform circles in the Kremlin had become fascinated by the possibility that, while retaining its sovereignty and independence, a more pliant, liberalized Socialist community in Eastern Europe might provide a bridging function in the construction of Europe's new common home.

3

Soviet deputy Roy Medvedev asserted, for instance, that the USSR would not lose its status as a superpower through relaxation of control over its satellite states. On the contrary, the Soviet Union would "live better" with a burden shed in Eastern Europe and a lessening of the U.S. presence on the western half of the continent.[16]

For Soviet reformers, the easing of cold war tensions and the continent's ensuing demilitarization would permit Moscow to redirect, at least in some measure, the USSR's spending from a bloated military sector to its dramatically overstretched, ailing civilian economy. Moreover, the inevitable result of a reduced U.S. military presence in Europe would offer Moscow immeasurably greater access to the rich reservoir of Western capital, technology, and financial skill on the continent deemed crucial to the success of Soviet *perestroika*.

The Soviet expert on Germany Vyacheslav Dashichev writes that the "end of the Cold War" on the continent was intended to liberate the Soviet economy "from the heavy burden of confrontation with the West."[17] In June 1990, defending the Gorbachev regime against charges that the Kremlin had "lost Eastern Europe," Shevardnadze, in fact, argued that Gorbachev had based his policies on the unacceptable reality that "ideological confrontation" with the West had cost the Soviet Union in his estimation more than 700 trillion rubles over the past two decades.[18]

Gorbachev's stated objective of overcoming Europe's division through contact and cooperation while preserving two distinct social systems, one capitalist and one Socialist, was powerfully reminiscent of former West German chancellor Willy Brandt's postulate on the German question.[19] Brandt and his advisers had argued that traditional concepts of reunification had been rendered obsolete not only by the unalterable presence of Communist rule in Moscow and East Berlin but also by the inculcation and widespread acceptance of Socialist values throughout the East German populace. Brandt's concept of one German nation, with ever-intensifying cooperation between two independent German states, may have perhaps even represented a microcosm for Gorbachev's thinking on Europe as a whole.

Germany, to be sure, lay at the heart of Gorbachev's pan-European concept. In his 1987 book *Perestroika*, the West Germans are the only citizens of Europe Gorbachev chose to single out specifically. "In our relations with the Federal Republic of Germany," Gorbachev wrote, "we take into account its potential and possibilities, its place in Europe and in the world and its political role. . . . Europe's development is impossible without active cooperation between our two states. Solid relations between the FRG [Federal Republic of Germany] and the USSR would be of truly historic significance."[20]

4

The asymmetries between West Germany and Moscow's Socialist German ally had doubtlessly become evident to many within the Gorbachev reform circle. The Federal Republic, with 62 million inhabitants—nearly four times the population of the GDR—occupied a territory more than twice as large as its East German neighbor. For years the Soviet Union's principal Western trading partner, West Germany, possessed superior deposits of natural resources, better waterways, natural ports, and, not least of all, one of the West's most highly developed competitive economies.[21]

Under Gorbachev, Soviet analysts were beginning to admit that East Berlin had lost its competition with Bonn. In a stunning 1989 report by the Institute of the Economy of the World Socialist System, one policy expert lashed out at the Honecker regime's "ideological primitivism," while praising in unqualified terms West Germany's "standard of living, social security, [and] development of democratic institutions."[22] The report recommended that East Germany should engage in a "step-by-step, controlled reform" that would lead to new forms of cooperation and perhaps even confederation between the two German states. As it took shape, then, a provocative new script for Soviet foreign policy toward Europe cast the West Germans in a central role, with the Communist East Germans relegated to understudy.

Honecker has noted that as early as 1987 he began receiving information from his ambassador in Moscow, Gerd König, that important Soviet strategists, including Foreign Minister Shevardnadze, were coming to the position that overcoming Germany's division, through confederative structures, for instance, "would constitute a contribution to the construction of the 'European Home.'"[23] Honecker fully understood, though, what Soviet reformers failed to grasp—that overcoming Germany's division would be feasible only through a "change of system," and hence a "sell-out of the GDR to the FRG."[24] Although Soviet officials have steadfastly denied any active role in exporting reform to East Germany, Honecker has hinted at an intimate link between Moscow reformers and the demise of his regime. He cryptically observed that his "fall as party and state chief was the result of a large scale maneuver, [and that] those who actually pulled the strings remain in the background."[25] It would be a great mistake "to assume that those who chorused in Leipzig: We are the People [are the ones] who brought about the upheaval in the GDR," observes the former East German head of state.[26]

Inside East Germany, Gorbachev's vision of reform socialism had crucial support, support that was certain to have given Soviet reformers confidence in their cause. First, there was the East German Evangelical Church, under whose protective wing the country's peace, environmental, and human rights activists had been permitted to operate during the years before the revolution. Unlike opposition in Poland, Hungary, and even Czechoslovakia, East Germany's dissident movement was to a great extent sympathetic to Marxist ideals and intensely skeptical of what they perceived to be the values of democratic capitalism. This attitude was at least in part due to the influence of the GDR's Evangelical clergy and its often transparent hostility to an alleged immorality of the market. In addition, East Germany's intelligentsia were dominated by a group of writers, artists, and academics whose Marxist orientation led them to argue fervently, even in the late stages of the 1989 revolution, in favor of socialism's reform and against an embrace of the West German system. Together with members of the clergy, they too had provided much of the intellectual capital and leadership for the GDR's opposition movement.

Finally, there was perhaps Gorbachev's most important ally in the GDR—the small but formidable cadre of would-be reformers within East Germany's Communist party, the Socialist Unity party (SED). For two years before the East German revolution, a number of SED officials, sympathetic to Moscow's reform course, had been quietly pushing for modification of East Berlin's hard line.

After his premature retirement as head of East German espionage in 1987, Markus Wolf, one of the most powerful men in the GDR, had emerged as the most prominent and provocative of Communist party advocates of reform. With close ties to Soviet reform circles, Wolf worked, at times surreptitiously, to exert influence on developments inside the GDR. But Wolf was not alone in advocating the Gorbachev line in the East German Communist party.

Klaus Höpcke, GDR deputy minister of culture, incurred the wrath of Erich Honecker by criticizing East Berlin's 1988 decision to ban the Soviet publication *Sputnik*, a monthly digest of the Soviet press. In 1989 Höpcke went a step further by voicing support for the imprisoned Czech playwright and later president, Vaclav Havel. In another instance of intraparty dissent, Rolf Henrich, a Communist party lawyer and functionary, published in the West his stinging critique of the East German state under the title *The Guardian State*.[27] Henrich tried to push himself to the forefront of the reform movement in the fall of 1989 as cofounder of the leftist, pro-GDR opposition group, New Forum.

An extremely important voice among the East German Communist reformers was that of Markus Wolf's friend Hans Modrow, the party's chief executive for the district of Dresden. Blocked from membership in the Politburo (Wolf, too, had been excluded by Honecker from East Berlin's ruling body) and, according to party insiders, "exiled" in Dresden for his proreformist sympathies, Modrow had been rumored by Soviet diplomats in East Berlin to be Gorbachev's candidate to replace Honecker.[28] His run in with the party's Central Committee in June 1989 (he was reprimanded for negligence in combating "bourgeois" and "hostile" anti-Socialist elements in his district) may have completed his credentials for his appointment as the GDR's reformist prime minister just weeks after Honecker's removal from power in mid-October of that year.

Such energetic, capable allies notwithstanding, Soviet calculations about reform communism in East Germany evaporated with astonishing speed. As popular pressure forced elections toward the center of the reform agenda, Communist reformers watched their leverage to negotiate change disappear. And when East Germans finally went to the polls on March 18, 1990, they embraced unification with West Germany's democratic capitalist republic just as fervently as they rejected Communist rule. The platforms of the party reformers and those independent activists who had advocated a "third way" to save the GDR were discarded with disdain.

The Soviets had indeed triggered the bloc's political transformation. In East Germany, as elsewhere, however, Gorbachev's vision of renewed socialism had been destroyed by the very process Soviet reformers themselves had cultivated and nurtured.

2

From a New World View to a New Europe

Gorbachev's new thinking on Germany and Europe, what in the end led to his unintentional loss of the Soviet Union's East European empire, derived from his concept of the relationship between the economy and the Soviet Union's international relations.

Gorbachev's Links to the Past

Before Gorbachev, other leaders had made major attempts to restructure the Soviet system to respond to new domestic and political challenges: Lenin's New Economic Policy after 1921; Malenkov's "new course" after Stalin's death in 1953; and Khrushchev's de-Stalinization and détente promoted with the West in the late 1950s and 1960s.[1] Gorbachev's realization, then, that expanded ties with Western nations would create demonstrable benefit for the Soviet economy was in itself nothing new. Nor was it surprising that initially, under Moscow's new reformer, the USSR's links to the Socialist community of states remained the Kremlin's first priority.

Thus the first stage of Gorbachev's foreign policy thinking showed a strong continuity with the past, as he vowed to maintain the "strategic line" of policies inherited from his predecessors.[2] Like his mentor, Yuri V. Andropov, a former KGB chief and party leader, Gorbachev placed economic modernization of the Soviet Union at the center of his agenda. As the six previous Soviet leaders before him had done, in his first address as general secretary to the Communist party's Central Committee Gorbachev pledged that he would "do everything . . . to expand cooperation with socialist states, to enhance the role and influence of socialism in world affairs."[3] At the time, Soviet Foreign Minister Andrei Gromyko praised the new general secretary's intuition in international affairs. Gorbachev had the ability, reported Gromyko, "to grasp the essence of a problem and draw conclusions—correct conclusions, Party conclusions."[4] Nevertheless as one analyst observed, from the beginning of his tenure Gorbachev displayed perceptible signs of a "sense of urgency about foreign affairs."[5]

Even before his appointment as general secretary of the Soviet Communist party, Gorbachev had been able to devote considerable time to questions regarding the relationship between economics and ideology, and how this relationship affected competition between capitalist and Socialist states. Brezhnev's foreign policy may have achieved for a moment what the Soviet Communist party viewed as "military-strategic parity between the USSR and the USA, the Warsaw Treaty Organization [the Warsaw Pact] and NATO."[6] These goals, however, had been pursued at the expense of an underdeveloped, foundering economy. Gorbachev had become convinced that only through a fundamental reconstruction of the economy could the Kremlin ensure the Soviet Union's "solvency and credibility" as a world power.[7]

In a speech given on December 10, 1984, at a meeting of Communist party ideologues—a frequently cited starting point of Gorbachev's new thinking—the scarcely known secretary of agriculture first articulated this position. Gorbachev stressed his belief that "profound transformations must be carried out in the economy and in the entire system of social relations" to ensure a "qualitatively higher standard of living."[8] More important, in Gorbachev's view,

> only an intensive, highly developed economy [would] guarantee the consolidation of the country's position in the international arena, [and] permit the country to enter the new millennium as a great and flourishing state.[9]

Gorbachev's analysis applied to more than the Soviet economy's deficiencies: it applied to the Soviet-style economy. In the words of Zdenek Mlynár, an official in Alexander Dubcek's reform Communist regime in Prague and a former law school classmate of Gorbachev's at Moscow State University, the Soviet leader's deep-rooted commitment to economic reform reflected a "belated response" to world developments "ignored" during the Brezhnev era. These developments encompassed "the rapid progress of the advanced industrial nations . . . in contrast to the crisis in the Soviet-type systems."[10] Gorbachev himself later described the results of the East-West competition in astonishingly candid fashion:

> We remained in what can be described as a past technological
> era in a number of important spheres and directions, whereas
> the Western nations entered an era of high technology with
> fundamentally new links between science and production and
> new forms of working and living conditions.[11]

Gorbachev's realization that the Communist world was unable to compete with the West—in technology but also in "working and living conditions"—had come, to be sure, not without prompting. By the time the new general secretary had assumed power, the primitive state of Soviet industrial and technological development had been laid bare by the seemingly insurmountable challenges posed by the rebuilding of American defense systems during the first half of the decade. In a meeting with Willy Brandt in May 1985, Gorbachev had acknowledged that the Soviet economy had been unacceptably overtaxed by cold war confrontation.[12] The arms race had become the greatest "objective" burden hindering development of the Soviet economy.[13]

The Strategic Defense Initiative (SDI), a program that, according to a scholar at the Brookings Institution, Ed A. Hewett, had "linked [economic problems] directly with the Soviet Union's status as a superpower," represented a particularly vexing problem for Soviet policy makers.[14] In fact, at the very time of Konstantin Chernenko's death and the transfer of power to Gorbachev, a Soviet delegation to the United States was busy fulfilling what had become a routine mission on trips by Soviet officials to the United States. As Vladimir V. Shcherbitsky, the Politburo member leading the group, described it, they were once again "trying to prove" to the U.S. president that SDI was simply "not worthwhile."[15]

Gorbachev's principal opposition to Reagan's SDI was unquestionably based on economic concerns. Even if Moscow were able to hold its own in this new phase of the arms race, Gorbachev was well aware that it would cost the Soviet Union considerably more than the West in time and share of gross national product. In the mid-1980s at the height of the Reagan arms buildup, the United States was spending approximately 6 percent of its $5 trillion GNP on defense, compared with Soviet spending of between 19 and 25 percent of its $1.4 trillion GNP.[16] Such costly competition, as Michael J. Sodaro observed, would "impose severe strains on the Soviet budget at a time when Gorbachev was resolved to concentrate Soviet resources on economic modernization."[17]

To compound Soviet frustrations, NATO's increased sensitivity to COCOM restrictions on technology transfer to the East during the

1980s had reportedly begun to cost Moscow billions of dollars each year.[18] If Soviet confidence about the USSR's technological prowess *vis-à-vis* the West was already waning, the April 1986 accident at the Chernobyl nuclear reactor did little to reverse this sentiment. (The Soviets subsequently felt compelled to turn to the International Atomic Energy Agency for assistance.)

In the international arena, Soviet third world client states and "national liberation movements" from Afghanistan to Nicaragua, from Mozambique to Angola and Ethiopia had come under increasing pressure in the 1980s to open political processes and cede to democratic procedures. Reevaluation of Soviet third world policy had led Gorbachev to the conclusion, at least in his rhetoric, that the promotion of revolution had become "futile and inadmissible."[19] On May 6, 1986, Gorbachev told Angola's president that every step toward disarmament would "make it possible to free resources for overcoming backwardness, including backwardness in African countries."[20] The following December, Soviet Foreign Minister Eduard Shevardnadze followed suit when he bluntly conceded in a meeting with Franz Josef Strauss, a leading West German politician, that Soviet involvement in Angola, Mozambique, and Ethiopia had ceased to produce anything of value to the Soviet Union, militarily, politically, or economically.[21]

In the European theater, NATO's 1979 two-track decision to counter the installation of Soviet SS-20s with its own Pershing and cruise missiles and to offer negotiations simultaneously had launched a heated debate that sent tremors through Western Europe's political landscape in the first half of the decade. But Gorbachev's 1987 signing of the Intermediate-Range Nuclear Forces (INF) agreement—a vindication of the "zero-zero" option proposed by Ronald Reagan in 1981—signaled Soviet capitulation to NATO's long-standing position on the issue of intermediate-range missiles. It also served as a begrudging acknowledgment of respect for Western Europe's, particularly West Germany's, resolve and the continued strength and resilience of Atlanticism.

Rethinking the dilemmas linked to development of the Soviet economy, and coming to terms with new foreign policy challenges, clearly made its mark on Gorbachev's policy deliberations. During his first two years in power, the new Soviet leader engaged in a high-profile, hands-on approach to Moscow's international relations. At home Gorbachev reshuffled the country's national security leadership, bringing less orthodox members into the upper ranks of Soviet policy makers,[22] giving at least some optimism about an eventual shift in Soviet foreign policy. By the end of 1986, he had held three summits in the West, visited India, and concluded an extensive series of visits to the capitals of his East bloc satellites.

11

Gorbachev sought a new balance. He claimed a desire to assign "absolute priority . . . to cooperative links between fraternal [Socialist] countries," but he stressed this did not mean "limit[ing] economic contacts with the West."[23] In the economic sphere, Moscow began to explore prospects for foreign joint ventures, expressed interest in expanded trade ties with Japan, applied to participate in the GATT (General Agreement on Tariffs and Trade) negotiations in Uruguay, and tested the waters for Soviet membership in the International Monetary Fund (IMF).

Despite this flurry of diplomatic activity, much of it aimed at enhancing Western trade ties and procuring pledges of economic assistance, the initial phase of Gorbachev's foreign policy reflected more style than substance, greater links to the past than meaningful breaks from traditional dogma. Gorbachev insisted on praising Brezhnev's "success" in détente—no less than eleven pro-Soviet dictatorships had come to power around the globe under his predecessor's rule—and called for a strengthening "of the fraternal friendships with our closest friends and allies—the countries of the great socialist community."[24] Concerning Europe, Soviet commentators stressed the desire for "mutually advantageous cooperation"[25] in economic affairs between the European Economic Community and Comecon, and urged that Socialist members not "be excluded from technology exchanges" with the West.[26] Time and again, Gorbachev would emphasize that the existence of two social systems should not be an obstacle to unity on the continent.[27]

But although Gorbachev and Shevardnadze had begun to tout their concept of a "common European home," the real source of Europe's division remained untouched in Soviet discourse, the Brezhnev Doctrine unchallenged. In April 1986, Gorbachev pledged that the Soviet Union and the Socialist camp would continue to serve as a "counterweight" to Washington and "its zealous imperialist designs."[28] Considering Moscow's German ally, he affirmed his unequivocal support for the Honecker regime, while displaying grave concern that "the ruling class of the FRG . . . has still not renounced its revanchist dreams and continues to speak of an 'open German Question.'"[29]

At the Polish Communist Party Congress held in Warsaw in June of the same year, Gorbachev warned those who would interfere with the development of socialism and, implicitly, those within the empire who would stray from the Kremlin's course:

> Socialism now manifests itself as an international reality, as an alliance of states closely linked by political, economic, cultural and defense interests. To threaten the socialist system, to try to

undermine it from the outside and wrench a country away from the socialist community means to encroach not only on the will of the people, but also on the entire postwar arrangement, and, in the final analysis, on peace.[30]

Despite such signs of continuity in Soviet foreign policy, it was also evident that the Kremlin's reform project—*perestroika* had first been proclaimed at the Twenty-Seventh Party Congress, February 25–March 5, 1986—could have implications far exceeding the narrow scope of greater domestic economic efficiency and productivity.

One implication was the beginning of a shift that had become evident in important foreign policy circles, a shift away from Moscow's traditional concept of a bipolar world dominating foreign policy considerations. According to Jerry F. Hough, the Gromyko foreign policy of the previous three decades had been dominated by the fear "that an independent Germany and Japan could become militarily dangerous." When Gromyko was elected president of the Soviet Union in 1985 and was replaced as foreign minister by Shevardnadze, though, this move was coupled by what Hough observed at the time as initial signs of Gorbachev's departure from the Gromyko line. Of particular note, in Hough's view, was the fact that now the "theme of German revanchism and Japanese militarism was sharply downplayed."[31]

Of importance in this regard as well was the emergence of two policy experts in Gorbachev's reform circle, Valentin Falin and Aleksandr Yakovlev. Both men stressed that Japan and a united Europe would soon become important power centers, counterbalancing, conceivably to Moscow's benefit, Washington's dominance among the Western industrialized nations.[32] If traditional superpower rivalry had become a burden Soviet reformers were no longer willing to shoulder, the rise in prominence of Germany and Japan in international relations might assuage Moscow's distress.

Falin was an expert on Germany who had served as ambassador to Bonn from 1971 to 1978. In October 1988 he was chosen to head a newly reconstituted Central Committee department dealing with foreign policy. Highly regarded in the Federal Republic for his enthusiasm and grasp of German language, culture, and history, Falin had displayed in his writings on foreign policy a fascination with West Germany equal to his coolness toward the United States. (In an August 1988 *Pravda* article, Falin chose to revive in heated tones the long-standing Soviet position that the United States bore sole responsibility for starting the cold war.)[33] From 1978 to 1983, Falin had served as deputy director of the Central Committee's International Information Department. He worked as a political commentator for *Izvestiia* from 1983

13

to 1986 and since 1986 as director of the Soviet press feature agency, Novosti.

In the reorganized Central Committee apparatus, Falin's department reported to a foreign policy commission headed since September 1988 by the party ideologist Yakovlev.[34] Since Gorbachev had discovered him in Ottawa during a 1983 trip to Canada (Yakovlev was serving at that time as Soviet ambassador to Canada—banished from Moscow, according to some reports, for his unconventional views), Yakovlev had directed the prestigious Institute of World Economics and International Relations, joined the Politburo, and become one of the Soviet leader's closest advisers on foreign affairs. Yakovlev shared with Falin a deeply rooted aversion, even animosity, toward the United States.

As far as Germany was concerned—the heart of any question concerning Europe's ascendancy as a world power center—Yakovlev, Falin, and Vadim Medvedev, director of the new Ideological Commission of the Central Committee, all appeared more interested in improved relations with Bonn than they were worried "about antagonizing their hyper-sensitive East German allies."[35] (Just days after the Berlin Wall fell, as the GDR's reformist regime was frantically warding off discussion of German unity, Yakovlev calmly declared that the Soviet Union would not interfere in any eventual reunification—a matter to be decided among Germans.)[36]

The Primacy of Westpolitik

By mid-1986 Kremlin reformers had realized that Soviet *perestroika* dictated, contrary to early assessments,[37] a fundamental restructuring in Soviet foreign policy. As the Soviet Union's ambassador to Poland later remarked, "a strong economy" at home gradually became "the main objective" of Soviet policy abroad.[38]

Gorbachev appeared visibly disturbed by the slow pace of Soviet economic reform. While growth rates in some sectors of the economy had begun to register modest improvements, the Soviet oil industry fell short of growth targets, agricultural problems persisted, and the manufacture of machine tools—a key to Gorbachev's long-term strategy for modernizing Soviet industry—was proceeding far slower than expected by the Soviet leadership.[39] Moreover, after the first year and a half of Gorbachev's reforms, the party's position of authority was beginning to suffer, with the deterioration of the supply of consumer and agricultural goods eroding the Soviet public's initial support for *perestroika*.[40]

Moscow had started to ponder ways in which a restructured foreign policy might serve *perestroika*. In shaping its foreign policy to serve its program of domestic *perestroika*, Soviet interest was naturally drawn to Europe. Divided Europe remained the heart of East-West competition and confrontation and, as a result, the primary drain of Soviet energy and resources.

Through his concept of a common European home, Gorbachev anxiously sought assurance, in the words of London's *Financial Times,* "that the conventional disarmament process would go ahead swiftly, and be radical, and that just as he [Gorbachev] starts to open up the Soviet economy (and Comecon with it) he will not be frozen out of the EC after 1992."[41] Unquestionably, Gorbachev's reform project could not afford to be excluded from a new club of 320 million united Europeans with its common market, highly developed industry, and deep capital reserves. Yet Gorbachev appeared to understand that the gradual unfolding of his plans for his common European home ran the risk of being eclipsed by the intensifying pace toward West European unity.

As a result of Moscow's fears that it could lose vital links to the continent just when the Soviet leadership needed them the most, Soviet foreign policy toward Europe underwent dramatic revision. In a speech given in Vladivostok in July 1986, Gorbachev demanded a "fundamental break with many customary approaches to foreign policy, a break with traditions of political thinking and of views on the problems of war and peace, on the defence and security of individual states and international security."[42] The Soviet Union was entering, as Gorbachev put it, "the most difficult period of restructuring."[43] If "economy" were to become the new "cement of international relations,"[44] the Soviet Union faced the formidable task of dislodging its system from isolation in order to join the international community of finance and trade. An economically unified Europe that included the Soviet Union, then, became a central preoccupation of Gorbachev's *Westpolitik.*

The Soviet Union's aggressive pursuit of rapprochement with Western Europe, particularly West Germany, designed to create opportunities for Soviet access to large capital and technology resources was not without precedent. In this instance, however, Moscow encountered unparalleled success. In October 1988, for example, the Soviet Union was able to conclude its largest credit line ever with the West, including agreements worth more than $5.5 billion with West German, British, Italian, and Japanese banks.[45]

But as the Soviets courted the West to win wider support for their reforms at home, Gorbachev's reformers were growing sharply critical of their subsidy relationship with their partners in Eastern Europe. By some estimates Moscow was spending at least $11–15 billion annually—excluding the cost of Soviet military forces in the region—to

15

subsidize the East European economies.[46] Even Soviet *Izvestiia* lamented the fact that the Soviet Union's burden of support for Eastern Europe was far greater than the U.S. contribution to the Atlantic alliance.[47] At a time when the financing of *perestroika* had become a central concern in Moscow, Kremlin reformers were becoming increasingly irritated with the continuous flow of substandard products from Eastern Europe in exchange for potential hard-currency-earning raw materials.

Thus, the genuinely "fundamental break" with the past Gorbachev had referred to in Vladivostok was to be found not in Moscow's *Westpolitik* but in new Soviet thinking toward its East European empire. The first manifestations of this new thinking were signs that Soviet policy makers wished to encourage economic reform in Eastern Europe, while distancing Moscow from responsibility for the burdensome, unproductive economies of its satellites. Soviet reform circles now openly and explicitly acknowledged that the Soviet-style economy was no longer viable.

A paper by Oleg T. Bogomolov's influential Institute of the Economics of the World Socialist System in mid-1988 argued that "the administrative-state model of socialism, established in the majority of East European countries during the 1950s under the influence of the Soviet Union, has not withstood the test of time, thereby showing its socio-political and economic inefficiency."[48] The same year Radomir Bogdanov, deputy director of the Institute for the Study of the USA and Canada, contended that the Soviet bloc had not only fallen behind the Western industrialized nations but also was in the process of becoming a "different civilization." Bogdanov asserted that if the trend were not reversed, the ever-widening technological gap between East and West would eventually preclude interaction and cooperation between the two systems.[49]

In Moscow's new view, individual countries in the bloc would be responsible for the essential restructuring of their economies. While praising Hungary's development, which Moscow "follow[ed] with respect," Gorbachev warned that some East bloc nations had yet to prove they were "capable" of introducing necessary reforms.[50] Gorbachev began to attack Comecon during this period for its bureaucratic intransigence.[51] If the Soviet economy was to be rebuilt, it had become increasingly obvious that "the bloc's economic union . . . [would have to] be turned into an asset for Moscow instead of a burden."[52] At a banquet held in his honor in Bucharest in 1987, Gorbachev issued an instructive warning to his hosts: "It is not just a matter of exchanging goods. . . . Trade must more and more be judged on whether it leads to production of higher quality."[53]

Arguing now that the Kremlin's approach to international relations should be dictated primarily by economic considerations, Shevardnadze observed that "at the present stage what is assuming crucial importance is the ability to increase the supply of material goods more rapidly on the basis of scientific advance and the latest technology."[54] (Even amid the tumultuous autumn of 1989, Gorbachev himself calmly noted that the changes in Eastern Europe were essential because the Eastern bloc lagged so far behind the West in economic development and technology,[55] though Shevardnadze had to admit that the tempo and intensity of developments had been unanticipated.)[56] Society, in Gorbachev's view, had become "increasingly aware that commodity production, economic methods of management are indispensable elements of socialism."[57]

Transformation of the East European economies had a clear economic purpose—to relieve Moscow of its onerous subsidy relationship with its Warsaw Pact neighbors. In addition, though, the emergence of liberalized, "democratic" Socialist states in this region could render, in the view of Soviet reformers, an important bridging function between East and West Europe. In the words of Zdenek Mlynár, Moscow's new foreign policy sought specifically to transform these East European satellites from instruments of hegemony into "instruments of beneficial cooperation between East and West Europe."[58]

There were practical concerns as well, political imperatives that dictated Moscow's encouragement of the bloc's reform, East Germany included. The Soviet Union's policy of *glasnost* had begun to awaken expectations among the citizens of rigidly Communist East European states that liberalization might be introduced in their native lands. New seeds of unrest were being sown. In fact, *glasnost*'s effects notwithstanding, according to Shevardnadze, the Kremlin had already begun to receive reports in the early 1980s from its embassies in Eastern Europe that the continued presence of Soviet troops in the bloc could lead to renewed conflict.[59]

In Czechoslovakia, a model of orthodoxy since the 1968 Soviet invasion crushed Dubcek's liberalization programs, there was the rich irony that Czechs and Slovaks would now wish for Soviet political intervention on the behalf of reform. Since the advent of Gorbachev's new thinking, Czechoslovak viewership of Soviet television, available via satellite, and radio listenership to Soviet stations registered significant increases.[60] (In Romania, information-starved citizens would queue up at the Bulgarian Embassy in Bucharest to copy program information for the Bulgarian Russian TV station.) When Gorbachev paid his first visit to Prague as general secretary of the Soviet Communist party in April 1987, some 5,000 Czechs spontaneously poured into the cobblestone streets near Hradcany Castle to greet the Soviet leader and his wife, Raisa. While members of Charter 77, the country's leading dissident organization, waited anxiously as Gorbachev's own plans for a "socialism with a human face" unfolded, Prague's orthodox Communist regime recoiled, attacking those within their own country who attempted "to take parasitical advantage of the changes in the Soviet Union and thus conceal their activity against the people and socialism."[61]

In East Germany, where some 85 percent of the population could track events in the Soviet Union via West German television, there were numerous signs of the restlessness inspired by Gorbachev's reforms. During an open-air concert held in June 1987 in West Berlin featuring Western rock star David Bowie and the band Genesis, for example, crowds of several thousand East German youths at one point pushed precariously close to the area near the Berlin Wall. When the East German Volkspolizei, or Vopos as they were known, and members of the state security forces (the notorious Stasi) began to use force to disperse the crowds, scuffles broke out, and dozens were arrested as East Germans gathered near the Brandenburg Gate, chanting, "The wall must go" and "Gorbachev, Gorbachev!" The East German press chose to play down events, claiming that any suggestion of confrontation was part of the typical "horror tales" invented by the Western press.[62] "As is usual on such occasions," reported East Berlin's news service, "the people's police took steps to guarantee public order and the free flow of traffic in the area."[63] But the message was inescapable: the Gorbachev effect was in force.

Although the orthodox regimes of the region continued to use repressive measures to stifle dissent in their own countries, it was becoming increasingly difficult for these regimes to shield their populaces from the destabilizing effects of reform elsewhere. The problem was certain to become only worse. The Soviet desire for rapid modernization of its industry demanded the massive importation of Western technology.

The growth of a Soviet computer culture with dramatically increased computer literacy, especially among young people, was a prerequisite for the competitiveness of the Soviet economy. Such steps would inevitably provide the catalyst for a telecommunications and information revolution inside the entire East bloc far exceeding the leakage taking place in 1988 and 1989. Computers, modems, faxes, cellular phones, video-cassette recorders, photocopiers—in a word, all the devices inimical to the totalitarian control of a society—were destined to be a part of Gorbachev's new world.

In a speech to the International PEN Congress of writers in New York in January 1986, Secretary of State George P. Shultz summed up the paradoxical situation faced by Gorbachev's reformers:

> Regimes that try to stifle the new information technologies may
> find themselves falling behind economically; and if they permit
> them, they risk losing their monopoly of control over informa-
> tion and ideas.[64]

Of course, the Soviet Union and its reform programs were not
the sole impetus to disruption in the bloc. The pluralizing societies of
Poland and Hungary, themselves precursors of *perestroika*, were posing
their own challenges to the so-called "gang of four"—East Germany,
Czechoslovakia, Bulgaria, and Romania.[65] They represented the core
of what Charles Gati aptly described as the Soviet Union's East
European "economic burden, ideological embarrassment and foreign-
policy handicap."[66]

Rumors were afloat that Honecker and other opponents of reform
in the bloc were constructing an anti-Moscow axis.[67] Eastern Europe's
orthodox recalcitrants placed their faith in time. Although in 1989 East
Berlin's Honecker and Gustav Husak in Czechoslovakia were both
already seventy-five, Romania's Ceausescu was seventy, and Bulgaria's
Zhivkov was seventy-six, these men remained stubbornly convinced
that the reformers in Moscow, Budapest, and Warsaw would fail and
disappear from the scene long before their own retirement.

Letting Eastern Europe Go

In late 1986 and early 1987, according to former Politburo member
Yegor K. Ligachev, the Kremlin leadership adopted a position of
"noninterference" in Eastern Europe's affairs. The spokesman for the
Soviet foreign ministry, Gennadiy Gerasimov, termed this new approach
the "Sinatra doctrine," that is, the freedom for each Socialist country
to choose its path its own way.[68] Gorbachev's embrace of the principle
of "freedom of choice" signaled Soviet abandonment of the Brezhnev
Doctrine, the most crucial development for Eastern Europe's road to
freedom.

This dramatic shift in policy was predicated on the rather astonishing new belief that Soviet security no longer demanded an iron
grip on the region, a question Gorbachev and his advisers had been
grappling with for some time. Instrumental in this process was the
Soviet leader's gradual realization that capitalism could in fact operate
economically without militarism and colonial conquest and that contemporary capitalist countries like West Germany and Japan could
prosper peacefully with minimum military expenditure.[69] Gorbachev
further acknowledged that Marx had

19

underestimated capitalism's ability to self-develop. Capitalism managed to assimilate the advances of science and technology to form such socio-economic structures that assured its viability and created a relatively high level of well-being for the majority of population in industrialized countries. [Moreover] social reforms . . . led to improvements in the living standards and social protection of working people in many capitalist countries of the West.[70]

It was in this new context of Soviet foreign policy thinking that Shevardnadze, in a speech to the Soviet diplomatic service in July 1988, was able to repudiate what had been a key principle of Soviet foreign policy—the principle of "peaceful coexistence" as a method of class struggle. In one of the most radical foreign policy statements to date, Shevardnadze explicitly rejected this notion. "Coexistence," Shevardnadze argued,

that relies on such principles as non-aggression, respect for sovereignty and national independence, non-interference in internal affairs and so on cannot be identified with class struggle. The conflict between two opposing systems is no longer the decisive tendency in the present age.[71]

Gorbachev's first implicit acknowledgment that the Brezhnev Doctrine was no longer in force came in a speech delivered in Prague in April 1987, when the Soviet leader commented on important aspects of the new character of Soviet–East European relations:

First and foremost we proceed from the premise that the entire system of the socialist countries' political relations can and must be built on the basis of equality and mutual responsibility. No one has the right to claim special status in the socialist world. We consider the independence of every party, its responsibility to the people of its own country, and its right to decide the question of the country's development to be unconditional principles.[72]

That same year in his book *Perestroika* Gorbachev had referred to those principles. "Every nation," he wrote, should be free to "decide which system and which ideology is better. . . . Relations between the socialist countries must be strictly based on absolute independence."[73] Gorbachev affirmed this new principle of Socialist autonomy in a joint declaration issued during his trip to Yugoslavia in March 1988. The two countries agreed that neither party had "pretensions of imposing their concepts of social development on anyone" and expressly rejected "any threat and use of force and interference in the internal affairs of other states."[74] The scene of Yugoslavia—ousted from the Soviet bloc in 1948 during a bitter dispute between Tito and Stalin—for Gorbachev's declaration was important, as it recalled the meeting between Tito and Khrushchev in Moscow in June 1956 where the Soviet leader accepted the Yugoslav road to socialism as legitimate.

At the same time, Oleg Bogomolov was taking the question of what the Soviets would and would not permit head on. In February 1988, Bogomolov startled an interviewer on Hungarian television with his assertion that Soviet security would not be threatened if Hungary were to evolve "into something like . . . Austria [or] Sweden."[75] In July of the same year Bogomolov argued that "diversity" was not a "weakness of the new system, but a quite normal phenomenon—even evidence of strength."[76]

Bogomolov painted an even broader picture of Soviet policy in September 1988 when he told an interviewer for *Moscow World Service* that "the Brezhnev Doctrine of limited sovereignty [is] now being eliminated. The command method which prevailed in relations between the socialist countries has ended."[77] According to Hungary's Prime Minister József Antall, in the spring of 1988 the Soviets privately made it explicitly clear to the Communist party boss, János Kádár, that he could no longer count on Soviet support in the event of a major internal crisis.[78] More than that, Károly Grósz, the Gorbachev follower who replaced Kádár in May 1988, reportedly received complete Soviet support for further political and economic liberalization in Hungary, including permission for the implementation of a multiparty system.[79]

It was not only Hungary that appeared to be free to pursue its own course. Much closer to the heart of the empire, reform-minded forces in Poland gained new room for maneuver. In September 1988, Nikolay Shishlin, a Gorbachev protégé from the Communist party's Central Committee, affirmed for *Le Monde* Bogomolov's assertion that Moscow had abandoned the Brezhnev Doctrine. The Kremlin no longer possessed a "right of veto in Polish internal affairs."[80]

In fact, according to one Soviet official, the Soviets "would not be afraid if Solidarity reemerged." "Marxism-Leninism," in Shishlin's words, "is not the highway code but a theology produced by the realities of life, which are themselves changing. . . . [In the Soviet view] trade union pluralism is not heresy."[81] By no means had Moscow grown indifferent to the fate of its East European allies. In Hannes Adomeit's view, Gorbachev's reformers still envisaged for Eastern Europe "an evolutionary path between the neo-Stalinist, centralized, bureaucratic 'socialist' system in the East, and the pluralist, social democratic, market-oriented 'capitalist' system in the West."[82] Gorbachev's doctrine for Eastern Europe, according to Angela Stent, was "pursued on the assumption that Eastern Europe [would] be able to

21

create entirely new, viable models of reform socialism, a 'third way' between Soviet-style socialism and Western democracy."[83] Ligachev conceded that the Kremlin presumed that "radical renewal of socialism" in the East bloc would emerge to supplant Communist orthodoxy.[84]

In July 1989 on the eve of revolution, Gorbachev warned explicitly against expectations in the West that East European nations would "return to the capitalist fold."[85] Later, in the midst of the bloc's upheaval, Gorbachev observed that some advocated "the administrative command system and rigid planning and control . . . not only in the economy but also in culture," while others promoted the view that "we must make our society capitalist. . . . We reject them both. . . . We have a different way in mind, the one that leads to social progress."[86]

How did Soviet reformers think the character of the new Soviet–East European relationship would evolve? At first Gorbachev may well have had in mind the sort of tie that he hoped would emerge as the new relationship between the Kremlin and the Soviet republics: a release of the dynamic "initiative of the different republics . . . [with] a regulated role of the center."[87] But in time it had become clear that Soviet leaders had a relationship of a different character in mind: the relationship between the Soviet Union and Finland. Gorbachev frequently referred to Soviet-Finnish relations as "a model for relations between states belonging to different systems."[88] His adviser Yakovlev had also observed that "relations between the Soviet Union and Finland could serve as a very interesting model for the construction of a common European home."[89]

In the past, when Soviet officials had lavishly praised the character of Soviet-Finnish relations, they were urging West European states to consider this model worthy of emulation. Now, though, the "Finlandization" of Eastern Europe had entered Soviet discourse. Soviet Marshal Sergey Akhromeyev argued that Soviet-Finnish relations were, in principle, simply an exemplary model of friendly relations between a great power and a smaller state.[90] More pointedly, in an article in *Moscow News*, one analyst at the Institute of the Economy of the World Socialist System embraced Eastern Europe's "Finlandization," referring to the advantages of "integration with Western markets [and] the achievements of Western science and technology."[91]

The liberalizing Communist states of Poland and Hungary reveled in their newly granted room for maneuver in 1988 and 1989. But for the region's orthodox states, Soviet disengagement from empire irrevocably undermined the status quo. Far from being exempt from this process, East Germany lay at the heart of Soviet design. During this time Ligachev alluded to Moscow's hope that East Germany's Honecker would eventually "wake up" and follow Moscow's lead on reform.[92] For East Germany, however, the question of reform posed a formidable challenge not only to the legitimacy of East Berlin's orthodox regime but to the longevity of the German Communist state itself.

3

East Germany and the Dilemma of Legitimacy

The question of the GDR's legitimacy as a sovereign German Socialist state had always been a concern of the highest order for East Berlin's orthodox Communist regime. And over the four decades since the founding of the two German states in 1949, East Germany frequently performed a balancing act responding to pressures, not only from its West German counterpart but also from its Soviet benefactor.

The Challenge from Bonn

In its founding document, the *Grundgesetz*, adopted on May 23, 1949, the Federal Republic made clear that Bonn would henceforth assert the right to speak for all Germans, including "those . . . to whom participation was denied."[1] The very term *Grundgesetz*, or Basic Law, was chosen by West German framers (rather than *constitution*) to underscore the provisional nature of Germany's division. Indeed, the Basic Law's last article stipulated that the document would "cease to be in effect on the day on which a constitution adopted by a free decision of the German people comes into force."[2] Even the choice by West German officials of sleepy, inconspicuous Bonn on the west side of the Rhine as the Federal Republic's capital was to add further testimony to the temporary status of Germany's division.[3]

The rule of Christian Democratic Chancellor Konrad Adenauer from 1949 to 1963 was characterized by a determined desire to deny the GDR—and for a time the other Soviet East European client states as well—any degree of formal diplomatic recognition. Bonn's Hallstein

Doctrine best symbolized the West German state's early commitment to isolate East Germany. Named after Walter Hallstein, state secretary of the Foreign Office, and first articulated by Adenauer's Foreign Minister Heinrich von Brentano on December 9, 1955, the Hallstein Doctrine proclaimed Bonn's refusal of diplomatic relations with any state that opened an embassy in East Berlin.[4]

Even before the Hallstein Doctrine had been formally discarded in the late 1960s, Bonn's *Ostpolitik* had begun to change in a variety of ways. Following Adenauer's retirement in 1963, a subtle shift in the Federal Republic's policy toward the East bloc under Christian Democratic chancellors Ludwig Erhard (1963–1966) and Kurt Georg Kiesinger (1966–1969) had already become evident with Bonn's establishment of trade missions in Eastern Europe and diplomatic relations with Romania in January 1967.[5]

In spring 1967, Chancellor Kiesinger became the first West German chancellor to exchange formal correspondence with an East German head of state.[6] Seeking contact and cooperation with his East German counterparts, Kiesinger proposed a sixteen-point program for easing tensions between the two states. As foreign minister in Kiesinger's "grand coalition," Social Democrat Willy Brandt had become the most vocal and influential advocate of a new *Ostpolitik*. Brandt's policy toward East Germany, which urged cooperation with GDR officials, rested on the assumption that confrontation had not weakened the GDR's resolve, as Adenauer had hoped, but in fact had deepened Germany's division.

Under Brandt's chancellorship from 1969 to 1974, the West German state's rapprochement with East Germany was predicated on Bonn's ability to forge closer, more comfortable ties to the GDR's patron, the Soviet Union. To this end, Brandt distanced himself from what he saw as the unconstructive anti-Communist rhetoric of Adenauer and the Christian Democrats. To enhance Bonn's favor with Moscow, Brandt's government displayed increasing reluctance to address directly issues such as the Soviet Union's arms buildup, its expansionist policies in the third world, and its abysmal human rights record.

Conservative critics charged Brandt's *Ostpolitik* with subordinating freedom to peace, with blurring the lines between Western democracy and totalitarian dictatorship. In doing so, Brandt introduced a dangerous form of distortion and self-censorship into West Germany's political debate, in their view, a first step toward "Finlandization" or the limiting of West Germany's sovereignty in foreign policy.[7] Brandt, however, hoped Bonn's less confrontational course would eliminate the threat of war in Europe and create an environment conducive to improving relations with, and conditions within, the second German state.

The Social Democrats' policy of *Wandel durch Annäherung*, or change through rapprochement, had been first conceptualized during Brandt's tenure as mayor of West Berlin from 1957 to 1966. Brandt's close adviser Egon Bahr—at the time head of West Berlin's Press and Information Office—had first articulated the major elements of this new *Ostpolitik* in a speech in July 1963 at the Tutzing Protestant Academy. Brandt and Bahr rejected Adenauer's Hallstein Doctrine, claiming that it was based on the illusionary view that pressure and isolation would bring the East German state to collapse. In his Tutzing Academy speech, Bahr criticized Adenauer's uncompromising insistence on elections for East Germany, a position he dismissed as "hopelessly antiquated [and] unrealistic."[8] Brandt and Bahr proposed instead their policy of "small steps" intended to induce change in East Germany's behavior through détente with the Communist regime.

In the context of Bonn's rapprochement with East Berlin, Brandt began to argue that while the existence of a single German nation endured, the legitimacy of two independent, German states was undeniable and deserved recognition. Brandt's *Ostpolitik*, administered by Foreign Minister Walter Scheel (Free Democratic party/FDP) and the chancellor's principal negotiator Bahr, provided the framework for Bonn's August 1970 treaty with Moscow, the Four Power Agreement on Berlin in 1971, and the Basic Treaty signed by the two German states in 1972. The Basic Treaty was by far the most important for East Berlin, as it offered the GDR de facto recognition and opened the door to membership in the United Nations for both German states.

In May 1974 Brandt fell victim to his own policy of good will toward East Berlin when he was forced to resign in the wake of a spectacular scandal. Günter Guillaume, an East German spy who had managed to become an aide and confidant to Chancellor Brandt, was unmasked in April of that year, just months after he and his wife had vacationed with the Brandts in Norway. It was a rich irony, to be sure, that this bit of East German mischief had caused the downfall of, in Michael Balfour's words, "the most sympathetic chancellor [GDR officials] were ever likely to have."[9] In fact, East Germany's head of espionage, Markus Wolf, later apologized for planting Guillaume in the chancellor's office. Guillaume's discovery jeopardized the Social Democrats' *Ostpolitik*, which Wolf had viewed as thoroughly constructive and favorable to GDR interests.

Indeed, Brandt's fatalistic acceptance of Germany's division had offered East German authorities indispensable leverage in their quest for full international legitimacy. In his first published memoirs, Brandt quietly conceded he had come to view unification of the two German states as unrealistic:

I was well aware that, throughout its phases of historical development, Germany had never entirely corresponded to the "classic nation-state." I nevertheless remained convinced that the nation would live on, even under differing political systems, because nationhood is a matter of awareness and resolve—Germany had always existed as a "cultural" entity and it was as a "cultural nation" that it would retain its identity.[10]

Brandt later argued in another volume of memoirs that his ever-ambiguous concept of *Deutschlandpolitik* had not represented a policy of resignation, but rather a new beginning to effect the "peaceful change of the situation in Europe and in Germany."[11] But Brandt's policies had in effect accepted what East German officials had always insisted on: that Germany's political division into two states be recognized and respected by Bonn. Even once the Berlin Wall had fallen on November 9, 1989, Brandt warned that "no one should act as if he knows in which concrete form the people [in East and West Germany] will find a new relationship," although he conceded that "the moving together of the German states is taking shape in reality in a different way than many of us expected."[12]

There were indeed fruits from Brandt's *Ostpolitik*. Détente had ameliorated certain hardships connected with Germany's division, and as a byproduct it may have weakened the totalitarian grip on East German society. Increased opportunities for inter-German travel, expanded telephone lines, cultural exchanges, and city partnerships all augmented, for example, the reservoir of information GDR citizens already enjoyed via West German television. Because of these gains, key elements of Brandt's *Deutschlandpolitik* did not disappear under the leadership of "conservative" Social Democrat Helmut Schmidt from 1974 to 1982, nor subsequently under Christian Democratic Chancellor Helmut Kohl. The continuity of Bonn's *Ostpolitik* was, of course, in part also attributable to Free Democrat Hans-Dietrich Genscher, a devoted advocate of détente who has served as West Germany's foreign minister since 1974. But even Chancellor Kohl's Christian Democrats—who had demanded a restoration in policy of the morally clear boundaries between Western democracy and Soviet-style communism—had come to acknowledge and value détente's *menschliche Erleichterungen*, or humanitarian improvements, for citizens on both sides of the wall.

In the progession of events, the Kohl-Genscher government permitted East Germany's campaign for legitimacy to reach a new milestone in 1987 when Erich Honecker became the first East German head of state ever allowed to pay an official visit to the West German capital. Honecker's long-awaited trip to Bonn seemed to ratify in the eyes of much of the world the seemingly unalterable status of Germany's division. The fact that Honecker's hosts were not the West German Sozis (Social Democrats) but Helmut Kohl's conservative-led coalition sweetened his welcome, an occasion replete with much of the pomp and circumstance normally accorded the head of state of a legitimate, independent country.

Under the watchful eyes of nearly 3,000 journalists, Helmut Kohl's government awkwardly attempted to maintain at least some distance between itself and Honecker's delegation, wanting desperately not to relinquish fully the conservatives' traditional denial of the East German state's legitimacy and their demand for "unity in freedom." The GDR anthem ("Arisen from Ruins"), played on Honecker's arrival in Bonn, was referred to by West German officials as a hymn, not a national anthem, and East Germany's Foreign Minister Oskar Fischer, who was part of the Honecker entourage, was greeted not by his West German counterpart, Hans-Dietrich Genscher, but rather by Dorothee Wilms, Bonn's minister for inter-German relations. Nonetheless, the stark symbolism of the occasion was lost on no one. Honecker's quest for the GDR's legitimacy had won its most important victory.

For disillusioned conservatives, the Kohl government had perpetuated, contrary to its own stated objectives, the unforgivable diplomatic weakness of the Social Democrats' policy toward East Germany. The "consciousness," wrote political commentator Eduard Neumaier, "of the difference between freedom and repression, between democracy and totalitarian dictatorship, indeed between good and evil in politics had been weakened to a disturbing degree."[13] American columnist Flora Lewis summed up the international implications of the Honecker trip to Bonn. Writing in the *New York Times*, she observed that the Honecker visit confirmed the fact "that there are two Germanys in postwar Europe and there will continue to be as far as the eye can see."[14]

The Honecker regime thrived on its success, and East Berlin's *Westoffensiv* expanded. In 1987 Honecker became the first GDR leader to visit the Netherlands and Belgium; in January 1988, he was the first to pay an official visit to France. The same year the GDR managed to initiate negotiations with the European Community on commercial relations.[15] And yet despite this intensifying campaign for legitimacy, the full diplomatic equality the GDR sought remained elusive. East German authorities were still left to lobby Bonn to close the Salzgitter Center, the West German office that monitored human rights violations in the GDR. Likewise, East Berlin struggled to persuade West Germany to recognize GDR citizenship.

In the early 1980s leading members of the Social Democratic party had led, to East Berlin's delight, a parliamentary campaign to amend

the Federal Constitution by eliminating the objective of German unification.[16] Although both German states had agreed in their Basic
Treaty of 1972 to exchange official representatives, Bonn had never
relinquished its insistence that these not be full ambassadors. West
German diplomatic offices carried the designation *"ständige Vertretung"*
(permanent representation) rather than "embassy."

The question of citizenship was no small matter. The prelude to
East Germany's revolution, the refugee crisis of the summer of 1989,
was precipitated by East Germans' awareness of their automatic en-
titlement to West German citizenship once they reached West German
territory (which included diplomatic facilities in Budapest, Prague,
and Warsaw).

East Germany's clouded legitimacy continued to be reflected, to
the utter frustration of GDR authorities, even in West German jour-
nalistic practices. The conservative daily, *Die Welt,* had maintained the
practice—dropped by other West German papers years before—of
always placing hostile quotations around the acronym "DDR." Ironically, in the winter of 1989 *Die Welt* was moving toward abolishing
its own last vestige of denying the East German state legitimacy.[17]

The Soviet Union and Its German Ally

The German Democratic Republic is forever and irrevocably
allied with the Union of Soviet Socialist Republics [from Article
Six of the GDR's 1974 amended constitution].[18]

The closer the friendship with the Soviet Union, the better
socialism in one's own country develops. . . . We adhere to the
well-established principle that the attitude toward the CPSU
and the USSR is a touchstone of faithfulness to Marxism-Leninism and to the revolutionary cause of the working class [from
Erich Honecker, *The German Democratic Republic: Pillar of Peace
and Socialism,* 1979].[19]

East German leaders had always understood that their very existence
depended on the presence of Soviet troops on GDR soil. In the years
before Mikhail Gorbachev's ascendancy to power in March 1985, the
Soviet Union's relationship with the GDR was characterized by immensely profitable cooperation in a number of ways.

Ideologically, the GDR had established itself as the most loyal of
Moscow's East European client states, a model of orthodox communism.
The fact that Moscow had concentrated in East Germany its greatest
number of troops outside the boundaries of the USSR underscored
the country's strategic importance. Economically, since the 1960s the

GDR had been the Soviet Union's most important trading partner (providing 10 percent of Soviet trade) and a major supplier of chemical products and industrial equipment. In the international arena, the East German state had become, next to Cuba, Moscow's most important proxy in providing economic, military, and security assistance to Communist allies from the Sandinistas in Nicaragua to Marxist movements and regimes across Africa and Asia.[20]

Nevertheless, the GDR's position of relative security in its relationship with the Soviet Union had not come easily. And after four decades of political and economic consolidation, the longevity of an East German Communist state still precariously depended on the good offices of Soviet interest and power. Honecker never lost sight of the unshakable fact that the GDR's friendship with the Soviet Union was, as he put it, "decisive for the foundation of our existence," a "vital necessity."[21] Thus more than anywhere else in Eastern Europe, as Timothy Garton Ash later observed, in East Germany Gorbachev's effect was most critical.[22]

Even before the end of World War II, Soviet officials had been engaged in laying the groundwork for a Communist administration in the Soviet zone of occupation in Germany. The country's division was by no means a self-evident tenet of Moscow's initial postwar policy on Europe, as Soviet authorities first sought to project their power across the entire country.[23] Even once the sovereignty of the GDR appeared ensured by the mid-1950s, East Berlin's relationship with Moscow was subsequently marked at times by suspicion, distrust, and ambiguity.

At the Potsdam conference held in July and August 1945, the United States, Great Britain, and the Soviet Union agreed to treat Germany as an economic whole and to administer it jointly. For the course of an interim period of unstipulated length, five or more central departments were to administer the Allied Control Council's policies.[24] During this time within the Soviet leadership two schools of thought on the future of Germany soon became evident.

One faction within the Soviet leadership, represented by Politburo member Andrei Zhdanov and Sergei Tiul'panov, chief of the information bureau of the Soviet Military Administration in the occupation zone from 1945 to 1949, advocated vigorous and rapid communization of the Soviet-occupied territory. They believed that Soviet security interests would be best served by two Germanys, not one, no matter the conditions.

A second faction was represented by Vladimir S. Semenov, political adviser to the supreme commander and military governor of the zone, and KGB chief Lavrenti Beria (later, posthumously, accused by Khrushchev at the Twentieth Party Congress of the CPSU of attempting to sell out the GDR). They favored a less confrontational policy that appeared to leave open the possibility of a unified but neutralized Germany that would secure a dominant Soviet influence in Europe, minimally through a Rapallo type of agreement[25] and maximally through the communization of a united German state.[26]

After the war the Semenov-Beria faction sought to exploit fertile ground in the western zones for the idea of Germany's neutralization. The Social Democratic party's leader, Kurt Schumacher, though a virulent anti-Communist, was nonetheless a determined advocate of a united, neutral Germany and represented a prospective partner for this Soviet group. Even members of what eventually became Konrad Adenauer's Christian Democratic Union—chief advocate of Western integration—were initially sympathetic to the idea of a neutral German government as a bridge between East and West.[27]

Precisely because these competing views within the Soviet leadership were becoming increasingly evident, the East German Communists learned from the beginning that a sense of insecurity was neither paranoid nor overreactive. Just seventeen months after the founding of the Socialist Unity party (in April of 1946), the East German Communists were treated to their first hint of Moscow's ambivalence. The Soviets stung their East German comrades when they not only failed to invite them to the first meeting of the Cominform in September 1947, a meeting to which even the French and Italian Communists were invited, but also neglected to inform them that the meeting was scheduled to take place.[28] Even two weeks before the GDR's founding on October 11, a delegation comprising the East German Communists' top leadership—Walter Ulbricht, Otto Grotewohl, Wilhelm Pieck, and Fred Oelssner—made a secret twelve-day visit to Moscow. During this time the East Germans may well have worked to gain assurances that Moscow was firmly committed to East Germany's sovereignty.[29]

When the German Democratic Republic was finally founded on October 11, 1949,[30] "Stalin sent the GDR a telegram of congratulations," writes British historian David Childs, "but not much else."[31] It is true that Stalin praised the founding of the East German state as a "turning point in the history of Europe," whose existence along with that of the Soviet Union excluded "the possibilities of new wars in Europe."[32] But that Soviet diplomatic representatives still kept the door open for some form of German unity, however, at least suggests that the Soviets had not fully decided on one Germany or two.

The historian Norman M. Naimark argues that both before and after Stalin's famous proposal of March 10, 1952, to the Allied Powers for the creation of a neutral, demilitarized, united Germany, the Soviet

31

Union may have been prepared "under the appropriate circumstances to cashier its East German partner in exchange for a neutral Germany."[33] Indeed, in the early years of its existence, the GDR appeared to serve the Soviet Union principally as a source of desperately needed war reparations and as an instrument of political leverage in shaping the landscape of the new Europe. Interestingly, only after 1955 did the Soviets, long after having formalized their relations with the other East bloc states, sign a state treaty with the GDR.

In this atmosphere of uncertainty the East German Communists had felt compelled to work all the more intensely to win the favor and confidence of their Soviet patrons to justify their existence. Since the 1948 rupture between the Soviet Union and Yugoslavia, Ulbricht had vigorously purged the party to decimate internal opposition but also to assure the Soviets of the unconditional loyalty and reliability of the East German Communist regime in the Socialist camp. According to the East German party's own accounts, although party membership was on the rise, some 150,696 unreliable individuals, either party members or candidates for party membership, were expelled from the ranks between 1948 and 1952.[34]

Stalin's death on March 5, 1953, triggered a new episode in Soviet–East German relations. Ulbricht responded to the death of "the greatest human being of our epoch"[35] with a flurry of publications of the writings and speeches of Stalin. From Mecklenburg to Saxony, new monuments were erected, and bleak and sparsely supplied East German shops became inundated with souvenir busts and other memorabilia of the great Soviet leader. GDR authorities changed the name of the city Eisenhüttenstadt, near the Polish border, to Stalinstadt (it was later renamed Eisenhüttenstadt).

The difficulty was, though, at the same time Ulbricht was raising the Soviet dictator's personality cult in the GDR to new heights, a power struggle had broken out within the Soviet leadership. The faction of the Soviet Communists that advocated a more moderate German policy, a course that would endanger the security of hard-liner Ulbricht (perhaps even the GDR itself), was maneuvering to gain advantage. And indeed this Soviet faction, by no means averse to meddling in the internal politics of the East German party, had already found a compatible group within its leadership. The Soviet Semenov-Beria group began to offer direct support to Ulbricht's rivals, Rudolf Herrnstadt and Wilhelm Zaisser, editor in chief of *Neues Deutschland* and minister of state security, respectively, who were also committed to slowing the GDR's increasingly rapid march to socialism.[36] It is in fact "tempting," as Martin McCauley has observed, to see the work of these Soviet–East German collaborators as devoted to "a plan to prepare the way for a united Germany."[37]

Of even greater, more immediate concern was the charge of Ulbricht's critics that East Berlin's overly aggressive industrialization policies, first announced at the Second Party Congress in July 1952, were destabilizing the country. Evidence of this, anti-Ulbricht forces argued, was the rising number of East Germans fleeing to the West, depleting an already listless, debilitated work force. In 1951, 165,648 East German refugees were registered by West German authorities. Despite efforts by the Communist regime to secure the internal German border in the summer of 1952, the number still rose by the end of the year to 182,393—over half the refugees were under twenty-five years of age. In 1953, 331,390 East Germans were received in the West, though many thousands more undoubtedly entered West Germany without bothering to register with refugee officials.[38]

During the spring of 1953, the Soviet "moderate" line, seizing opportunities afforded by Stalin's death in March, was inching toward greater leverage in Moscow. At this time, the Soviet faction led by KGB chief Beria began to exert pressure on East Berlin to "halt [its] accelerated construction of socialism."[39] A New Course, announced by the East German Communists in June, conceded party and government errors and promised amnesty for those who had left the GDR illegally. East Berlin suggested a softening of the policies of forced collectivization of agriculture and nationalization of artisans and small businesses, price increases were withdrawn, and persecuted members of the intelligentsia had ration cards returned to them.[40] In this sudden shift, East Germany's "moderate" Communists were bolstered, while Ulbricht's position seemed to hang in the balance.

East German workers, however, starting what at first appeared to be a series of small strikes in East Berlin on June 15, provided the catalyst for large-scale antigovernment demonstrations, which within forty-eight hours had spread to over 270 cities and towns throughout the GDR. Whether in East Berlin or Leipzig, demonstrators demanded a far-reaching program of change, including everything from reduced work norms to free elections. This spontaneous anti-Communist eruption proved more than the party and its security organs could handle, forcing Moscow to use Soviet forces stationed in the GDR to crush the uprising. Twenty-one demonstrators were reported killed, seven later executed, and as many as a thousand imprisoned.[41]

Ironically, the June uprising may have helped save Ulbricht's career. If the Soviet leadership—itself still enmeshed in its own power struggle—had replaced Ulbricht at the time, that decision could have been viewed only as a victory for East Germany's restive populace. Rather than risk further destabilization, the Soviets chose to back off, allowing Ulbricht time and maneuvering room to consolidate his position.[42]

On May 14, 1955, the GDR was admitted to the Warsaw Pact, and in September of the same year the first treaty between the Soviet Union and the GDR was signed. The Soviet occupation troops were converted, semantically, into allied forces, and the GDR received by Soviet definition its full sovereignty. The Soviet Union did retain the right to fulfill its international obligations regarding "Germany as a whole," in particular regarding the special status of Berlin. And although the GDR was granted permission to manage civilian transit between Berlin and West Germany, the Soviets continued to oversee air traffic in the three corridors between West Germany and Berlin as well as Western allied–related traffic. Nevertheless, the self-image of the GDR's leadership soared. For the first time East Germany felt confident enough to consider itself on equal terms with the other Communist states of the region. The power of the new state was consummated on January 18, 1956, when the National People's Army was founded.

Another potential setback in relations with the Soviet Union was averted the very next month. In February 1956 at the Twentieth Party Congress of the Soviet Communist Party, Stalin fell into disfavor, and the entire personality cult surrounding the late Soviet dictator received its first public censure. This reversal demanded reaction from East Berlin, and Ulbricht, the cunning and hitherto quintessential Stalin loyalist, was not remiss in responding. It was quite clear now, according to the East German party boss, that Stalin's personality cult had caused "significant damage," and by no means could the Soviet leader be "counted among the classic [architects] of Marxism."[43] Almost overnight in East Germany, monuments to Stalin were demolished, his name was removed from street signs and from names of towns, and his publications were banned. At this stage of his career, Ulbricht's loyalty to his Soviet masters, whichever direction the wind might blow, was beyond reproach.

In the period after 1956 Walter Ulbricht gained prestige and political capital with Moscow, as signs of the GDR's own economic development became evident. The Soviet Union had not given up, however, on its *Deutschlandspiele*. On November 27, 1958, Khrushchev provoked a minicrisis over the Berlin problem by calling for the Western powers to withdraw from West Berlin. The new "free city" would have its security guaranteed, according to Khrushchev's proposal, by the four occupying powers and the two German states. In March 1959 Khrushchev, over the heads of the government in East Berlin and the conservative-led government in Bonn, made reunification overtures to Erich Ollenhauer, head of the West German Social Democrats. The Social Democrats, in turn, published their own plan for German unity to be achieved through a step-by-step rapprochement of the two German states.[44] Not surprisingly, the idea soon faded, having found little resonance in Bonn and East Berlin. A far more concrete, formidable challenge of a different nature, though, lay just ahead for the East German state.

From a certain point of view economic conditions in East Germany should have improved in the 1950s. Reparations ended in 1954, occupation costs ceased to be levied after 1959, and food rationing ended in 1958.[45] But the command economy—although the most productive in the bloc—could only sputter, and while West Germany's system had begun to generate wealth, East Germans were left behind, their portion of the country mired in poverty. During the latter half of the decade a steady stream of East German citizens continued to flow westward in search of political freedom and economic opportunity.

Between 1949 and 1961 over 2½ million East Germans fled to the West, draining the GDR's work force. Nearly 50 percent of the refugees were under twenty-five years of age; only 10 percent were retired.[46] Communist authorities tensely watched the number swell during the three years before the construction of the Berlin Wall. In 1959, 144,000 East Germans emigrated from the GDR; in 1960 the number reached 199,000. In the first half of 1961, 207,000 East Germans left for West Germany.[47]

Rumors had begun to emerge in the West that the Communist regime was preparing to undertake a violent response to the mass flight of its citizens, and in fact the Western allied powers had received intelligence early in the summer of 1961 indicating that the GDR might intervene to abate the flow of refugees. On June 15, 1961, East Germany's Communist party daily, *Neues Deutschland*, printed a statement given by Walter Ulbricht in East Berlin in response to the rumors circulating in the West:

> As I understand your question, there are people in West Germany who wish that we mobilize the construction workers of the capital of the GDR in order to build a wall. I have no knowledge that such an intention exists. The construction workers of our capital are occupied with building apartments, and this takes their entire energy. No one has the intention of erecting a wall.[48]

Refugees continued to pour out. During the first two weeks of August alone, over 47,000 fled. Ulbricht had indeed organized a contingency plan to stem the GDR's hemorrhaging. In the early hours of the morning on August 13 East German construction workers under the supervision of the People's Police and the National People's Army began to seal off passage to the West as they laid the foundation of the Berlin Wall. The West expressed indignation but mustered little else. West Berlin's mayor, Willy Brandt, desperately appealed to U.S. President John F. Kennedy to guarantee the territorial integrity of West Berlin, which remained precariously embedded in the heart of East Germany.

Ulbricht's sealing of the East–West Berlin border crushed much of the spirit of dissent inside the GDR. And as the flow of refugees began to subside, the GDR's economy showed signs of stabilizing. Beyond its domestic effect, Ulbricht's action in Berlin brought about a kind of redemption in the eyes of the Soviets. Times had changed since the Soviet Union had been forced to intervene on behalf of the East German Communist regime to crush the uprising in 1953. Now the East Germans were able to demonstrate their own competence and capability in the handling of their internal affairs.

Indeed, Moscow seemed to approve. In 1964, the first Treaty of Friendship, Mutual Assistance and Cooperation between East Berlin and Moscow was signed (again, long after friendship treaties had been signed by Moscow and the other East European states). The Soviet-GDR treaty acted as a military supplement to the Warsaw Pact, guaranteeing among other things that the GDR's borders would henceforth be considered "inviolable and a basic factor of European security."[49] For Ulbricht the treaty had the double function of strengthening his position within the East bloc and further building the GDR's case for international legitimacy.

If the new climate did in fact help shore up Ulbricht's position with the Soviets, however, the situation did not last long. New seeds of conflict were sown by the East German leader himself. In October 1964, when Khrushchev was removed from power, Ulbricht insisted on praising Khrushchev's "great contributions," even as the Soviet Communist party was moving to illuminate the former Kremlin chief's grave mistakes, converting him into a "non-person."[50] Ulbricht's lavish praise of Khrushchev cannot have endeared him to the new Soviet leader, Leonid Brezhnev. To aggravate matters, an overconfident Ulbricht had begun to boast at international Communist gatherings that the GDR (by inference not the Soviet Union) should now be considered the contemporary model of Socialist economic development. Ulbricht even bragged that since he was the only East bloc leader to have known Lenin personally, it was he who was best informed as to what the character of the relationship should be between the different Communist parties.[51]

The Soviets decided to rein in the GDR. With trade the central topic on the agenda, Brezhnev traveled to East Berlin in November 1965, paving the way for a new Soviet-GDR trade agreement. This agreement forced an increase in the GDR's trade with Moscow, negating the essence of the New Economic Policy, which had been designed by East Berlin to increase the GDR's trade with the West to improve the country's lagging standards and also to raise the GDR economically to the status of a Socialist vanguard country.[52]

Ulbricht's perceived arrogance, though, was not easily checked. On June 30, 1968, Ulbricht celebrated his seventy-fifth birthday in unbridled, extravagant style, with the GDR press heaping praise on its head of state in a manner that would have befitted Stalin. Yet as Ulbricht's public confidence appeared to soar, there were ominous developments. First at home, Ulbricht's rival Erich Honecker had begun to enhance his authority by forging strong ties to Brezhnev. Second, in Czechoslovakia Ulbricht's colleague and soul mate Antonin Novotny, first secretary of the Czechoslovak Communist party and head of state, had been forced to step down in March, giving ground to the reformer Alexander Dubcek. The Honecker challenge was not yet imminent, and the Czechoslovak problem was eventually "solved" by the Warsaw Pact's August intervention. Some speculated that Ulbricht—fearful that the Czech "virus" would spread to the GDR—was among the first to argue in Moscow in favor of an invasion. But Moscow itself had meanwhile become the central challenge to Ulbricht's authority.

In 1968–1969, Brezhnev had begun to contemplate the virtues of détente and rapprochement with Bonn. Through access to Western technology and credits, Soviet leaders believed that their concerns about parity in East-West technological competition, accentuated by the American success in putting the first man on the moon in July 1969, could be effectively addressed.[53] The Soviet Union was also preoccupied at the time with tensions along the Sino-Soviet border and had little interest in anything even suggesting conflict with NATO. Moreover, Moscow sought to enhance the prospects of a conference in Helsinki, which held promise of formal Western acceptance of the European status quo.

If the Soviets wished to enjoy the fruits of Bonn's new *Ostpolitik*, however, an obstinate and arrogant Ulbricht threatened to hinder the process. The East German Communists feared the destabilizing effects of détente at home and the adverse impact any domestic disruption could have on the GDR's legitimacy campaign abroad. The Soviets appeared to be less concerned about these consequences. East Berlin's fears were confirmed when Chancellor Brandt traveled to Erfurt in March 1970. When the chancellor and his entourage arrived at the

Erfurt train station on March 19, thousands of East Germans turned out to greet the West German leader. To the intense embarrassment of GDR officials, the crowds of East Germans chanted, "Wil-ly, Wil-ly"—not for East German President Willi Stoph but for Willy Brandt. (Western observers had speculated at the time that Ulbricht might have helped organize a portion of the demonstration to impress Moscow of the dangers of inter-German détente.)[54]

Things did not improve from the GDR's perspective. Ulbricht cannot have been pleased by the August 1970 signing of a renunciation of force treaty by Willy Brandt and Leonid Brezhnev, which, in the East German leader's view, failed to take into proper account GDR interests. The treaty stressed that the Soviet Union and West Germany would respect the territorial integrity of current borders in Europe but did not require Bonn to recognize the GDR under international law. A more imminent problem for Ulbricht was an indication that Moscow wished to see a negotiated solution on the status of divided Berlin.

A. James McAdams describes the conflict over Berlin in the following way:

> [Ulbricht's] demands for the city's neutrality and for East German control over its access routes were linked directly to the SED's claims that the GDR enjoyed total sovereignty over its territory. The only way to stabilize the country internally, so Ulbricht and others in the party leadership reasoned, was to convince its skeptical citizenry that there were no other legitimate pretenders to control over eastern Germany. Ulbricht had good reason to think that he enjoyed Moscow's complete support on this issue. In previous years, Leonid Brezhnev and other Soviet leaders had repeatedly assured the SED that there would be no compromise with the West on Berlin. Thus, in Ulbricht's eyes, Moscow's new course in 1970 showed an incomprehensible disregard for the GDR's interests.[55]

Ulbricht overestimated his own security. One month before his removal from office, writing on April 1, 1971, in *Neues Deutschland*, the East German leader again alluded to his personal acquaintance with Lenin, noting with supreme confidence that the Soviet revolutionary hero had been aware that even the "Russians" had "things to learn."[56] For Brezhnev this assertion appears to have been quite enough.

The Soviets—Moscow's Ambassador Pyotr A. Abrassimov was said to have played a pivotal role[57]—in collaboration with members of the East German Communist party's ruling Politburo forced Ulbricht from power in May 1971, although they chose to do so in a manner that did not risk destabilizing the GDR. Ulbricht was persuaded to step down "voluntarily." In a face-saving measure, the East German leader announced his own resignation as a first secretary to the Central Committee on May 3, 1971, citing reasons of age and health. He was allowed to keep his ceremonial titles as chairman of the party and the *Staatsrat*, but with his resignation the Ulbricht era had unmistakably come to an end.

With Ulbricht gone, Moscow proceeded with the negotiation of a treaty on Berlin, the contents of which—Soviet supervision over traffic to Berlin and absence of a provision guaranteeing West Berlin's neutrality, for instance—confirmed that East German sovereignty was to remain subordinate to greater Soviet foreign policy objectives.[58] In the context of warming relations between Moscow and Bonn, Brezhnev traveled to Bonn in May 1973—the first time a Soviet head of state had paid a visit to West Germany.

The GDR's new leader, at fifty-seven, the younger but no less dour Erich Honecker, went to great lengths to avoid the friction experienced between Moscow and his predecessor. Imprisoned by the Nazis in 1935, the Communist activist Honecker had been liberated in 1945 and the following year charged with the near-sacred task of guiding the Communist youth movement in Germany as chairman of the Free German Youth. He had served on the Communist party's Central Committee since 1946, becoming a candidate member of the Politburo in 1950 and a full member in 1958.

In the 1960s Honecker had gained a reputation for his unwavering fidelity to the Soviet Union (he had first visited the Soviet Union with a German Communist youth delegation in 1931) and an unremitting commitment to Communist orthodoxy. As the man responsible for security matters within the Central Committee, he had played a key role in the construction of the Berlin Wall in 1961. In the mid-1960s, he had led the GDR's campaign in the cultural purge of dissident writers, artists, and other "anti-state" intellectuals. In 1968 he was, not surprisingly, a vociferous supporter of the Warsaw Pact's crushing of the Prague Spring.

Like Ulbricht, Honecker was not at ease with the new coziness between Moscow and Bonn. Honecker's answer, however, was to use the setting of East-West détente for his own purposes—seducing the West German government into according the GDR greater legitimacy and economic privileges, while implementing a regimen of strict ideological vigilance at home. The December 1970 strikes in Poland had reminded GDR leaders that any relaxation of authority could lead to disturbance and destabilization. In addition to intensifying East Berlin's policy of *Abgrenzung* (the stressing of political, ideological, and cultural differences with the West German state), Honecker tightened the party's grip on GDR society by nationalizing the remaining private and semiprivate enterprises—accounting for nearly 2 million workers and 14.4 percent of the national income.[59] To consolidate his own power, Honecker reshuffled the country's leadership, making certain that any remaining Ulbricht loyalists were replaced by his men.

Honecker's brand of *Westpolitik* met with success, and during his tenure the GDR transformed itself into a committed convert to détente. For the next decade and a half, the GDR's promotion of détente and inter-German rapprochement—from the medals brought home by the GDR's Olympic machine to the economic and political rewards produced by a constant stream of diplomatic offensives in Europe—provided fresh confidence for the Communist regime.

When Moscow called for its allies to cool ties with Western Europe in 1983–1984 in response to NATO's deployment of Pershing II and cruise missiles, Honecker postured about the threat of a "new ice age"[60] in East–West German relations, a way of punishing Bonn for cooperating with Washington. In reality, though, East Berlin found itself in a position similar to that of the West Germans—trying to insulate inter-German détente, albeit for different reasons, from the new chill in superpower relations. In 1983 the GDR had just received a DM 1 billion guaranteed credit from the West German government. In July the following year, Bonn provided an additional government-guaranteed credit to East Berlin for DM 950 million.[61] GDR authorities were unprepared to relinquish these benefits of inter-German détente.

When Gorbachev ascended to power, however, Moscow refocused attention on Soviet–West German relations. And suddenly the GDR regime again felt neglected, its interests jeopardized in the process. The East Berlin–Moscow relationship then faced its most severe test.

Gorbachev's Deutschlandpolitik

Although the Soviet Union's policy of deliberate disengagement from Eastern Europe gradually became evident, as did Moscow's encouragement of reform in the bloc, by no means was it initially clear whether East Germany was to be exempted from Gorbachev's policy.

Most poignantly, behind any discussion of reform in East Germany lurked the question of Germany's division, and with that the balance of power between East and West. As *The Economist* remarked in August 1989, for all the dramatic change in Soviet foreign-policy thinking, East Germany remained "the great unanswered question in the communist half of Europe."[62] In the unsettling climate created by Gorbachev, the GDR's legitimacy and longevity had been placed in a precarious new position.

During its initial phase, Gorbachev's thinking on Germany and the German question yielded little difference from that of his immediate predecessors. When Gorbachev and Honecker first met in May 1985, a joint communiqué declared that both leaders firmly rejected "all concepts . . . which proceed from the postulate of an unresolved German Question."[63] In February 1986, *Neues Deutschland* reported business as usual between the GDR and the new Soviet leader, who had "impressed" East Berlin with his "creativeness" and "historic optimism." According to the East German Communist party daily, the GDR would "fully and entirely" support Gorbachev's proposals. They represented "the triumphant advance of socialism in the Soviet Union [and remained] the strongest argument" in favor of the GDR's course.[64] At the East German Party Congress of April 1986, Gorbachev affirmed in principle the Soviet Union's support for its German ally and, to Honecker's pleasure, took time to express grave concern that "the ruling class of the FRG . . . has still not renounced its revanchist dreams and continues to speak of an 'open German Question.'"[65]

During an official visit to East Berlin in early February 1987, Soviet foreign minister Shevardnadze underscored the position that Germany's division was a desirable anchor in Europe's political landscape:

> We believe that the stability and inviolability of existing borders, which have emerged after World War II and are enshrined in international law, provide the most reliable guarantee for the peaceful and tranquil development of Europe. This is demonstrated by the existence on German soil of two German states, the GDR and the FRG.[66]

During the visit by West German Foreign Minister Hans-Dietrich Genscher to Moscow in July 1986 and the subsequent visit by President Richard von Weizsäcker the following year, Gorbachev publicly showed little sympathy toward Bonn's broaching of the German question. During Weizsäcker's visit, though, the Kremlin chief could not resist what appeared at the time as a traditional Soviet tease. While Gorbachev made it unambiguously clear that the German question was not open to discussion, the door to German unity remained slightly ajar, as "history" would still decide, according to the Soviet leader, "what would come in the next 100 years."[67]

Nevertheless, when President Weizsäcker insisted on presenting Bonn's position on the unity of the German nation in a speech at the Kremlin, both the Soviet news agency Tass and the Communist party daily *Pravda* took care to censor the unwelcome passages.[68] Gorbachev's expert on Germany, Valentin Falin, first explained the deletions as a technical error but then later provocatively claimed they reflected differences of opinion in Soviet leadership circles.[69]

As Gorbachev's new thinking began to take hold in foreign policy, it became apparent to most observers that West Germany figured prominently. Because the Federal Republic functioned as the linchpin of NATO's strategic force, the idea of driving a wedge between Bonn and the Atlantic alliance had always been a prized objective of Soviet foreign policy. In this regard there was little evidence of change under Gorbachev's leadership. More than this, though, at a time when the Soviet Union was increasingly concerned with its internal economic problems, West Germany represented—as Khrushchev had once recognized and explored—Europe's primary repository of the capital, technology, and know-how deemed essential for the modernization of the Soviet economy.

The success of Ludwig Erhard's *Wirtschaftswunder* (economic miracle) and West Germany's vibrant and sturdy capitalist welfare state had undoubtedly made an impression on Soviet reformers. In a conversation in March 1987 with former chancellor Helmut Schmidt, Valentin Falin, a past Soviet envoy to Bonn, insisted that implementation of what he vaguely referred to as the "socialist market" had become the Soviet Union's economic objective.[70] Three years later, Shevardnadze conceded that "one can learn something from capitalism."[71] Gorbachev suggested, in fact, that aspects of Bonn's "social market economy" might be worthy of Soviet emulation.[72]

By no means did Gorbachev encounter an uninterested audience in the Federal Republic with his policy of intensified rapprochement. In fact, "no other West European state," wrote Jochen Thies, a speech writer for former chancellor Schmidt, approached "Gorbachev's reform attempts as positively as the Federal Republic."[73] Schmidt himself noted how Gorbachev offered Europeans the possibility of shedding their bystander role as a "friendly, applauding audience" when Soviet and American leaders met.[74] For his countrymen, he advocated the cultivation of the Federal Republic's "privileged" relationship with Moscow. "We can assume," said Schmidt, "that it will continue to provide opportunities to use Moscow's interest in expanding Soviet-German economic relations to promote German national interests."[75]

Not the least of German interests to the east was the economic aspect of Soviet-German ties: indeed, the Federal Republic was eager to gain advantage over other countries competing to modernize the Soviet economy.[76] Before Bonn's minister of research, Heinz Riesenhuber, traveled to Moscow to conclude the first German-Soviet nuclear agreement in the winter of 1987, he found it difficult to conceal his enthusiasm for the profits awaiting German business: "With our world-leading technology we want to help assure that there will not be another Chernobyl. It's a question of billions in contracts for the revamping of some 78 reactors."[77]

In a speech given in East Germany at Potsdam in November 1988, Foreign Minister Genscher, always fond of recalling the close ties shared by German industrialists and Czarist Russia over 100 years ago, appealed for an intensification of East-West economic and technological cooperation. "We want to reactivate," proclaimed Genscher, "the once so varied and fruitful bonds between Germans and Russians."[78] Interest in expanding German trade ties with Gorbachev's Soviet Union transcended partisan political lines in Germany. Bavaria's conservative governor and chairman of the Christian Social Union, Franz Josef Strauss, usually at odds with Genscher, found himself in complete agreement with Bonn's foreign minister.

When Strauss arrived in Moscow in December 1987, he proclaimed his enthusiastic support for a new stage in Soviet-German cooperation. In Moscow at the invitation of the State Foreign Economic Commission of the USSR, Strauss stated the preparedness of Bavaria, one of West Germany's most industrially advanced states, for this important endeavor.[79] "Mars, god of war, should step aside," said Strauss, "and Mercury, god of commerce, should come to the fore."[80]

As West German political dignitaries began to stream into Moscow,[81] the Soviets initiated an expansive, robust "charm offensive" in West Germany itself. During the first six months of 1988 eighty-three separate Soviet-German sporting events were held; a *Blitzkrieg* of Soviet-sponsored cultural, political, and business meetings took place; student exchanges flourished; and twenty-six Soviet-German city partnerships were established. The Soviet Embassy in Bonn augmented its cultural staff, and Soviet spokesmen regularly began to appear at cultural and political meetings sponsored by even the most conservative political parties and organizations. Meanwhile, Gorbachev himself did not remain satisfied with delegating responsibilities. As James Dobbins, chargé d'affaires at the U.S. Embassy in Bonn observed, the Soviet leader had "spent more time with German politicians [in 1987–1988] . . . than with all other West Europeans put together."[82]

Helmut Schmidt's advocacy of using the climate of Gorbachev's reforms to promote German national interests went beyond considerations of economy, trade, and diplomacy. In his 1987 book, *Perestroika,* Gorbachev broached the German national question by quietly reminding his readers who did, and who did not, hold the key to its solution:

> Regardless of what Ronald Reagan and other Western states say in this regard, they are not in a position to make the FRG any realistic offer in regard to the "German Question." That which has been historically created, should best be left to the

43

course of history. This applies also to the question of the German nation and the forms of sovereignty.[83]

Franz Josef Strauss acknowledged the accuracy of Gorbachev's inference in his posthumously published memoirs: "Without deep-rooted change in the Soviet Union, as one hopes and dreams of under Gorbachev, unity [cannot be] . . . a realistic, accomplishable reality."[84] Thus for this reason too Gorbachev was able to capture the imagination of West German political elites and large segments of the Federal Republic's populace.

Perestroika landed on the best-seller charts in West Germany where it remained for months. The Soviet Union under Gorbachev was rapidly transforming itself, in West German eyes, from adversary to indispensable partner. A poll conducted by the West German Defense Ministry in the autumn of 1988 found that 75 percent of those asked no longer believed in a "Communist threat" from the East; 82 percent placed complete faith in Gorbachev's desire for peace and reconciliation with the West.[85] In 1989, nine out of ten West Germans said they trusted Mikhail Gorbachev—compared with 58 percent who could say the same of President Bush.[86]

A crowning moment of Gorbachev's *Westpolitik* came in October 1988 when Chancellor Kohl set off for Moscow accompanied by five cabinet members, 70 business and banking leaders, and an entourage of 400 aides and journalists. During this visit, a West German consortium headed by Deutsche Bank signed an agreement with the Soviet bank, Vneshekonombank, providing a DM 3 billion ($1.7 billion) bank line of credit for exports to the Soviet Union.[87] For the Soviets, the roots of a long-term, lucrative partnership appeared firmly planted.

On the surface, the chancellor's 1988 visit to Moscow seemed remote from the problem of East Germany and the unresolved question of national unity. When Kohl insisted on raising the issue of Germany's division at a Kremlin dinner in his honor, an irritated Gorbachev pushed aside the prepared translation of Kohl's speech (though this reaction may also have been a deliberate reflection of Gorbachev's lingering resentment over the chancellor's comments in 1986 when he compared the Soviet reformer to Nazi propaganda minister, Joseph Goebbels).[88] When Kohl pressed the question of Germany's division, Gorbachev warned that "attempts to force developments through unrealistic policies," in his view, were an "unstable and dangerous undertaking."[89] Yet while Gorbachev's public posture may have appeared unflinching, a sequence of articles and statements by Soviet officials had already begun to suggest stirrings of a new Soviet thinking on Germany.

"Soviet German experts," Egon Krenz wrote, referring to this period, "saw at this time that we [the GDR] had ideas about cooperation with the FRG in specific areas, [but] did not have a concept for dealing with the national question."[90] What later emerged as Gorbachev's new *Deutschlandpolitik* and Soviet reexamination of the national question can be traced to an article by Nicolae Portugalov, an expert on Germany in the CPSU Central Committee, in January 1987. In a commentary in *Moscow News*, an important forum for Soviet reformers, Portugalov lit a fuse when he pointed out that, despite the existence of two German states, "the people of the GDR are still German and belong to the same nation [as citizens of the Federal Republic]."[91] Inoffensive at first glance, Portugalov's statement about East and West Germans being members of a single nation nonetheless represented a quiet, but unmistakably significant challenge to the Honecker regime.

The GDR's first constitution had maintained the concept of national unity, the first article stating that "Germany is an indivisible republic . . . [and that] there is only one German citizenship."[92] Like his West German counterparts, East Germany's first president, Otto Grotewohl, stressed that his "provisional government" would remain committed to the "reunification of Germany."[93] But the GDR's rhetorical commitment to national unity did not last. Although East Berlin's new constitution of 1968 reaffirmed that the Communist state would shoulder the "responsibility to guide the entire German nation on the path into a future of peace and socialism," legislation had been passed the previous year governing the question of a separate GDR citizenship.[94] As a consequence, Ulbricht's 1968 constitution spoke of the GDR as a "socialist state of the German nation" whose "national task" was articulated as the reestablishment and cultivation of "normal relations" between the GDR and the Federal Republic. By the end of the next year, the East German Central Committee was demanding that all business with the Federal Republic be conducted in strict accordance with international law; that is, henceforth the West German state was to be treated by East Berlin as a foreign country like any other.

Ulbricht's shift on the national question was in part a response to the international climate of détente at the end of the 1960s. For a regime still searching for legitimacy and full diplomatic equality with the Federal Republic, the trend toward intensifying inter-German rapprochement held both promise (for economic subsidy) and peril (of ideological damage and instability). When Chancellor Willy Brandt referred in his 1970 meetings in Erfurt to the "special nature" of the "two states in Germany," his host Willi Stoph recoiled. The GDR's chairman of the Council of Ministers chided the West German leader for persisting in his illusionary view about the "unity of the German nation." "You know as well as I," responded Stoph, "that [such utterances] do not conform with the social and political reality."[95]

To undersore the GDR's distinctiveness from the Federal Republic, Erich Honecker intensified the GDR's defensive policy of *Abgrenzung* or demarcation in the early 1970s.[96] When the Berlin Wall went up in 1961, an estimated 17 percent of the GDR's populace owned television sets and were able to tune into "hostile" broadcasts on West German TV. By the time Honecker assumed power a decade later, the figure had risen to 85 percent. This development, along with the GDR's acceptance of Willy Brandt's overtures toward friendlier relations, convinced Honecker of the increased need to shield his state from the destabilizing effects of these tears in the iron curtain.

So that no ambiguity might linger on the national question, Honecker had the GDR's constitution amended in 1974, deleting all references to "Germany" and "unification." The GDR would no longer be considered a Socialist state of the German nation but, as Article 1 now promulgated, a "socialist state of workers and peasants."[97] "Sentimentalizing about being German," in the words of one party official, had become nothing more than "an old trick of certain circles in the FRG for covering up imperialist class interests."[98]

For Honecker's regime, then, the fiction of two German states *and* nations—one Socialist, one capitalist, their respective citizens with different values and consciousness—became inextricably linked to the heart of the German Communist state's *raison d'être* and conflicted directly with West Germany's "revanchist" concept of "two states" within "one German nation." Honecker's two-nation postulate provoked no objection in Moscow.

Nicolae Portugalov, the author of this subtle but startling shift of Soviet perspective now advocating the unity of a single German nation, was a seasoned Germanist who had represented the Soviet news agency Novosti in Bonn between 1972 and 1979 before becoming an adviser on German affairs to the party's Central Committee. Given his position of relative prominence among Soviet policy analysts, Portugalov had likely—despite the breakdown of hierarchy at this time under *glasnost*—discussed his comments with his superiors.[99]

One individual with whom Portugalov was almost certain to have consulted was Falin, one of Gorbachev's closest advisers on foreign affairs. The two men were by no means strangers to each other. Falin, who had served in the Soviet Control Commission in Germany (1950–1952) at the beginning of his career, returned as Soviet envoy to Bonn in 1971. As Moscow's ambassador to West Germany for the next seven years, Falin had maintained regular contact in Bonn with Portugalov.

Since 1986 Falin had served as director of Novosti, an institution closely linked to another leading reformer and Gorbachev associate, Aleksandr Yakovlev.

Indeed, Portugalov's remark did not go unnoticed. In a 1987 interview with West Germany's weekly *Stern*, the GDR's chief ideologist, Kurt Hager, was confronted by his West German interlocutors with the suggestion that Portugalov's commentary was a sign of new Soviet thinking on Germany. Hager fired the first warning shot in what soon emerged as the ideological battle between East Berlin and Moscow. If *Stern* interpreted Portugalov's contention about a single German nation as a sign of conflict between the GDR and the Soviets, the West Germans were mistaken and, as Hager suggested, in need of a better translation of the article in question. After all, did Portugalov cease to speak of two, independent German states?[100]

Portugalov was not deterred from further provocation. In May, speculating about the design of a common European home, he referred to future opportunities that "should please" the West Germans, including the prospect of a withdrawal of foreign military presence from both German states. In July, an article by Leonid Potshchivalov in *Literaturnaya Gazeta*, another publication controlled by pro-Gorbachev reformers, affirmed Portugalov's thesis that despite the existence of two separate states, the German nation endured.[101] After Franz Josef Strauss visited Moscow at the end of 1987, the Bavarian was able to report with pleasure that, although at the time it might be "senseless to direct negotiations toward reunification . . . nonsense about the theory of a capitalist nation in the West and a socialist nation in the East had evidently been abandoned" by the Soviets.[102]

Portugalov was still postulating a single German nation in an early 1988 interview broadcast on West German television, asserting in addition that it was not the Soviet Union that had "caused the partition of Germany." Portugalov "wholly support[ed]" the constantly improving relationship between the two German states, though "history [would still] make the ultimate decision about the national destiny and about the form of Germany's existence as a state."[103]

The semantic reflection of this subtle shift in Soviet thinking was not altogether concealed during Kohl's fall 1988 trip to Moscow. At that time Gorbachev expressly referred to *Germans* in the GDR and the Federal Republic, rather than to the standard "GDR- and FRG-citizens."[104] Gorbachev warned against "strong-arm" attempts "to erase the borders between the sovereign German states" but also stressed that "there can be no two opinions about the fact that the fate of the Germans is indissolubly bound up with the fate of Europe [and] with the prospects for building the 'European Home.'"[105]

Several weeks later East Berlin, undoubtedly wishing to send a signal to Moscow as well as to Bonn, released its pit bull of ideologists, Karl-Eduard von Schnitzler, in the pages of *Neues Deutschland*, where he vociferously attacked Chancellor Kohl's State of the Nation Address. Bonn persisted in an illusionary obsession—it raised in von Schnitzler's mind, in fact, "the question [of Kohl's] political competence"—with a single German nation.[106]

During Gorbachev's reciprocal visit to Bonn in June 1989, traces of new Soviet thinking on the question of German unity were still to be found. The Russian-language version of a Soviet–West German joint declaration referred to the West German state as *Federativnaya Respublika Germaniya* rather than *Germanii*—the change in Russian from "i" to "a" emphasizing one single Germany with a federal structure rather than two Germanys, one with a federal structure. As Hannes Adomeit points out, this was no small matter since the West Germans had attempted in vain for some time to convince the Soviets to make this modification.[107]

Was there something more afoot in Soviet thinking on Germany than mere shifts in semantics? In the fall of 1987 Ottfried Hennig, parliamentary state secretary with the federal minister for inter-German relations, referred to reports that Gorbachev had commissioned a special committee in January 1987 to explore alternative ways of dealing with the German question. The committee was said to include Nicolae Portugalov and Valentin Falin, as well as the elderly Germanist Daniil Melnikov and Georgi Arbatov, director of Moscow's Institute for the Study of the USA and Canada.[108]

That Gorbachev's advisers on Germany were intensely occupied with a serious reevaluation of the Soviet Union's relationship with the two German states is beyond dispute. Moreover, West Germany was unquestionably at the heart of this discussion, as Soviet officials explored new links with Bonn, "pondering," in Falin's words, "how long-term interests [between the Soviet Union and the Federal Republic] can be best served."[109]

Reevaluation of the Kremlin's *Deutschlandpolitik* had its logic in the grander scheme of Gorbachev's foreign policy thinking. Falin and Yakovlev, both implacably hostile in their writings toward the United States and virulent critics of NATO policy, viewed the transition from a bipolar to a multipolar system of international relations as advantageous to Soviet interests. New management of the German question might offer Moscow the two things highest on its agenda: West German largess in the form of capital and technology for its modernization program and a gradually diminished American military presence in Europe.

In 1987, following Portugalov's remarks on the unity of the German nation, a string of Soviet statements began to reflect this new thinking in Moscow. Falin, for example, added to Portugalov's musings with provocations of his own. In a September 23 interview with a West German television station, Falin asserted that a "constellation with two German states in which no foreign troops were stationed" was not only "possible" but would eventually become "a fact."[110] Regarding the special problem of Berlin, the Four-Power Agreement governing the administration of the divided city would no longer be considered, according to Falin, "the last word" in a new common European home.[111] Falin pursued this thought in an interview with a West German newspaper, suggesting that Europe's common home should entail "possibilities" for the "normalization" of Berlin.[112] Not the least bit impressed with such disruptive speculation, nor consoled by *Pravda's* assertion that attempts "to 'amend' the four-power agreement . . . were unwelcome and futile,"[113] Honecker wasted no time in chiding "Mr. Falin" (not *comrade*) for his unsolicited and unwelcome opinions. The current agreement on Berlin, in the East German party's view, was one with which the GDR lived quite comfortably.[114]

Still further agitation from other Soviet sources exceeded Portugalov's theorizing about a single German nation and Falin's speculation on the Berlin question. On September 28, Soviet mission adviser in Geneva, Stanislav Cherniavskiy, made a rather startling comment to members of the World Lutheran Federation: The "[Berlin] wall will cease to exist very soon. Its last days have come."[115] A flurry of official Soviet statements followed with damage control, Foreign Ministry spokesman Gennadiy Gerasimov claiming Cherniavskiy's remark was simply a "slip of the tongue which was enlarged into a statement"[116] and subsequently "distorted"[117] by the Western media. Falin, when asked about the comment by a West German interviewer in mid-October, played the innocent, knowing nothing of the alleged utterance.[118] But neither the East German nor the West German leadership could be fully convinced that such an apparent indiscretion was not without its purpose.

Whatever one wished to make of Cherniavskiy's comment, unqualified Soviet justification of the Berlin Wall had begun to recede quietly. In fact, according to Falin, during this period both Gorbachev and his adviser Yakovlev had confronted East Germany's leaders with their opinion that the Berlin Wall did not represent "a pleasant decoration of the city" but rather a "tragic tribute" to the past.[119] Honecker splenetically responded with his declaration that the Berlin Wall would still be in place in "50 or 100 years."[120]

Another Soviet expert on Germany, Vyacheslav Dashichev, also played an important role in shaping the new Soviet concept of German policy. In an interview with the West German weekly *Der Spiegel*, published in the summer of 1988, Dashichev drew heat from the Honecker regime for speculating that greater "trust between the socialist and capitalist states of Europe" would bring a rapprochement between "social structures," which in turn might produce "closer interaction between the two German states, in whatever form."[121] *Neues Deutschland* subsequently pointed out how Dashichev's remarks were misinterpreted and manipulated by reactionary circles in the West, which insisted on believing the fiction of a rift between East Berlin and its Soviet patron.[122] But Dashichev's fascination with the dynamism of the West German economy, and its importance both as a model[123] and as an engine for Soviet *perestroika*, led to remarkable conclusions about the GDR's position in the Socialist community.

In April 1989 Dashichev produced a stunning report in which he concluded that the GDR had lost its competition with the Federal Republic. Dashichev, who had spent two years as a visiting professor at the University of Dortmund in West Germany, credited the West German political elite for having correctly concluded that the "economic, scientific-technological, and intellectual progress of a society" is not possible without "democracy based on the rule of law" and the "market economy."[124] In his comparative observations, Dashichev spared little in his unfettered praise of Bonn's capitalist republic:

> The regulating role of the state was sensibly restricted. The strict centralization of political power was subordinated to the principle of political pluralism, reflected in the federal system. . . . Thanks to this came the economic miracle of the FRG in the 1960s and 1970s. [This society] allowed the full use of the scientific-technological and information revolution to create an atmosphere and standard of living, which made the majority of the population politically and socially entirely content.[125]

Dashichev went to lengths to emphasize that the GDR had been outpaced by the Federal Republic not only in "standard of living, social security, development of democratic institutions, the rights and freedoms of [its citizens], but also in the possibility for further dynamic development."[126] Further, he ominously predicted that without reforms in the GDR the economic and technological gap between East and West Germany would only grow greater and that the "social and political situation in the GDR [would become] more complicated, [and] the German Question more urgent."[127]

At a press conference at the Soviet Embassy in Bonn in 1988, Dashichev had referred to the Berlin Wall as "a relic of the Cold War," whose presence "damages the existence and psychology of people."[128] While the Kremlin was certain to have gathered Dashichev's observations for careful study, the GDR reacted angrily with a ban on travel to East Germany for the Soviet foreign policy pundit. Perhaps most pivotal—and most disturbing—of all in Dashichev's study was his conclusion that the "complicated" triangular relationship among the USSR, the Federal Republic, and the GDR prevented the Soviet Union from "effectively realizing the national interests of our country."[129] The way out was reform for the GDR, which, in Dashichev's view, could be achieved with the help of West Germany's political elite, a group that had, in the author's judgment, no interest in destabilizing the GDR. The result might be "a confederation of the two German states . . . or [eventually] a unification under conditions of guaranteed security for all the countries of Europe."[130] Specifically, a reformed East German Communist party and the West German Social Democrats (the largest Social Democratic party of Western Europe, as Dashichev noted) would find a "historic opportunity" to unite in the service of "very similar objectives and ideals."[131]

When Gorbachev traveled to Bonn in mid-June 1989, Soviet–West German rapprochement reached dizzying new heights. The Soviet press was aglow. While *Moscow News* dwelt on the importance of the generational affinity between Gorbachev and Kohl,[132] even *Pravda*, the one-time refuge of Soviet hard-liners, had begun to speak of the West German republic in warm, conciliatory tones. "Times have changed," wrote one correspondent just weeks before Gorbachev's visit, as Chancellor Kohl had begun to speak "with growing interest and respect about restructuring, glasnost, and openness in the USSR." "Relations with the USSR," observed the Soviet paper, "have gradually become 'central' to Bonn."[133]

As Michael J. Sodaro points out, Gorbachev's summer trip to Bonn came at a critical time, when the pace of the bloc's democratization was intensifying and Communist ideology was under fire around the globe. On May 25, the Congress of People's Deputies, pressing forth with its reform agenda, held its opening session in Moscow. In early June, Gorbachev visited Beijing, the site of the bloody crackdown at Tiananmen Square. The Hungarian Communist party announced its intention to hold multiparty elections, while in Poland non-Communist candidates won landslide victories in partially free elections on June 4.[134]

To pave the way for the Gorbachev visit, Kohl's friend and personal adviser, Alfred Herrhausen, chairman of Deutsche Bank, had traveled to Moscow at the beginning of June. Under the auspices of Politburo member Yakovlev, Herrhausen met with Soviet officials to discuss ways of improving Soviet–West German economic cooperation.[135] Although trade with the Soviet Union still represented less than 2 percent of West Germany's total trade, the relationship was improving. Exports to the Soviet Union rose by 36 percent in value in the first quarter of 1989; imports went up 12 percent.[136] In addition, larger firms such as Siemens and Daimler-Benz and more than fifty mid-sized companies announced their involvement in joint ventures during this period.[137]

Economic interests appeared to have paved the way for improved political ties. In a Soviet–West German joint declaration issued during Gorbachev's visit to Bonn, the Soviet leader and his West German counterpart lamented the fact that the European "continent had been divided for decades" and declared it "their paramount objective to contribute toward overcoming the division of Europe." While the German question was not addressed (nor even more specifics like the question of free elections for East Germany), the communiqué referred to the "right of all peoples and states" to self-determination, in full accordance with "international law in domestic and international politics."[138] In an article published in *Der Spiegel* just before Gorbachev's trip to Bonn, Portugalov wrote that "nothing speaks against pushing ahead construction of the central part of the common European home more quickly—in other words, in central Europe. Without infringing on the interests of the other 'tenants,' this could take into account the concerns of the two German states—that is, of all Germans in Europe."[139]

Gorbachev had never given up on his German Socialist ally. (In fact, under Gorbachev, responsibility for the GDR had been moved from the German division—where the affairs of the Federal Republic and other German-language–speaking countries were handled—to the department for European Socialist states.) Gorbachev reportedly assured his West German interlocutors during his June visit to Bonn that Honecker would "start to move soon."[140] But the Soviet leader sought nothing other than the legitimization of East Germany's Socialist system. Later in the wake of the euphoria surrounding the opening of East Germany's border in November 1989, Gorbachev would in fact emphatically declare that "reunification is not on the agenda," warning against the "patronizing and know-it-all attitudes" in the West of those who contended that "socialism has failed [and] that we should take over other models."[141]

Portugalov's comments about the unity of the German nation were instructive in this regard. While he promulgated the view that a single German nation endured, Portugalov constantly stressed the need to respect the "reality" that two German states of different social orders existed side by side in the heart of Europe. Just days following the collapse of the Berlin Wall on November 9, 1989, Portugalov himself emphasized his belief that although there was no GDR nationality, he did not "believe in reunification." "I proceed from the fact," he wrote, "that socialism is not negotiable for most GDR citizens."[142]

Again in a November 17 interview in *Frankfurter Allgemeine Zeitung*, Portugalov expressed his pleasure that "the breezes of perestroika [had finally] reached the GDR." The East German upheaval represented, in Portugalov's view, "a crisis of the administrative command system in its GDR incarnation. . . . [but] by no means a crisis of socialism. . . . The majority of the GDR population are not willing to put humane socialism, reform socialism, if you like, up to disposition." Portugalov added that reunification, at least for the "foreseeable future . . . is incompatible with the geopolitical and geostrategic requirements of stability."[143] In December, Portugalov continued to insist that, while a confederation to maximize "economic, environmental, and cultural" cooperation between Bonn and East Berlin was highly desirable, "both Germanys [would] continue to exist as sovereign and equal states."[144]

4

Prelude to Upheaval

As Soviet experts on Germany were busy laying the theoretical basis for a shift in Soviet thinking, disputes between Moscow and East Berlin had begun to break out. Moscow's desire for East Germany to soften its approach to Bonn in the interest of greater détente implicitly demanded domestic liberalization of the GDR regime. But as Vladimir Tismaneanu put it, for East Germany's orthodox rulers "ideological relaxation [meant] erosion of legitimacy rather than popular acceptance,"[1] a prospect that seemed to elude the architects of Gorbachev's policy on Germany.

Between 1987 and 1989, as the Moscow–East Berlin conflict steadily grew in intensity, East German dissidents and reformers within the Communist party gained confidence. Thus by the fall of 1989, much of the regime's strength had been sapped, and crucial elements were converging to bring about a revolution both from above and from below.

Moscow versus East Berlin

High-ranking Soviet and East German officials (including Aleksandr Yakovlev and Valentin Falin on the Soviet side) meeting in Moscow in February 1990 acknowledged publicly for the first time that Moscow and East Berlin had been at odds because of the Soviet Union's movement toward new thinking in domestic and foreign policy under Gorbachev. In a report published in *Neues Deutschland*, Gregor Gysi, head of the Party of Democratic Socialism (the successor to the East German Communist party), observed that "after 1985, the relationship between the leaderships of the CPSU and the SED [East German

54

Communist party] showed ever more irritations."[2] This was putting it mildly.

Initial signs of friction between the Soviet leadership and the Honecker regime, although at first quite undramatic, were linked to the economy and were already visible when Gorbachev attended the Eleventh Party Congress in East Berlin in April 1986. The good news for East German leaders was that Gorbachev unambiguously affirmed that Moscow could not "imagine the future without the close cooperation" of the GDR.[3] East Germany's Communist party boss Honecker, however, who expressly refrained from mentioning the Soviet Union's reforms in his own speech, waited in vain for Gorbachev to champion East Germany as a model of Socialist economic progress and achievement.

For some years the GDR had been permitted to take credit as East Europe's premier economic success story. By mid-1986, though, Gorbachev's reformers may have come to regard East German innovations (such as the *Kombinate* or combines) as obsolete variations of the unsuccessful centralization they viewed with increasing skepticism.[4] In fact, under Gorbachev, managers of Soviet industry had begun to observe, certainly to the dismay of East German officials, that "the German comrades were faced with the same problems" as the Soviets themselves.[5] Soviet reformers doubtlessly understood that any success of the GDR economy was in large part due to the generous subsidy relationship the East German state enjoyed with its West German neighbor.[6]

Former Politburo member Günter Schabowski reports that Gorbachev and Honecker appeared to have built a "normal relationship" with each other until the Soviet leader asked at the Eleventh Party Congress: "Erich, why is it that you [and your comrades] do not discuss social-economic acceleration?" Honecker was incensed. The newcomer Gorbachev presumed to make suggestions for the GDR?

> Did he not know that since 1971 a comprehensive social program existed in the GDR? That there existed a unity between the GDR's social and economic policies? Why would Gorbachev encourage the GDR to embrace 'social-economic acceleration'? East Berlin would never presume to advise the Soviet Union to adopt GDR policies.[7]

Although Soviet reforms very soon became a frequent topic of discussion and debate at the various levels of the political apparatus below the Central Committee, according to Schabowski, "in the politburo the topic of Gorbachev was [henceforth] a taboo."[8]

Following the January Plenum of the Soviet Communist Party in

1987, Honecker directed Egon Krenz to analyze Gorbachev's speech on economic development, not, according to Krenz, because Honecker was interested in Gorbachev's remarks but because he was interested in finding out what Krenz thought of Gorbachev's agenda for reform.[9] Once the report had been prepared, Honecker's only reaction to his deputy (if Krenz's account is to be believed) was curt but revealing: "Industrious work. But I have doubts about what you have written— that Gorbachev's policies go back to Lenin."[10]

Honecker's claims notwithstanding, the GDR's economy was beginning to suffer acute problems. By many estimates, foreign trade had stagnated, and economic growth had stalled. In addition, according to some assessments, since the beginning of the decade the GDR had experienced an absolute decline in goods and services.[11] Economic difficulties were aggravated by the reduction in oil exports to East Germany from the Soviet Union since 1982. And after Gorbachev's arrival exports of lead, zinc, ammonia phosphate, cellulose, and other raw materials had been reduced as well, a fact Honecker was careful to point out.[12]

It was not long before dissatisfaction from East Germany's disgruntled workers made itself felt,[13] prompting the GDR press to concede at least minor economic difficulties, such as the ineffectiveness of the GDR's distribution system.[14] Nevertheless, the GDR regime held firm on its defense of the status quo. If problems in the economy indeed existed, they were aberrations that could be easily dealt with, in East Berlin's view, within the context of GDR-style socialism. Experimentation with features of the market economy remained out of the question. Otto Rheinhold, the Communist party theorist and rector of the Academy of Social Sciences of the party's Central Committee, explained the GDR's view on deviation from the tenets of Marxist-Leninist economic planning:

> In the world of socialism it has come about from time to time, unsuccessfully, that attempts have been made to guarantee the inseparable connection between economic and social policy through pricing or salary policies. The unity of economic and social policy cannot be achieved through the principles of the so-called market economy.[15]

In April 1987 an East German official for the first time publicly addressed the question of a GDR response to Soviet reforms. In a now famous interview in West Germany's largest circulation news weekly, *Stern*, Kurt Hager made clear that East Berlin had no interest in following the Soviet lead in *glasnost* and *perestroika*. A veteran of the Spanish Civil War and a long-time friend of Honecker, Hager was responsible for party ideology (culture and science) in the Politburo, where he had sat as a full voting member since 1963. When asked whether the East German Communist party would eventually emulate Soviet-style reforms in the GDR, Hager snapped: "Just because your neighbor puts up new wallpaper, does that mean you'd feel obliged to do the same?"[16] Gorbachev's indirect response to Hager's remark— that the Soviets were not merely changing wallpaper but were involved instead in the fundamental reconstruction of their home—reflected the seriousness with which Hager's comments were taken in Moscow.[17]

The East German regime was in no mood for outside disturbance or interference, certainly not from the Soviets, particularly if the reports in West Germany's tabloids were true that the aging Honecker was contemplating retirement following the attainment of his desperately sought-after goal—to be received in Bonn on an official visit as the GDR's head of state.[18] There were also rumors at this time that the virus of Soviet *glasnost* was beginning to infect the ruling *nomenklatura*. Twenty-four children of prominent GDR officials—including the nephew of the minister for state security, Erich Mielke—were said to have expressed a desire to emigrate to the Federal Republic.[19]

The East German Communists held course. Honecker's wife Margot, a Central Committee member and GDR minister of education, called for stiff resistance to any and all attempts at tampering with existing socialism in the GDR. In a speech to young pioneer leaders in Dresden, Mrs. Honecker called for a renewed commitment to "socialist patriotism," consisting of tireless work in the party, "without ifs and buts for the GDR fatherland." The great tasks set before GDR society could never be tackled, in her words, "without a firm socialist awareness, without an unshakable class standpoint." Her husband followed up, remarking specifically on Soviet reform in an interview with a Danish newspaper. It was not the case, according to Honecker, that the GDR no longer had anything to learn from the Soviet Union. All Socialist countries continued to learn from each other. But there was no such thing, in Honecker's view, as a "prescription" or "model" that one country would copy from another.[20]

Recognizing the unique opportunity offered them by Gorbachev's new thinking, East German dissidents pushed their agenda with ever-increasing confidence. In 1987, as public protests became more frequent, so too did the presence of "Carry on Gorby" signs and the like. Church groups began delivering appeals for assistance to the Soviet Embassy in East Berlin addressed to the Kremlin leader.[21] In June of that year, when East German police forcibly dispersed hundreds of rock fans crowded near the Brandenburg Gate to hear music from a concert on the west side of the Berlin Wall, youths began singing the "Internationale," shouting "Die Mauer muss weg" (The wall must go) and chanting Gorbachev's name.

When in November 1987 police stormed the rectory of East Berlin's Zion Church to confiscate underground publications,[22] *Neues Deutschland* carefully assigned blame for the incident to "fascist hooligans . . . controlled from West Berlin."[23] But much of the impetus for East German dissident action now clearly stemmed from the East, not the West. Some members of the Politburo, themselves sympathetic to the Gorbachev line, reportedly argued that the Stasi raid on the environmental library at the Zion Church had only caused greater social tension at home, while generating damaging negative headlines in the West.[24]

The party's vigilance did not taper, however. Two months after the police action at the Zion Church, dozens of dissidents were arrested in January when they attempted to join an official march in East Berlin commemorating German Communists Rosa Luxemburg and Karl Liebknecht. Again the Communist party daily published an article accusing the West, specifically "imperialist intelligence agencies . . . connected with antisocialist centers and forces in the FRG" of trying to organize "a so-called opposition" inside the GDR.[25] But at this time the GDR's authentic, indigenous dissident movement seemed more interested in support from Moscow than from Bonn.

In the wake of a wave of censorship of Protestant church newspapers in early 1988, GDR clergy, often citing Gorbachev's reforms as their model, insisted on continuing their own appeals for liberalization. Manfred Stolpe, president of the East Berlin Church Consistory, sought to ensure that the church's desire to fulfill "its responsibility in its entirety" was "not in conflict with the state."[26] The regime was not persuaded, however. According to Günter Mittag, Politburo member and minister of economics (reportedly Honecker's closest friend and adviser in the Communist leadership), the church was clearly overstepping its bounds.[27]

In March, while the Conference on Security and Cooperation in Europe (CSCE) was meeting in Vienna, East German oppositionists took their efforts abroad, joining dissidents from Poland, Hungary, Czechoslovakia, and the Soviet Union in an appeal for conscientious objector status in their countries.[28] That GDR citizens were now coordinating their efforts with dissidents elsewhere in the bloc was a particularly disturbing development for the Honecker regime and orthodox rulers elsewhere in the bloc.

Honecker was no longer able to conceal his displeasure with the Soviet leadership. At the GDR's annual international trade fair in Leipzig in September 1988, the East German leader snubbed the USSR's delegation, creating a painfully amusing embarrassment. The GDR daily *Sächsisches Tagesblatt* reported that Honecker "took the floor" at the Soviet pavilion to deliver his customary remarks when, in fact, the East German leader had refused to speak following remarks by the head of the Soviet delegation who pleaded for "new political thinking" throughout the Socialist world.[29]

East Berlin increased its state of ideological vigilance throughout 1988. A number of those associated with the January protest in East Berlin were (many actually against their will) expelled to the West in an attempt to dissipate the opposition leadership. In a search for its own scapegoats, some criticism within the Communist party was directed at Eberhard Aurich, the forty-one-year-old head of the Free German Youth. Aurich was an easy target to blame for what was generally viewed in leadership circles as disorderly and unruly behavior among the GDR's youth.[30] GDR officials also stepped up censorship of the presses of other Socialist countries, Gorbachev's Soviet Union at the top of the list.

There was a particularly rich irony to this reaction. With the exception of the GDR's southeastern corner around Dresden (colloquially known as the "valley of the unknowing"), some 85 percent of the East German populace could follow the progress of Gorbachev's reform movement in great and textured detail every day via West German television. Nevertheless, this access to the news did not stop GDR officials from busying themselves futilely with the careful editing of speeches and articles by Soviet and other East bloc reformers before dissemination inside East Germany.

When, for example, in May 1988 János Kádár was ousted in Hungary after thirty-two years as Communist party chief, the GDR media paid scant attention to the transition, offering virtually no commentary. The East German press failed altogether to report that eight of thirteen Politburo members had been replaced (new members were simply listed without comment) and that the 108-member Central Committee had accepted 33 new members.[31] In June censors shifted their sights to the remarks of West German Foreign Minister Hans-Dietrich Genscher, who sought to make the most of the new atmosphere in the bloc generated by Kremlin reformers. *Neues Deutschland* insisted on striking offending passages from Genscher's speech at a conference in Potsdam, with references to the "German nation," human rights, the Berlin Wall, and travel restrictions among the casualties.[32]

Still, Moscow remained Honecker's worst problem, not Bonn. The catalyst of the first East German–Soviet dispute of serious consequence came in October 1988 with the appearance of an issue of *Sputnik*, a German-language monthly digest of the Soviet press. The issue of

Sputnik in question featured a historical essay that raised questions about German Communist culpability for Hitler's rise to power. This accusation, according to astonished editors at *Neues Deutschland*, was usually heard from quite a different end of the political spectrum.[33] In grappling with this aspect of the legacy of Stalinism, the article posited the following thesis. "The German Communists," wrote the author, "refused to join the Social Democrats in their struggle against Hitler. Had they done so, Hitler would not have been able to win the *Reichstag* elections and European history probably would have run a very different course."[34]

Although ultimate responsibility for the stance of the German Communist party in 1932 rested with Stalin, this postulate regarding German Communist complicity in Hitler's success struck a nerve in the GDR's regime, which drew on a purported tradition of antifascism as a central source of its moral legitimacy. The situation was undoubtedly exacerbated by the fact that Honecker and his associate Hermann Axen were veterans of Nazi prisons and concentration camps. Both men were reportedly irate over this unsolicited Soviet commentary on the history of the German Communists during the Hitler period. Almost in anticipation of this controversy, party ideologist Kurt Hager had already stated that the East German Communists "saw no reason to undertake a search for 'blank spots' in official history." Hager referred specifically to the alleged "errors" of the German Communist party during the Weimar Republic, a topic that in his view had already been sufficiently analyzed by party historians.[35] But now the topic was being reopened by the GDR's patron.

Neues Deutschland was quick to indict the Soviet publication for its "historically false analysis." Then in an unprecedented move the East German regime imposed a ban on *Sputnik*—reportedly on Honecker's personal orders[36]—making the gravity of the situation from East Berlin's point of view abundantly clear. As far as the East Germans were concerned, *Sputnik* no longer fulfilled its purpose, to "strengthen German–Soviet friendship."[37]

This was not the first time East Germany had banned dissident voices from the fraternal presses of other Socialist countries. During the Prague Spring of 1968, East Berlin interrupted delivery of *Volkszeitung*, a German-language weekly from Czechoslovakia. With the advent of Solidarity in Poland in the 1970s, the GDR blocked circulation of the German-language supplement to the Warsaw daily, *Zycie Warszawy*.[38] And as previously mentioned, articles and speeches by Soviet and other East bloc officials during the Gorbachev era had been carefully edited by GDR censors before their release inside East Germany. The case of *Sputnik*, however, was the first instance the GDR had banned a Soviet publication outright. The *Sputnik* decision proved enormously important, not only as a catalyst for open dispute between East Berlin and Moscow but also for dissent within the GDR.

The fact that East Berlin now openly viewed information from and about the Soviet Union as heretical propaganda angered and, at the same time, darkly delighted many East Germans. After all, had they not always been taught that "to learn from the Soviets is to learn victory"? A new, unprecedented hunger for information from Soviet sources led to the extraordinary and ironic twist that the GDR's well-disciplined border guards were now compelled to stand by helplessly and watch a new form of subversion—German-language editions of *Pravda* and *Moscow News*, "smuggled" from West Germany to meet the growing East German demand.[39]

East Berlin's ban on *Sputnik* was followed by a flurry of ideologically protective measures leveled against the Soviet Union. Initially, five Soviet films were withdrawn from GDR movie theaters.[40] Ironically, while the East German press launched a diatribe against Tengiz Abuladze's "Repentance" (a satire on the excesses of the Stalinist period), GDR citizens were still able to judge the much discussed Soviet film themselves on West German television.[41] In an even greater irony the film had been made in Georgia years earlier with the blessing of none other than Eduard Shevardnadze, first secretary of the Georgian Communist party at the time and now Gorbachev's ally for reform in Moscow.[42]

As if to punish the Soviets for their *Sputnik* transgressions, in December East Germany's Society for GDR-Soviet Friendship—the second-largest mass organization in the country after the Communist-led trade union—interrupted publication of its weekly magazine *Freie Welt* (with a circulation of 300,000), ostensibly because of a paper shortage.[43] Meanwhile, the Politburo's ideologist Kurt Hager took the offensive. Responding indirectly to those who insisted on looking to Moscow for inspiration in such uncertain times, Hager argued that East Germans "need not feel ashamed of our democracy. We have nothing to catch up to."[44]

Meanwhile, the East German Communists' own frustration with Soviet behavior became increasingly evident. "As if to mock" events in the Soviet Union, observed the *Wall Street Journal,* the East German party rehabilitated East Germany's Stalinist Walter Ulbricht, who had otherwise been erased from the Communist party's memory since Honecker assumed leadership in 1971.[45] Honecker himself, while carefully reaffirming the GDR's support for the policies of the Soviet Communist party in general, began to lash out publicly at specific byproducts of Moscow's new thinking. The rehabilitation of Stalin's enemies in the Soviet Union was, for example, according to Honecker, "the croaking of the petit bourgeois run wild."[46] In November 1988 Honecker staged a flashy summit in East Berlin with another Gorbachev nemesis, Romanian dictator Nicolae Ceausescu, who received the prestigious Karl Marx Order from the East German Communist general secretary.

After Christmas of that year East German demonstrators were again in the streets. This time the protests coincided with the meeting of the foreign ministers of the nations of the Conference on Security and Cooperation in Vienna. On January 15, the same day the CSCE accord was adopted, some 190 prodemocracy activists were arrested in Leipzig, while in neighboring Czechoslovakia an estimated 2,000 demonstrators in Prague were dispersed by police using water cannons, tear gas, and truncheons.[47] The GDR was not the only orthodox state under fire.

Still the GDR's attempted interdiction of undesirable Socialist influence did not let up. East German Communist theorist Otto Rheinhold acknowledged the growing "discussion among social scientists in socialist countries as to whether there are not in socialism differences in pace of development characterized by periods of stagnation and periods of basic restructuring prophecies." But Rheinhold unambiguously stated that "we reject such a concept." Addressing more specifically the issue of Gorbachev's reforms in the Soviet Union, Rheinhold rather boastfully argued that because the East German economy was far more successful than the Soviet economy, it had no need for renewal or restructuring. In addition, Rheinhold rejected out of hand recent claims by Hungarian authorities that unemployment should be accepted as an inevitable part of the reform process of Socialist economies.[48] The topic of *glasnost* remained wholly untouched.

Underscoring this point, the February issue of the Soviet German-language publication *Neue Zeit* was not permitted by East German censors to circulate in the GDR because it included an interview with Polish Solidarity leader Lech Walesa.[49] In the spring of 1989 the pace of GDR-Soviet conflict intensified. In March, GDR authorities refused to grant permission for an exhibition of work by an East German painter, Joachim Buhlmann, which was to be held on a Soviet military base near Potsdam. The exhibition, to which some 100 East German guests had been invited, was entitled "Glasnost and Perestroika in the Name of Gorbachev." Invitations to the event had been provocatively inscribed with the words: "Gorbachev, the messenger of hope, the liberator from fear."[50]

While East Berlin's regime moved to counter Soviet influence inside the GDR, the regime was taking action in Moscow as well to circumvent the undesirable effects of *glasnost*. During the spring of 1989, the GDR's Foreign Ministry decided to reshuffle the personnel at the Moscow Embassy for fear of unwanted influence by Soviet agents of *perestroika*.[51] At home the party later announced an attempt to cleanse itself by a thorough review of its 2.3 million members, with the declared intention of strengthening the "political, ideological, and organizational unity and solidarity" of the East German Communist party.[52]

In a quiet though public display of dissatisfaction with Moscow's behavior, on May 1 of that year *Neues Deutschland* celebrated international workers' day by publishing forty-nine political slogans in which for the first time the Soviet Union received no mention.[53] The GDR press continued to ignore the continuing roundtable talks in Warsaw between the Polish government and Solidarity. Nonetheless, the success of their Polish and Hungarian counterparts and particularly the Soviet tolerance of change in the bloc undoubtedly inspired East German dissidents to lodge formal protest with GDR authorities over the fraudulent local elections in East Germany on May 7, in which the Communists claimed 98.5 percent of the vote.

Such a disturbance remained a mere aberration for Honecker, who preferred to focus on the GDR's façade of security and achievement. As Politburo member Günther Schabowski later observed, Honecker quite literally "considered and understood [state-organized] parades like the 'May Day' festivity as actual reality." Since the official May Day activities "took place without 'extracurriculars'. . . . [Honecker believed this was] a convincing barometer to indicate the fundamental agreement with his . . . policies."[54]

Even if Honecker ignored the stranglehold that had come to embrace his GDR, others within the leadership found it increasingly difficult to deny trouble. During the summer of 1989 a series of dissident actions and repressive government counter-measures continued to heighten the tension in the country. In the words of one oppositionist, regular marches had begun to occur, but "police presence [was] so great I think we [were] always outnumbered by them."[55] On July 7, ZDF television of West Germany reported more than 1,000 members of the state security organs patrolling Alexander Square in East Berlin before the start of an announced demonstration. Once the demonstration began, participants were dispatched with violence. The ZDF crew was forced from the scene, their cameras sprayed with varnish by Stasi officers to prevent filming of the event.[56] Evidence of a showdown between the state and its citizens appeared imminent. Although reports of frustration among the Communist ranks suggested that the party apparatus was less than secure,[57] Egon Krenz's unqualified support of the Beijing regime following the massacre at Tiananmen Square in June suggested the leadership's enduring resolve.[58]

Against this backdrop the daunting challenge of Gorbachev's reform agenda was still pressing the Honecker regime for a response. In the beginning of June Gorbachev was scheduled to travel to Bonn. A visibly nervous Erich Honecker, fearful of collusion between his class enemy in Bonn and the Soviet reformer, was quick to request a meeting with the Kremlin chief before his meeting with West German officials. To Honecker's exasperation, Gorbachev was not able to schedule even a short visit in East Berlin on his way to Bonn but sent Foreign Minister Shevardnadze instead to extend the Kremlin's "brotherly regards" on June 9.[59] While Shevardnadze stopped in East Berlin to affirm the "fraternal and trusting nature" of Soviet–East German relations,[60] Gorbachev was on his way to Bonn where he reportedly assured his West German hosts in confidential talks that "Honecker will start to move soon."[61] For his part, the East German leader promptly announced his intention to visit Gorbachev in Moscow by the end of the month—an effort to set the record straight.

In addition to Gorbachev's alleged remarks concerning Honecker, the Soviet leader gave GDR officials other reasons during his Bonn visit to be attentive. Gorbachev's joint communiqué issued with Helmut Kohl in Bonn on June 13 stressed "the priority task . . . [of] overcoming the disunity of Europe," recognizing that this could be achieved only in the context of the "right of all peoples and states to freely determine their fate." For the West Germans and East Germans alike there could be no question that this statement represented an implicit reopening of the German question. Soviet Deputy Defense Minister General Valentin Varennikov made a far bolder, more explicit remark several weeks later when he told a BBC interviewer that German reunification was entirely "a matter for the German people."[62]

During the summer of 1989, the editors of *Moscow News* were involved in their own exploration of new thinking on Germany and the character of its division. A poll taken in July, but made public only in late November after the breach of the Berlin Wall, asked Muscovites if they believed that the fortified division of Berlin continued to contribute to peace and progress (the poll did not ask about stability) in Europe. Most respondents were unfavorably disposed toward Honecker's cherished "anti-fascist Defense Wall."[63]

Honecker's trip to the Soviet Union did little to mend deteriorating relations with the Kremlin. Rather than attempt conciliation with Soviet reformers, Honecker simply demonstrated his own obstinacy. In a June 29 speech at a rally in Magnitogorsk, the industrial city where he had once worked as an eager young Communist in 1931, the East German leader unambiguously expressed his complete satisfaction with existing socialism in the GDR. Amid the "current complicated international situation,"[64] the East German party would by no means consider "allow[ing] well-tried things to be changed." In Honecker's view, "The ideas of Karl Marx and Friedrich Engels [had] been honorably fulfilled in their native land." Thus Honecker claimed that

> as the result of a great process of revolutionary restructuring, the GDR today is a modern socialist state with developed industry, agriculture, science, and culture. It is marked by stability and dynamism, a high material and cultural living standard of the people, developed democracy and the rule of law, as well as social security for all.[65]

Upon Honecker's return to East Berlin, many within the party leadership realized that the desire to shield their state from the infection of reformist impulses in the bloc was becoming simply untenable. East Berlin had watched with dismay as Hungary rehabilitated Imre Nagy on June 18 (Nagy was the Hungarian leader executed by the Soviets after their 1956 invasion). The East German news service (ADN) did what it could to carry the ideological torch, berating the Nagy memorial services in Budapest for their subversive, anti-Communist character. That the services were attended by an estimated 250,000 people was serious enough. Far more distressing to GDR authorities was the attendance of the diplomatic delegation from Moscow at the reburial on June 16—an unofficial ceremony that did not require diplomatic presence.[66] Hungary was the source of still another problem. *Junge Welt*, the chief publication of East Germany's Communist youth organization, expressed its "serious concern" in early July over the Hungarian decision to allow Radio Free Europe to open an office in Budapest.[67] For its part, the Kremlin offered tacit support to liberalizing trends, wherever they occurred.

At a meeting attended by the seven Warsaw Pact nations in Bucharest on July 7–8, Gorbachev continued to champion diversity in the bloc. "Independent solutions of national problems" were to be, according to the Soviet leader, a new cornerstone of relations among Socialist countries.[68] A wary Honecker fell ill, suffering from gallstones and, perhaps fortuitously, was forced to return early to East Berlin. Krenz reports in his memoirs that, with the exception of the Romanian hosts, the GDR delegation had received an icy response from other participants at the Warsaw Pact meeting, many of whom actually sought to avoid their East German comrades during coffee breaks between meetings.[69]

Honecker's theorist Otto Rheinhold again affirmed the obvious, namely that an ideological split had indeed emerged within the bloc. Rheinhold wrote:

> In the Soviet Union and Hungary the idea exists that what are needed are great changes in conditions relating to property, a development of market relations, a broad development of socialist democracy, and competition in the hope that these changes will lead to faster development of science and technology and greater efficiency.[70]

But the regime insisted on the right of orthodox Communist states to pursue their own independent solutions to national problems. "The SED follows a different strategy," reiterated Rheinhold, "and with it some other socialist countries, for example the CPCZ [Communist party of Czechoslovakia]."[71]

At the end of July *Neues Deutschland* surprisingly published an interview with Hungary's reform-minded Communist leader Károly Grósz, a decision that may have suggested a grudging acceptance of the right of the Hungarians to follow their own unorthodox course.[72] Yet the GDR still rejected any deviation from its own course. In an article published in the party's theoretical journal, *Die Einheit*, Hager outlined East Germany's course for "socialism in the colors of the GDR."

Hager rejected experimentation with aspects of the market economy and in foreign policy ruled out anything but the traditional forms of peaceful coexistence with the "imperialist" West. He observed what he characterized as "strong reactionary trends" in West Germany, which were whipping up a dangerous "attack on socialism." He deplored the "imperialist countries" in general where the "legitimacy of the October Revolution is frankly disputed, socialism is described as a 'wrong track of history,' and counterrevolution is propagated."[73] Looking to the East, *Neues Deutschland* alluded to the proposals of some reform circles that would mean "in reality the elimination of the socialist system."[74]

Developments in Poland were continuing to unnerve GDR leaders. On August 11, the Solidarity-controlled Senate in Warsaw passed a resolution expressing "sorrow" over Poland's participation in the 1968 Prague invasion, a "violation," in the words of the Polish lawmakers, of Czechoslovakia's right to "self-determination."[75] On August 22, Polish premier-designate Tadeusz Mazowiecki bluntly told an Italian newspaper that Poland intended to move "from a communist system of ownership to capitalism."[76] Meanwhile, in the Soviet Union historical revisionism was still on the march. On August 18 Gorbachev's adviser Yakovlev admitted for the first time that there had been secret protocols to the 1939 Hitler-Stalin pact, a move that prompted GDR historians to rewrite their own history in this instance.

Soviet spokesmen constantly restated Moscow's policy of noninterference and the right of each Socialist country to pursue its own path. Yet the Soviets knew well that their reforms had found a strong constituency in the GDR. Pleasure in this awareness was evident when, for example, the editors of *Sputnik* responded to the GDR ban by printing a letter from a reader in Dresden: "By all means carry on in the same manner . . . the youth of the GDR is enthused about perestroika and glasnost."[77] In surveying the scope of reforms then under way Gorbachev confidently predicted during a visit to Paris in July that the "process of democratization" would soon spread to all of Eastern Europe.[78]

Indeed in considering the course of Socialist reform in the GDR, Gorbachev had several important constituencies inside the country itself: the Evangelical Church, whose clergy was to a large extent sympathetic to Gorbachev's concept of Socialist reform; the Marxist-oriented dissident movement sheltered by the church; and the country's leading dissident writers, artists, and academics, whose criticism operated, in the main, within the framework of improving, not rejecting communism. Finally, Gorbachev's most important ally was a clique of Communists within the party who had begun to express, whether out of conviction or opportunism, signs of their proreform sympathies as early as 1987. These groups provided the ingredients for what Soviet reformers presumed would be a Socialist revolution in the GDR.

East German Dissent and Kremlin Allies for Reform

The GDR's opposition movement paled in comparison with Solidarity in Poland or Charter 77, the human rights organization that had carved out a niche for itself in Czechoslovakia. This was in part, no doubt, because of the proficiency of the GDR's Ministry for State Security (Ministerium für Staatssicherheit, MfS) and its astonishingly well-crafted surveillance apparatus.

Under Erich Mielke, the elderly general and Politburo member in charge of state security since 1957, the MfS (colloquially known as the "Stasi") was staffed at its peak by at least 85,000 full-time employees who managed the thirty-nine departments headquartered in the massive office complex in the Normannenstrasse in East Berlin. In addition to its core staff, the Stasi empire included an estimated 109,000 active informers and 500,000 to 2 million part-time informers,[79] as well as over 2,000 properties, an arsenal of weapons, and a budget envied by even the best intelligence services in the West.[80]

In line with Mielke's conviction that "everyone is a potential security risk,"[81] the "Shield and Sword" of the party went to extraordinary lengths to ensure the integrity of the East German state against anti-Socialist subversion. Factories, offices, homes, restaurants, concert halls, gas stations, even confessionals in Catholic churches—no place was immune from the eyes and the ears of the Stasi. More than 2,000 staffers were employed full time to censor mail and another 1,500 to monitor telephone calls.[82] The Stasi maintained an estimated 4 million files on GDR citizens—about one-third of the state's adult population—with an additional 2 million files on citizens of the Federal Republic.[83]

By no means was the Stasi's unrelenting campaign to control and monitor dissent restricted to the territory of the GDR or to GDR citizens and their contacts. Following the imposition of martial law in Poland, the Stasi reportedly set up a surveillance network to monitor the activities of Catholic church authorities and Solidarity leaders. Impatient with the Polish security organs' attempts to contain the Solidarity virus, Honecker, it seems, had commissioned a special Stasi unit to work out of the East German Embassy in Warsaw and GDR consulates in Szczecin, Gdansk, and Wroctaw. At the same time Stasi officers deployed in the West were directed to provide information to the Polish secret police about Solidarity's organization and activity in West Germany, France, and Holland—Honecker wanted his Stasi to "show the Poles how it's done," according to one East German official. From 1985 on, Stasi activity was expanded in the East bloc to include Czechoslovakia, Hungary, and Bulgaria, where Stasi agents were assigned chiefly to observe the activities and contacts of GDR citizens abroad.[84]

The Evangelical Church. In this context of severe state-sponsored repression, dissidents managed to form organizational cells in the 1970s and 1980s. The core of East Germany's dissidents rallied around peace and environmental issues. Eschewing state-sponsored organizations, they frequently found shelter for their independent activities under the protective wing of the Lutheran or Evangelical church. With an estimated 5 million members and a formidable infrastructure (some 4,000 clergy in over 7,000 parishes),[85] the East German Evangelical Church had created a place for itself as the only quasi-autonomous social institution in the GDR. In this capacity the church was able to create a forum for open discussion and debate, particularly for the country's disenchanted youth.

A continuing dialogue between church and Communist party leaders in the early 1970s had supplanted the state's confrontational policies of the 1950s and 1960s, reflecting the Communist party's own interest in developing what it viewed as a necesary and constructive relationship. Although Ulbricht's rhetoric had always stressed the absence of contradictions between socialism and Christianity, only under Honecker did the regime begin to claim it had "erred" in neglecting for two decades the role of the church in the development of socialism.[86] Honecker's secretary for church affairs, Klaus Gysi, for example, spoke explicitly of a party strategy aimed at "gradually winning over [the church's] potential for the stable development of our society."[87]

In exchange for its limited autonomy, the church could fulfill, in the regime's view, two important functions. First, the moral authority of the church could help legitimate the East German state both at home and abroad. Second, the party recognized that the church's empathy with the social and political concerns of its members created the basis for a dialogue among church, state, and citizenry, which, if properly controlled, could serve as a useful vent for the country's socially discontented. The question of an alternative military service, disputes over paramilitary education in secondary schools, nuclear and environmental issues, and travel and emigration rights dominated the agenda of most church-sponsored "cultural" gatherings.

Not surprisingly, the church frequently found itself performing a delicate balancing act between co-optation and opposition. The church's own view of its position within GDR society was probably best characterized by the often cited formula of Bishop Albrecht Schönherr, the first chairman of the Federation of Evangelical Churches in East Germany. In 1971, anxious to strike a compromise of coexistence with the Communist state, Schönherr stated that the Evangelical Church leadership wished to see neither "a Church against socialism, nor a church alongside of socialism, but [rather] a church in socialism."[88] In defense of its independence and integrity, Thuringian Bishop Werner Leich later asserted in 1983 that "the Church [was] neither a camouflaged regime party nor a camouflaged opposition party."[89] Nevertheless, the church had certainly been granted its limited autonomy by the state by "oppos[ing] anything that might appear to destabilize the GDR or cast doubt on its international legitimacy."[90]

Many church leaders, considering themselves champions of humane socialism, made it known in the late 1980s that they felt more at ease with Mikhail Gorbachev's reform agenda than with the Federal Republic's system of democratic capitalism. Bishop Leich, in his role as chairman of the Conference of Evangelical Church Leadership, had assured Erich Honecker in March 1988 that his congregation "in no way intended to turn away from the forms of socialist society."[91] In

69

fact, even in his campaign for *glasnost* in the GDR media, Leich reminded Honecker of the problem when GDR citizens felt compelled to inform themselves of political events through the selective "negative reports" of West German TV and radio. It was evident, according to Leich, that many GDR citizens "confused [these reports] with reality and objectivity."[92]

The church's influence on the dissident movement it sheltered was not insignificant. Partly as a result of the Socialist-oriented atmosphere in church-sponsored forums, the GDR's political opposition developed a basically "loyalist approach," refusing to "challenge the legitimacy of the existing regime."[93] During the Gorbachev era church-sponsored forums frequently assumed an explicit political dimension, and church leaders and oppositionists became bolder than ever in their criticism of socialism in the GDR. In the summer of 1988 church congresses held in Halle and Rostock issued twenty theses for domestic policy renewal in the GDR—a direct response to the reformist impulses generated from inside the Soviet Union.[94] The regime responded by attempting to restrict the church's politically linked activities. On October 10, 1988, the Stasi temporarily detained 80 among some 200 activists in East Berlin protesting a wave of antichurch measures, including numerous arrests and censorship of church newspapers.[95]

Manfred Stolpe, president of the Federation of Evangelical Churches in the GDR, was probably the most important church official linked to the GDR's opposition. Born in Stettin, an attorney (not a theologian) by training, the fifty-two-year-old Stolpe had become a skillful diplomat, who, through his artful balancing between opposition and regime, enjoyed significant maneuvering room for his activity. "Whoever wants to get people out of prison," Stolpe once said in response to those who criticized his closeness to government officials, "must negotiate with the prison guards."[96]

Concerning his own political values, Stolpe appeared to share the ideals of those linked to the apparatus who worked and waited for a viable, reformed socialism. In 1987 Stolpe argued that political liberalization, including expanded travel opportunity for East Germans, would only strengthen the solidarity and "national identity" of the GDR's citizenry.[97] Stolpe proceeded from the premise, held by Soviet experts on Germany, Falin and Portugalov, that "the majority of the GDR citizens do not want a fusion with the capitalist FRG, but a better socialism."[98] In encouraging the regime to embrace *perestroika*, Stolpe insisted that the new impulses from the church were "not hostility to the state but friendliness to the state."[99]

In a June 1989 interview with *Frankfurter Allgemeine Zeitung*, Stolpe appealed for respect of the Helsinki process whose Final Act bound

Western signatories, including West Germany, to accept the "existing European community of states, including the two German states." He called for a reinterpretation of the preamble to Bonn's *Grundgesetz* (with its mandate for unity), "taking into account the all-European peace process and the West European unification in the spirit of partnership relations between the two German states."[100] As a Socialist-minded reformer, Stolpe later assumed a leading role as a political organizer for proponents of a "third way" during the East German revolution. In an August 1989 interview with West German television, Stolpe cautioned against "hasty changes" in the GDR, by "emulat[ing] Poland or Hungary." On the question of political opposition Stolpe counseled that "the existing structures must first be thoroughly examined to see whether they do not permit [an] exchange of conflicting opinions." "For the time being," said Stolpe, "we do not need any new structures."[101]

Curiously, Stolpe was quick to announce in late October 1989 that Honecker's successor, hard-liner Egon Krenz, who lasted scarcely six weeks, was "Gorbachev's candidate . . . capable of introducing glasnost and perestroika into the GDR."[102] Later Stolpe himself was rumored to be a candidate for Hans Modrow's reform Communist government, at one time for minister of church affairs, and at another time for the post of foreign minister. Not surprisingly, during the fall revolution Stolpe called for "a strategic plan for the future coexistence of the Germans in two states."[103]

Echoing the appeal of East Berlin–Brandenburg Bishop Gottfried Forck for a "democratic and socialist prospect in the GDR," Stolpe asserted that the East German state had reached "a critical moment . . . a great chance to further shape the country by means of a joint consensus."[104] Stolpe again called for Bonn to reinterpret the preamble of the Basic Law and cease "beat[ing] on the drum of reunification."[105] Bishop Leich, who shared Stolpe's belief in a separate East German national consciousness, similarly urged preservation of essential GDR values at this critical moment.[106]

Before he was elected governor of the new federal state of Brandenburg in October 1990, GDR advocate Stolpe was ironically invited to deliver a speech to the Bundestag on June 17—the "Day of German Unity."[107]

Peace, the Arts, and Academia. The loyalist approach of East Germany's opposition was also linked to the fact that an active group of East German Marxist intellectuals provided a significant portion of the movement's leadership. This coterie of painters, poets, writers, and academicians (a number of whom were present or former Communist party members) firmly advocated socialism's reform in East Germany, not its abandonment.

In October 1989 Jens Reich, a biologist by profession who had cofounded the independent political organization New Forum, alluded to the "left-wing" nature of the country's opposition. This bent, Reich observed, had much to do with the strong influence of the country's "intellectuals who [had never] abandon[ed] Marxism." Reich was one of the few to caution at the time that East Germany's "silent majority" did not identify with the leftist orientation of the country's proliferating opposition organizations.[108]

Marxism traditionally had a strong constituency in artistic and intellectual circles in East Germany. In the 1970s the most visible symbol of East German dissent was the poet and songwriter Wolf Biermann. Biermann had left Hamburg in 1953 to take up citizenship in the GDR to devote his life's work, in his words, "to the purpose of advancing the development of a socialist workers' democracy."[109] Nearly two decades later, during a West German concert tour in 1976, Biermann was accused by party officials of slandering the Socialist state and prevented from returning home to the GDR. Biermann became a hero to many East German Marxist dissenters who wished to remain in the GDR and work for change. In the weeks and months following his expulsion, a number of writers, artists, and church activists were jailed for protesting the state action against Biermann. Among those placed under house arrest for several weeks was Biermann's mentor, physicist Robert Havemann, who in a sense also served as mentor for an entire generation of Marxist intellectuals in the GDR.

From the time of his simultaneous expulsion from the party and dismissal from Humboldt University in East Berlin in 1964 until his death in 1982, Havemann had been perhaps the most articulate spokesman for reform socialism in the GDR. Havemann maintained that the flaw of Stalinism was not only the repressive domination and control of all critical and oppositional tendencies in society but also the structure of the Stalinist-style economy. "Economically," wrote Havemann, "the socialist revolution under Stalinism was only half complete."[110] According to Havemann, "the first phase, the attainment of power and the capture of power from the bourgeoisie" had been completed in the GDR.[111] But the means of production had not been transferred from the capitalists to the workers and farmers but rather to the state, with stifling consequences. Havemann praised Dubcek's 1968 liberalization programs and called for free speech and free expression in the GDR, principles that he ascribed to Rosa Luxemburg.

Havemann's critical views extended to the character of inter-German relations as well. His letter to Leonid Brezhnev before the Soviet leader's visit to West Germany in the fall of 1981 presaged the views of Gorbachev's advisers concerning a possible German confederation. Havemann wrote at the time:

> Originally, it seemed that through the partition [of Germany] a dangerous aggressor had been deprived of power for good and that peace in Europe was insured. The result, however, has been the opposite. . . . In this connection, it is opportune to recall that up until the 1960s the Soviet Union called for the demilitarization and neutralization of all of Germany. Now, 36 years after the end of the war, it has become an urgent necessity to conclude the peace treaties and to withdraw all occupation troops from both parts of Germany. . . . After this, it should be left up to the Germans to determine how we will solve our national problem.[112]

A voice of criticism still closer to the party apparatus in the 1970s was that of Rudolf Bahro. Bahro had been sentenced to eight years in prison in 1978 for his dissident tract *Die Alternative* (published in the West in 1977) but was permitted to emigrate to the Federal Republic the next year, where he later emerged as a leader of the West German Green party. Like Havemann, Bahro, who claimed that "communism is not only necessary [but] possible," became a source of moral authority and encouragement to a large portion of East Germany's Marxist dissidents.[113] In *Die Alternative* Bahro foreshadowed the Gorbachevian tenet that existing socialism had created a system of "organized irresponsibility" through the strict centralized monopolization of economic and political power. Only political liberalization and decentralization of economic power could revive society's creative and productive impulses.

During the first half of his life Bahro, a member of the East German Communist party since 1954, had pursued a career rather typical of a bright, aspiring apparatchik. Following philosophy studies at Humboldt University, he edited several newspapers, including the prestigious *Forum*, a publication of the party's youth arm, the *Freie Deutsche Jugend*. As political frictions began to emerge between him and his political superiors, Bahro was transferred into industry where the potential for ideological harm was thought to be less likely by party authorities. The 1968 Soviet invasion of Czechoslovakia, however, brought Bahro's complete break with the East German Communists and a disillusionment that eventually culminated in *Die Alternative*.

Many GDR dissidents drew on the foundation and inspiration provided by Biermann, Havemann, and Bahro. In the summer of 1986, a dissident group calling itself "Initiative for Peace and Human Rights" began publishing a bulletin—at first sporadically, later monthly—entitled *Grenzfall*. In 1987 another independent publication, *Umweltblätter*, appeared. *Grenzfall, Umweltblätter*, and a spate of other new underground publications aligned themselves with Gorbachev's rhetoric concerning openness, restructuring, and democratization. For the most part the GDR's *samizdat* showed little sympathy with or interest in the value system of democratic capitalism but rather championed the cause of "Socialist democracy" and a return to the ideals of mythologized Communist heroes. Thus one author of an article in *Grenzfall* wrote: "This state is a caricature of socialism. . . . [It] has nothing in common with the ideas and the struggle of revolutionary spirits like Rosa Luxemburg."[114]

In January 1988, at an official rally in remembrance of the murder of two founders of the German Communist party, Karl Liebknecht (1871–1919) and Rosa Luxemburg (1870–1919), East German dissidents prepared a counter-demonstration of a size unprecedented in recent GDR history. Hundreds of demonstrators carried banners with slogans calling for freedom of travel and Rosa Luxemburg's assertion that "freedom is only freedom for those who think differently." Many of the leaders of the march were not anti-Communists but Gorbachev sympathizers. Yet the East German Communists viewed strict ideological vigilance to be of utmost importance, especially at a time when "imperialism's" goal to liquidate socialism was said to remain firmly in place.[115] The Stasi moved swiftly, arresting scores of dissidents, many of whom never managed to leave their apartments on the day of the event. Some of the arrested demonstrators were *Ausreisewillige*, those who sought emigration. But many, and in particular the organizers, were dissidents who wished to remain in the GDR and work for change from within. It was at this core of would-be GDR reformers that the regime struck most vigorously, expelling dozens from the country.

Among those deported to West Germany were folk singer Stephan Krawczyk and his wife, theater producer Freya Klier, both immensely popular among East German youth and leading organizers of the demonstration. Krawczyk and Klier had both been warned just weeks before by GDR authorities that they would face criminal proceedings if they insisted on continuing their dissident activity.[116] As in the past, the party leaders believed that expulsion of chief troublemakers would deprive the country's timid and sporadic opposition of any cogent, organized leadership. The strategy had proved successful in the past. In the late 1970s a long list of GDR Marxist intellectuals who openly sympathized with Robert Havemann's work were forced to emigrate— all potential leaders of a GDR opposition. In 1987 the regime had expelled the prominent folk singer Sascha Anderson, who, like Krawczyk, had strong appeal with East Germany's youth. But in 1988 the numbers of open dissenters within the GDR intelligentsia had swelled, and opposition groups like Initiative for Peace and Human Rights were proliferating. "For each group the state destroys," observed one exile in the West at the time, "five more spring up in its place."[117]

For writer Stephan Hermlin, Gorbachev's policies were nothing less than "a second October revolution," a historical occurrence the GDR could not possibly ignore.[118] Born in 1915, Hermlin was a senior party loyalist among the GDR's intelligentsia (a member of the East German Communist party since 1947) who now had suddenly come to believe that a policy of "openness," long overdue in his own country, was essential to the strengthening of socialism. Hermlin himself had strong Stalinist roots, to be sure, although ironically it was he who had organized a cultural evening at the Academy of Arts in East Berlin in 1962 that included poetry by Wolf Biermann, an event that resulted in the first ban on performance of Biermann's work in the GDR.[119]

Like many others, Hermlin believed that time was now on Gorbachev's side, not Honecker's, and his conversion to liberalization undoubtedly had much to do with strong opportunistic impulses. According to Hermlin's assessment of the East German Communist party, not everyone in the leadership supported Honecker's rejection of Gorbachev's course.[120] His appeal to GDR citizens for "one to two years credit" in patience implied an expected change in course by the next Party Congress scheduled for spring 1991.[121] Hermlin was optimistic that, contrary to Honecker's personal assessment, the Berlin Wall might in the foreseeable future be rendered superfluous.[122] Yet Western democratic capitalism and unification were not on Hermlin's agenda.

Likewise for the painter and peace activist Bärbel Bohley, later a cofounder of the opposition group New Forum in 1989, preservation of the GDR remained the single hope for a viable socialism on German soil. Bohley had first become active in East Germany's dissident movement as a leader of Women for Peace, founded in the beginning of the decade primarily to seek the right of conscientious objection for women subject to draft in East Germany since 1982.[123] Bohley's work, however, also encompassed issues connected to the larger peace and human rights movement during the 1980s.

Bohley firmly rejected the idea that "the GDR should . . . follow the capitalist path." "We want the situation in the GDR to change," she told an interviewer in October 1989. "A permeable border—yes; freedom to travel—yes; but reunification—no."[124] It was her own personal tragedy, Bohley later mused, that "I did not want to go to the West—but that the West is now coming to me."[125] This sentiment was shared by novelist Christa Wolf. Expelled from the party over her protest of Biermann's expulsion, Wolf had received attention for, among other things, her advocacy of unilateral disarmament by the Warsaw Pact. In the fall of 1989, Wolf joined Bohley in appealing for a patient process of reform in East Germany that would circumvent unification by fostering a new "development of socialism" in the GDR.[126]

Another novelist, Stefan Heym, took the initiative to meet with reform Communist Prime Minister Hans Modrow in December 1989 to express his anxiety that the GDR's Socialist system was on the verge of disintegration. Days later, in Frankfurt am Main, Heym sharply criticized Helmut Kohl's ten-point plan for a German confederation, claiming that discussion of German unity could incite civil war–like disturbances in the GDR.[127]

In August 1989, against the backdrop of the burgeoning GDR refugee crisis in Hungary, the peace activist and Protestant minister from East Berlin Rainer Eppelmann—later minister of disarmament and defense in the GDR's elected government—demonstrated his own sympathy with reform socialism and the preservation of a separate East German state. He lamented, for example, the fact that so many people were leaving East Germany—the very people who, in his view, would be urgently needed for the GDR's restructuring in the coming years.[128] To underscore the GDR's sovereignty, Eppelmann signed a resolution with a group of civil rights activists and members of the Free Democratic party of Lower Saxony calling for "an independent and joint German identity." In Eppelmann's words such a resolution would affirm that while Germans "share the same history, language, and culture," they respect "the differences between the two countries."[129]

It is not clear to what extent opposition leaders—from church circles or the GDR's intelligentsia—who shared common cause actually cooperated with party reformers in the months before the East German revolution. Certainly the Stasi's guiding hand was always present in the opposition movement. Martin Kirchner, general secretary of East Germany's Christian Democratic party, had collaborated with the Stasi for at least fifteen years while serving as a member of the Lutheran Church High Consistory in Thuringia.[130] Other prominent casualties of Stasi affiliation from the opposition movement in 1989 and 1990 included Democratic Awakening leader Wolfgang Schnur and the Social Democrat's chairman Ibrahime Böhme, both forced to resign in the aftermath of the revolution. Even the leader of the East German Christian Democrats, Lothar de Maizière, who became the GDR's first elected prime minister in March 1990, was forced from office after allegations that he too had cooperated with the Stasi.

Regardless of the nature and scope of links between the East German Communists and the GDR opposition in the past, by the autumn of 1989 key dissident leaders had begun to work openly with party reformers who challenged the authority of the Honecker regime.

Reformers in the East German Communist Party. Despite the party's long-standing reputation as one of the most disciplined East bloc Communist parties, the phenomenon of internal dissent was not without precedent, nor was the phenomenon of Soviet links to party dissenters.

The nearly 1.3 million members in the East German Communist party by no means represented a political organization of unified opinion after its founding in 1946. Party historians later referred to a "process of ideological clarification" that took place after the creation of the party.[131] This process involved both the systematic attempt by party authorities to inculcate Marxist-Leninist values in its members and the eradication of any evident resistance within the party to Ulbricht's course.

While much of the party's so-called social democratic problem had been solved by the time of the GDR's founding in 1949, a dissident Communist faction nevertheless managed to remain. In the early 1950s, this faction centered around Minister of State Security Wilhelm Zaisser and the party's chief ideologist, Rudolf Herrnstadt. When Zaisser and Herrnstadt challenged Ulbricht's economic policies in 1953, they received explicit support from the Soviet representative to East Germany, Vladimir Semenov.

Semenov had met with East Berlin's Politburo in May 1953 to issue Moscow's orders for a new political course in the GDR. Ulbricht's rapid drive toward socialism—perhaps an attempt on his part to ward off any Soviet plans for overcoming Germany's division at the party's expense—had come under attack for its disruptive effects from the Zaisser and Herrnstadt faction.

Semenov was not the only Soviet official Ulbricht suspected of offering his rivals support. Lavrenti P. Beria, who as head of the KGB maintained close ties to Zaisser, was a far more dangerous threat in Ulbricht's eyes. Beria's dismissal in June 1953 following his abortive attempt to gain power in the Soviet Union strengthened Ulbricht's hand, however, while undermining the efforts of the Zaisser and Herrnstadt faction.[132]

Equally important to Ulbricht's survival was the fact that while Semenov and Beria were waiting for Zaisser and Herrnstadt to outmaneuver the East German leader,[133] the GDR's workers added a new factor to the power equation with their nationwide strikes in mid-June 1953. The country's civil unrest—partly a reaction to Ulbricht's policies of quickened industrialization and raised work norms—ironically may have helped Ulbricht save his job, as discussed earlier. Once order had been restored by the Soviets, Moscow appeared to believe that Ulbricht's removal at the time would have been viewed as a victory for the participants in the demonstrations.

As a result of this respite, Ulbricht won time and leverage to eliminate his main political rivals. At the Fifteenth Plenum of the Central Committee held in July, Zaisser and Herrnstadt were dismissed from the Central Committee and Politburo. Zaisser was released from his position as minister for state security; Herrnstadt was forced to relinquish his post as editor in chief of *Neues Deutschland*. A series of expulsions followed for a number of those who had sympathized with them. Within six months both leaders of the anti-Ulbricht faction were expelled from the party, as Ulbricht completed the final act of the purge.

Again in the late 1950s, this time influenced largely by the 1956 Hungarian uprising, another attempt occurred within the party to undermine Ulbricht's authority and moderate the party's course. During this period the reform-minded philosophy professor Wolfgang Harich, editor of the prestigious journal *Deutsche Zeitschrift für Philosophie*, enjoyed a close working relationship with several other important cultural functionaries in the party who shared his critical views of the rigid Stalinist system.

Their group sought, and may have in fact established, cooperative contacts with key Ulbricht rivals, including Politburo members Franz Dahlem, Fred Oelssner, Paul Merker, and Central Committee Secretary Paul Wandel.[134] In 1956 Manfred Hertwig, director of Aufbau Verlag (the GDR's chief publishing company) and economist Bernhard Steinberger (member of the Academy of Sciences) met together clandestinely with Harich in Harich's apartment to formulate an agenda for reform.[135]

The Harich group envisaged a "German path to socialism . . . a platform of Marxism-Leninism free from Stalinism, legally within the party."[136] Their plan purportedly encompassed the dismissal of the most important East German party officials linked to Ulbricht's Stalinist course, the restoration of "inner-party democracy," transformation of the *Volkskammer* into a democratic parliament, cessation of forced collectivization, and decentralization in management of the economy.[137] While Harich, Hertwig, and Steinberger were arrested for their activities and sentenced to lengthy prison terms in 1957 (as were others subsequently linked to the conspiracy), a power struggle reflecting this split in the party's thinking was played out at the highest level of the regime.

Led by Politburo member Karl Schirdewan (Central Committee

secretary responsible for cadre policy) party oppositionists wished to pursue reform by creating a "left-wing Marxist party which would have nothing in common with the Communist Party of the Stalinist type."[138] The Schirdewan oppositionists advocated a moderation of Ulbricht's economic policies and hoped to make conditions favorable for some form of German unity. As in the struggle against Ulbricht in 1953, the head of state security, Zaisser's successor, Ernst Wollweber, assisted the efforts of the opposition. As in the first case, Soviet support for the dissenters was evident. In fact, Nikita Khrushchev had assured Schirdewan of Soviet backing during his visit to Moscow following the Twentieth Party Congress of the CPSU with the caveat that the transition of power be implemented smoothly.[139]

But as Khrushchev's own power declined, so too did his ability and willingness to support the Schirdewan group. And one by one high-ranking East German Communists who had collaborated or sympathized with Schirdewan's faction were discredited and dismissed by Ulbricht. Schirdewan, Wollweber, and Wandel were expelled from the Central Committee; Oelssner left the Politburo; other minor officials were forced to recant (Kurt Hager, then a secretary of the Central Committee, later Honecker's chief ideologist, conceded his own mistakes in diverging from the party's orthodox course). Between March and June 1958 nearly a third of the party's chief functionaries connected with "opportunistic" and "revisionist" thinking at the district level had been removed through party elections.[140] The purge and subsequent power consolidation secured Ulbricht's position for the next decade.

At the end of the 1960s Ulbricht, plagued by economic problems at home, faced a foreign policy challenge from Willy Brandt's social-liberal coalition in Bonn. Although Brandt's *Ostpolitik* offered the GDR an opportunity to break out of its international isolation, of greater concern to Ulbricht was the threat it posed to East Germany's domestic stability. Moscow appeared less concerned. Frustrated by the East German regime's attempts to thwart the Kremlin's own efforts to benefit from Bonn's new policies, the Soviets intervened, with the help of Ulbricht rivals, to orchestrate a transition of power in May 1971.

Although Ulbricht's successor Erich Honecker stabilized the GDR's relations with Bonn and Moscow over the next years and maintained firm control of the party apparatus, signs of internal dissent again appeared by the end of the decade. The Final Act of the 1975 Conference on Security and Cooperation in Europe accord had heightened expectations for improvement in human rights among the GDR populace, for example. Moreover, the attractiveness and success of the liberalized Euro-Communist movement in Western Europe found resonance with a number of prominent East German Communists. In January 1978 (one year after the appearance of Rudolf Bahro's *Die Alternative*), an Alliance of Democratic Communists of Germany—purportedly a loose association of middle- and high-level party functionaries—published in *Der Spiegel* a "manifesto" representing the aspirations of oppositionists within the East German Communist party. (In retaliation government authorities closed *Der Spiegel*'s office in East Berlin.) The anonymously published text appealed for a "pluralistic communism," which would eliminate the principle of democratic centralism and implement free elections for an independent parliament.[141] In addition, the authors claimed dedication to unifying Germany under the joint leadership of Social Democrats, Socialists, and democratic Communists.

A minor disruption within the party leadership came later in 1985 when two Honecker rivals in the Politburo, Konrad Naumann (the party's chief executive for East Berlin) and Herbert Haeber (an expert on German policy), challenged Honecker's authority. Günter Schabowski reports that Honecker had been suspicious of Naumann and was particularly disturbed by his close relationship with the Soviet ambassador to East Berlin, Pyotr A. Abrassimov, whom Honecker did not trust.[142] Effortlessly, though, Honecker ejected both Naumann and Haeber from the Politburo as well as from the party.

At the Eleventh Party Congress in April 1986, Honecker resolidified his position, overseeing the promotion of four supporters to full Politburo membership and obtaining full Central Committee membership for three of his closet associates: Alexander Schalck-Golodkowski (who later managed GDR foreign trade), Günter Rettner (head of the FRG department in the party secretariat), and Ewald Molt (then the GDR's permanent representative to Bonn).[143] Nevertheless, the most serious internal challenge to Honecker's leadership lay just ahead.

The regime's ban on *Sputnik* of November 1988 had become a catalyst for oppositionist voices within the party. *Samizdat* literature reported at the time a wave of resignations from party membership over East Berlin's decision to ban the Soviet publication.[144] In the fall of 1988 GDR activist Werner Fischer, affiliated with the Initiative for Peace and Human Rights and a close friend of New Forum leader Bärbel Bohley, claimed acquaintance with "people in the apparatus . . . sympathetic to glasnost and perestroika."[145] Church official Manfred Stolpe even spoke explicitly of a "struggle inside the power apparatus," which, Stolpe predicted, would soon allow some things in the GDR to look "quite different."[146]

Dissident tones in prominent quarters within the Communist party had indeed emerged. Klaus Höpcke, the GDR's deputy minister of culture, criticized East Berlin's decision to ban *Sputnik*—a ban presumably issued on Honecker's personal orders. Although he later recanted and retracted his deviation from authorized policy, for a time Höpcke also lent his support to the imprisoned Czech dissident, playwright, and later president, Vaclav Havel. This was a turn of events. A decade earlier Höpcke had helped lead the charge in Honecker's crusade to crack down on dissidents in the GDR's cultural life. In 1980 he had denounced West German circles that, in Höpcke's view, worked to sabotage détente with their hostile contentions about the unity of German literature and culture.[147]

Party functionary Rolf Henrich, secretary of the Collegium of State Attorneys for the district of Frankfurt/Oder, caused a disruption as well with the 1989 publication in the West of his book *Der vormund-schaftliche Staat* (The guardian state), an unflinching critique of East German socialism. Born in 1944 in Magdeburg, Henrich had joined the Communist party in 1964. Until the publication of his proreform manifesto, he had credibly represented the party, leading the life of an ideal functionary—National People's Army, university education, attorney, party secretary, and medal of honor.

Henrich was a Marxist critic of GDR socialism in the tradition of Bahro and Havemann. The themes of *Der vormundschaftliche Staat* are purely Gorbachevian: the destruction of dogma, the empowerment of the individual, and the eradication of overextended oppressive bureaucracy. Henrich's proposed solutions to the GDR's problems reached into Gorbachev's arsenal of reform Communist methods. He supported in principle the idea of elections (although detail on the character of elections remained undiscussed) and openness in the press and other social institutions (though here, too, there are few specifics). Henrich's economic concept of a third way in economic life envisaged "free entrepreneurs" independent from the state but "who are not capitalists and do not wish to become such."[148]

In response to such developments the party initiated a campaign of internal vigilance. Höpcke was censured, and afterward he recanted; Henrich was dismissed, although surprisingly he was neither expelled from the GDR nor imprisoned (Egon Krenz claims to have intervened on Henrich's behalf).[149] The editor in chief of *Neues Deutschland*, Herbert Naumann, was replaced by Wolfgang Spickermann, presumably to charge the party paper with fresh ideological vigilance. In the summer of 1989, the party announced an effort to strengthen its "political, ideological, and organizational unity" by reviewing the 2.3 million members. (During the last such action in 1980 3,944 members were found unfit and expelled.)[150] But Honecker's authority, it appeared, was being weakened principally by a number of party opponents with close ties to Soviet reform circles.

Without question East Germany's renowned spymaster, Markus

Wolf, was the most unlikely and most important of East Germany's pro-Gorbachev Communists. Born on January 19, 1923, in Hechingen near Stuttgart, Wolf spent the Nazi years (1934–1945) with his parents in exile in Stalin's Soviet Union. After the war, Wolf returned to Germany, where he worked as a radio propagandist under the Soviet military administration in East Berlin. With the founding of the GDR in October 1949, he accepted an assignment with the new East German Foreign Service in Moscow. Wolf remained in the Soviet capital until 1952, when he returned to East Germany and became formally active in the GDR's espionage service.

Wolf served as East Germany's chief of foreign espionage from 1958 until his sudden and unexpected retirement in 1987. At sixty-four and reportedly in good health, Wolf was a youthful member of the East German party's gerontocracy. On February 6 *Neues Deutschland* devoted only a quiet, single sentence to Wolf—five years earlier warmly praised in the same pages on the occasion of his sixtieth birthday— noting that the general had stepped down "for his own personal reasons."[151] Wolf himself subsequently insisted his retirement was voluntary, a reflection of his desire to concentrate on writing a book about his deceased brother Konrad, an East German filmmaker. But a conflict with the Honecker regime over a proper response to Gorbachev's reforms was in fact the central source of Wolf's fall from grace.

Western intelligence sources have suggested that Wolf, prepared to throw in his lot with the Gorbachev course by late 1986, deliberately provoked Mielke into dismissing him.[152] According to one account, Mielke had forbidden Wolf to celebrate his wedding with his young Russian bride, Andrea, in a lavish, ostentatious manner. When he ignored Mielke's order (the wedding couple reportedly arrived in a white carriage for an extravagantly prepared fête), Wolf was suspended from office until his formal retirement could be announced three months later in February 1987.[153]

Wolf had always been a personal rival of Erich Mielke, the dour, elderly general who had served as the GDR's minister of state security since 1957. It was presumably because of Mielke that Wolf had been denied access to membership in the Politburo, a body Mielke had joined as a full member in 1976. A former officer of the GDR security service reported in his memoirs that "it was generally known within the MfS that minister Mielke always viewed . . . espionage chief Markus Wolf, despite his immense success, with a certain distrust."[154] For his part, Wolf's personal animosity toward Mielke was not concealed after the revolution. Although he was in fact the number two man in the security organization, Wolf resentfully denied he ever "deputized" under Mielke,[155] a man about whom "it's hard to find a good word to say."[156]

According to another account by a one-time Honecker adviser, Wolfgang Seiffert, the real provocation for Wolf's firing was a private meeting when the espionage chief "attempted to convince GDR defense minister Heinz Kessler . . . that one had, in some way, to take up the Gorbachev course in the GDR." "Factionalism," according to Günter Schabowksi, had always been in Honecker's eyes "the worst offense." Honecker had worked assiduously toward the "isolation of the individual politburo members," in Schabowski's words, creating an atmosphere of distrust that was so pervasive that one always feared that any candid discussion would be reported back to Honecker.[157] Indeed, Kessler refused to cooperate with Wolf, choosing instead to inform his friend Honecker of the espionage chief's disloyal behavior.[158]

Though he denies he was involved in any conspiratorial actions, Wolf has conceded that his house had become a gathering place for functionaries and "enraged" academics from Humboldt University. There they met to discuss "their concepts of modern socialism," which remained at the time completely unacceptable to the antireformist leaders in East Berlin.[159] In 1989, two years following his official retirement, Wolf first publicly began to reveal his sympathies for Gorbachev's reforms, which he characterized as "very important, very right and necessary" and, not least of all, fully applicable to the GDR.[160]

There is no mention of Gorbachev or Honecker in Wolf's 1989 book *Troika*—ostensibly the story of the author's brother Konrad and the evolution of his friendship with Viktor Fischer, an American, and a West Berliner named Lothar Wloch (the three had befriended one another during exile in Moscow). Nevertheless, *Troika* represented nothing other than a thinly veiled appeal for East Germany's emulation of Soviet new thinking.[161]

"Many attributes of socialism," wrote Wolf, "have become clear and recognized. [Yet] many decisive [qualities] remain to be proven in the *praxis*."[162] In tones reminiscent of Soviet Foreign Minister Shevardnadze's 1988 renunciation of class struggle, Wolf's characters in *Troika* eschew confrontation and embark on a search for reconciliation. Building new bridges between East and West is a major subtheme of the book.[163] In his artistic work the novel's protagonist, Koni, becomes intensely preoccupied with Gorbachevian themes such as the role of the individual in Socialist society and the need for greater tolerance and "transparency," that is, *glasnost*.[164] The author himself mused: "A little more courage for openness would certainly not hurt our cause."[165]

Wolf's role in the attempt to change the East German system from within was by no means restricted to literary theorizing. In a revealing interview with the *New York Times* two weeks after the fall of the Berlin Wall, Wolf implicitly conceded he had cooperated with the

Soviets in promoting East Germany's revolution from above, a "fight . . . to preserve socialism," in his words. "I was telling the Russians," Wolf reported, "we could still turn things around here in respect to glasnost and perestroika. . . . Even a half year ago there was still a chance for the party to take charge of these events. . . . But we were not able to act in time."[166]

A former acquaintance of Wolf's (a Nuremberg businessman who was sentenced to three years in prison for his contacts with the espionage chief) offered the following description of the most remarkable of East German Gorbachev enthusiasts: he was always "open-minded . . . the absolute opposite of a stubborn ideologist. But he always followed the party line 100 percent."[167] Without a doubt: and the party line Wolf chose to follow was Moscow's, not East Berlin's. Indeed, if the Soviet Union had sought support within the East German party to promote Gorbachev's new thinking, Wolf would have been the ideal candidate.

Mischa, as his friends call him, was a life-long, loyal Communist who had received his formative political training in the Soviet Union, the country he always treasured as his "second homeland." Honecker's former aide, Wolfgang Seiffert, speaks of Wolf's "double identity: German nationality, Soviet loyalty." A description of his brother Konrad's torn feelings in *Troika* may well have represented the author's own autobiographical reflections:

> Koni has his own problems. He is an officer in the Red Army and considers himself a citizen of the Soviet Union. At the same time, as the son of a German Communist and writer he is expected to see his future in the country in which he was born and where his parents live.[168]

Among East Germany's reform Communists, Wolf held a position of unparalleled power. In addition to Wolf's being able to offer the Soviets detailed assessment of the social climate inside the GDR, his relationship with Vladimir A. Kryuchkov, a wartime friend and Gorbachev's head of the KGB since October 1988, permitted him a unique view of what was happening inside the Kremlin. Wolf claims he had explicitly warned the East German Communist leadership of the dangers of rejecting reform and the possibility of unrest inside the GDR. In a January 1989 meeting with Honecker, which reportedly lasted more than an hour, Wolf asserts that he "bluntly" offered Honecker his assessment of the situation in the country: "If things go on like this, there will be an explosion."[169]

Reports from regional Stasi offices to headquarters presented a "precise portrayal" of the GDR's potential for internal unrest. And, according to Wolf, the dissatisfaction with the prevailing conditions in the country extended right to the top of the Ministry of State Security.[170] Mielke himself is said to have confronted Honecker with "critical" and "realistic" information about conditions in the country, reports that Honecker refused to take seriously.[171] Valentin Falin's assessment in August 1989—speculating on the probability of widespread unrest in the GDR—was certain to have been assisted by reports from Mielke at the time and influenced by Wolf's own characterization of the GDR's internal climate.

Wolf denies any personal involvement in what he later described as the "medieval conspiracy" that eventually toppled Honecker on October 18, 1989.[172] But it is unthinkable that Wolf was not well informed then about the developments inside the ruling apparatus. Later in November, during the process of revolution, he reportedly played a pivotal role in brokering the arrangements—through a series of meetings said to have taken place at the Soviet Embassy in East Berlin—for the transition of power from Honecker's successor, Egon Krenz, to the reform-minded Dresden party boss, Hans Modrow.

Modrow, who according to one Politburo member belonged to Wolf's close circle of friends,[173] had been viewed for nearly two years before the revolution as East Germany's most prominent reform-minded official (Wolf fondly described Modrow as his brother Konrad's friend in *Troika*). Like Wolf, Modrow was intensely enthusiastic about the Soviet Union (he, too, calls it his "second homeland"). In fact, at meetings of the Central Committee Honecker had chided Modrow at times for his penchant for "see[ing] everything only from the Soviet point of view."[174]

Modrow had first landed in the Soviet Union as a POW during the Second World War, though, in his own words, "during four and a half years of imprisonment, I never became homesick."[175] According to Modrow, it was in Stalin's Soviet Union that he "learned, grew, and became an independent personality."[176] Although his break with Stalinism took some time according to his own account, it later provided the basis for his personal aversion to Honecker, who, wrongfully in Modrow's view, had become the "central figure" in East German politics, "taking the place of the party."[177]

Modrow was born in 1928. He studied economics at Humboldt University, receiving a doctorate at the age of thirty-eight. His relatively modest life style during his tenure in Dresden (1973–1989), and his willingness to engage in dialogue with church leaders on social topics had won him the open respect of Evangelical officials in Dresden. For Bishops Johannes Hempel (Dresden) and Joachim Rogge (Görlitz), for example, Modrow represented a "reliable partner" who contributed "clear" thinking and perspective to politics in the GDR.[178]

As early as 1987 diplomats at the Soviet Embassy in East Berlin were circulating word that Modrow was considered favorably by Kremlin reform circles and was Gorbachev's candidate to replace Honecker eventually.[179] That same year, Soviet KGB Vice-Chairman Kryuchkov had visited Dresden, reportedly to discuss reform proposals with Professor Manfred von Ardenne, director of a prestigious institute for the social sciences. It is exceedingly unlikely that Modrow, the district's chief executive, would not have had contact with Kryuchkov at this time.[180]

Modrow's propensity for political openness was coupled with his fondness for experiments in economic reform. In May 1988 following a trip to China, Modrow could hardly conceal his fascination with Deng's reforms and the productive use of Western investment and technology.[181] In the summer of the next year, Modrow's apparent liberalism provoked the attention of the party's central authorities, who publicly reproached the sixty-one-year-old Saxon for his district's lack of ideological vigilance in combating anti-Socialist elements.

Some party insiders have speculated that Honecker had specifically seen to it that Modrow, who was never able to gain Politburo membership, had been left in "exile" in the provinces over the years, far from the center of power. During the weeks of revolution in the fall of 1989, however, Modrow's star rose rapidly. Elevated to the Politburo on November 8, he was appointed prime minister just five days later. Once in office, Modrow promptly offered Markus Wolf—rumored at one time to be a Soviet favorite to replace Oskar Fischer, the GDR's foreign minister—a position in the new government to revamp the country's security services.[182] Although Wolf declined, choosing to remain in the backgound, he did agree to serve as "an unofficial consultant" to his friend from Dresden. Wolf may well have offered his services to Modrow previously. Reports that the Stasi had monitored Modrow's proreform activities on orders from Honecker[183] led to speculation that Wolf had used his considerable influence to alert and protect Modrow during this time.[184]

If East Germany's political transformation was in the offing, the reformist, pro-Gorbachev allies Modrow and Wolf were well positioned and prepared to contribute. Wolf later asserted that it had been "the healthy nucleus in the party [which had] made a major contribution to the changes" in the GDR.[185] He called it the "tragedy of our development" that the various opposition forces, inside and outside the party, had not sought to cooperate, particularly after the introduction of *perestroika* in the Soviet Union.[186]

5

Revolution

On August 13, 1989, *Neues Deutschland* stubbornly insisted on cele-
brating with the regime's usual pomp and circumstance the twenty
eighth anniversary of the construction of the Berlin Wall. In foreign
policy, according to a lead article in the Communist party daily, the
wall had contributed to the peaceful coexistence between states of
differing social systems. It had paved the way for the Four Power
Agreement on Berlin (1971), the Basic Treaty between Bonn and East
Berlin (1972), and the Final Act of the Conference on Security and
Cooperation in Europe (CSCE, or the Helsinki Accords) signed in 1975,
which, in East Berlin's view, offered final legitimization of the postwar
borders in Europe.

In the domestic development of the German Democratic Republic,
the contribution made by Honecker's "anti-fascist defense wall" had
been decisive:

> For the GDR and its citizens the measures taken on August 13,
> 1961 have had a positive effect. Above all, [the measures] have
> brought peace, stability . . . security, [and] the continuation of
> socialist construction. . . . A decade after the conditions had
> been created . . . the VIII. party congress of the SED was able to
> introduce the phase of developed socialism in our country. For
> the well-being of the people, for the happiness of the nation, for
> the interests of the working class and all working people [the
> party congress] committed itself to unity of economic and social
> policy.[1]

Thus, by the Communists' own implicit admission, the "measures"
taken by the regime in August 1961 to seal in East Germans had in

fact provided the basis for the longevity and success of the GDR. In August 1989, members of the East German intelligentsia did not fail to add their homage to the wall and its apparent defensive character. Writer Stefan Heym posited the following in an interview on West German television:

> When I look at Mr. Schönhuber [leader of the right-wing Republikaner party in West Germany], and what is coming out of the brown abyss, which still remains there, and when I consider how this could spread, . . . then I think it's perhaps good that the GDR remains and the Wall protects a bit, so that one day a portion of Germany is still there to which Greens, Social Democrats and others may apply for asylum if they should be persecuted by fascists.[2]

Although the GDR itself continued to work diligently to control the movement of its citizens, its isolation from the West was being undermined by others during the summer of 1989. Some 200 miles south of Berlin, a gaping hole was being cut in the iron curtain. On May 2, Foreign Minister Gyula Horn of Hungary and his Austrian counterpart, Alois Mock, together clipped the first piece of Hungary's 150-mile, double barbed-wire fence with Austria. A modest action in itself, this initial crack in the East bloc's outer shell served as the catalyst for events that within weeks ignited a prodemocracy revolution in East Germany, a revolution that then swept through all of Eastern Europe.

East Germany, Czechoslovakia, and Romania were irate over this development in Hungary. Budapest's decision to open the Austro-Hungarian border directly threatened the internal security of these states, bent as they were on tightly controlling the movement of their citizens. It only added to their grievance that Gorbachev's adviser Valentin Falin could scarcely conceal his indifference to the concerns of the Soviet Union's orthodox Warsaw Pact allies. For Falin the opening of this portion of the iron curtain simply represented a "free decision of the Hungarian Government . . . a free choice of the Hungarian people," and nothing more.[3]

There can be little doubt, however, that Gorbachev and other Kremlin leaders understood the implication of Hungary's newly opened border, particularly for East Germany. No one had a better sense than Valentin Falin, for example, of the dissatisfaction prevailing within the GDR's populace. Falin knew as well that Hungary, long the favorite vacation destination of travel-frustrated East Germans, would be filled with thousands of restless citizens during the summer months. The chemistry for crisis, if not explosion, was evident.

By the beginning of August, at least 600 East Germans had crossed the border into Austria,[4] while several hundred others had taken refuge in West German diplomatic facilities in Budapest, Prague, and East Berlin. The numbers rose by the day. The possibility of any kind of refugee ordeal was an unsettling prospect for GDR authorities, particularly at this time. A record 44,263 East Germans, according to West German officials, had already emigrated to West Germany in the first six months of 1989. East Germany had always used selective emigration as a method of skimming disruptive elements from society, but the authorities believed it important for the state to remain in full control of this process. The emerging crisis was further complicated by the ill health of Honecker and the inability of the GDR leadership to act decisively. The elderly East German leader (he turned seventy-seven on August 25) had been forced to leave a Warsaw Pact summit meeting in Bucharest in July and had reportedly undergone surgery for the removal of gallstones on August 18.

As for Hungary, it felt itself squeezed into an uneasy position. On the one hand, as a member of the Warsaw Pact, bound by a twenty year old agreement with the GDR, Budapest's Communist regime was obliged to stop East German citizens attempting to leave for the West through Hungary. Officials in East Berlin frantically insisted that Hungary should honor its fraternal obligations to a Socialist neighbor, and, at least initially, the Hungarians seemed reluctant to disturb their bilateral relations with the GDR. On the other hand, though, as a recent signatory to the Geneva Convention on Refugees, Hungary was under pressure, particularly from West Germany, to accept responsibility for the East German citizens streaming south for access to the West.

A compromise of sorts at first resulted as Hungarian authorities approved the construction of refugee camps inside their country. But at the same time, to appease East German authorities, the Hungarians stamped the passports of GDR citizens turned back from the border after illegally attempting to leave the country (although frequently Hungarian border troops simply looked the other way as East Germans slipped into Austria). For those whose escape was blocked by border authorities, their stamped passports identified them as would-be escapees once back in East Germany. There, criminal conviction for the illegal attempt to flee could result in a prison sentence of up to eight years. Hungarian authorities also contributed a kind of passive assistance to the East German effort to stem the flow of refugees, remaining silent as scores of Stasi agents poured into Budapest and into towns and localities throughout the western Hungarian countryside. Often donning T-shirts and Bermuda shorts, Stasi agents sipped cool beers at campsites and local taverns, where they were able to pick up conspiratorial tidbits about GDR citizens planning to flee to the West.

From Sopron to Leipzig

Hungary's delicate balancing act became untenable. The temperature of East German–Hungarian resentment was raised a degree on August 19, when border guards gracefully stepped aside and in just several hours some 900 East Germans waltzed into Austria from the Pan-European Picnic (organized under the patronage of Otto von Habsburg and Hungarian Communist reformer Imre Pozsgay) near the town of Sopron. That Hungary was leaning westward was clear; the appeal of pleasing East Germany's rival, Bonn, was starkly evident. West Germany was, after all, the most important country in the new Europe that Hungary wished to join. A relic of sorrowful past ties, East Germany in contrast offered virtually nothing to command the attention of Hungarian authorities at this point. By the end of the month Budapest had acquiesced to pressure from Bonn—which held financial leverage over Budapest through credits and loans—to repeal the passport stamping policy.

On August 31, Foreign Minister Horn arrived at Schönefeld Airport in East Berlin in an unannounced visit to the GDR's foreign minister, Oskar Fischer. Officials in Budapest continued to hold that East Germany should lift this responsibility from the Hungarians by working directly with the Federal Republic to resolve the matter of the refugees. The same day that Horn was meeting with Fischer at East Berlin's Foreign Ministry, Hungary's minister of the interior, Istvan Horvath, expressed the hope in an interview on West German television that "an acceptable solution, conforming to Europeans' norms and culture" would be found soon. Horvath, in charge of the border facilities, stated bluntly that he found "the present situation at the country's borders highly unpleasant and inconvenient."[5] Although no agreements were announced between East Berlin and Budapest at this time, sources in the West German government claimed that Bonn, sidestepping negotiations with East Berlin, had already worked out a plan with Hungarian officials that would soon allow the free passage of East Germans through Hungary to the West.[6]

Pravda continued to offer unflagging support of the East German leadership during the August refugee crisis,[7] but statements attributed to Gorbachev's reform arm further undermined Honecker's position. Soviet officials, of course, persistently denied any rift between Moscow and East Berlin. Nicolae Portugalov adamantly refused to admit any attempt to "press the GDR to [emulate] reform according to the Soviet model."[8] Yet Falin, according to a report attributed to West Germany's intelligence service and published in *Die Welt*, was conceding at this very time the obvious: an unmistakable state of "alienation" between the East German regime and Gorbachev's leadership. While Falin insisted that the Brezhnev Doctrine of military intervention was dead, political influence from the Soviet side was not explicitly ruled out. Falin confirmed, for instance, that Soviet efforts to convince Honecker to implement even the smallest changes in the spirit of Moscow's reforms had to date continually "met with harsh rejection."[9]

Most damaging for the stability of the Honecker regime was Falin's speculation that widespread unrest could be expected by spring. Falin was certain to have been in close if indirect contact with Markus Wolf, who by his own accounts carefully briefed Soviet officials on the GDR's domestic mood during this period. Wolfgang Seiffert, a former economic adviser to Honecker living in West Germany, concurred with Falin's assessment of the gravity of the GDR's internal situation. "The many would-be emigrants [in Hungary]," Seiffert told an interviewer on Austrian television at the end of August, "[were] only the external sign of the internal crisis. . . . The GDR has slid into the most profound crisis of its existence."[10]

In spite of mounting evidence of widespread discontent and increasing agitation among the populace, Honecker insisted on holding course. At the end of September word of heated debates on the state of the economy at the East Berlin factory of Bergmann-Börsig became known, and Honecker and his confidant, the Minister of Economics Günter Mittag, asked Günter Schabowski for an evaluation of the problem. But when Schabowski tried to characterize the gravity of the situation, Honecker remained silent, while Mittag remarked that even back in June 1953 (the time of a workers' uprising) Bergmann-Börsig had shown distinct "counterrevolutionary tendencies."[11]

By the end of September, Soviet officials had already given the green light for a Western resolution of the refugee crisis—a devastating blow to Honecker's regime. Beginning in late August, the Soviets reportedly participated in discussions with Hungarian and West German officials to try to pave the way for East Germans to leave Hungary for the West.[12] It was, according to Western diplomats, a direct result of these three-way consultations that Foreign Minister Horn was able to announce on September 10 that Hungary would suspend a twenty-year-old agreement with East Germany that had required Hungarian authorities to block the passage of GDR citizens to the West. The Hungarian position had become clear. In Horn's words, the matter was simple: "Hungary could not afford economically to keep the East Germans here. Nor could we send them back."[13]

91

According to a *Washington Post* report, later confirmed by Hungarian officials, the actual decision to open the border for East Germans had been made in secret more than three weeks earlier.[14] Hungarian Prime Minister Miklos Nemeth later acknowledged he had met secretly with Chancellor Kohl in West Germany on August 24 to inform him of Hungary's decision to let the East Germans go. According to Nemeth's account, the talks with Kohl lasted two and a half hours and laid the foundation for a series of secret meetings that took place almost daily in Vienna between envoys of the two countries to iron out the diplomatic nuances of the arrangement. Foreign Minister Hans-Dietrich Genscher and Horn were also said to have taken part in the August meeting. Nemeth and Horn, according to the former Hungarian prime minister, flew to a U.S. military base near Cologne and from there were ferried by a West German military helicopter to Gymnich Castle, where their meeting took place.[15]

Nemeth avoided the question of explicit Soviet involvement in the process, stating at the time that Hungary had "taken a sovereign decision [and] the Soviets . . . [had] not said no."[16] He has acknowledged, however, that when Hungary first contemplated opening its border in early spring, the Soviet leadership was forthcoming with at least tacit approval and support. During his meeting in March with Gorbachev in Moscow, Nemeth claims the Soviet president assured him that Hungary was free to pursue its course and that East European opponents "would not move alone" to block Hungarian actions. East German officials were livid. The Soviets were sanctioning Hungary's decision. Equally stupefying was the fact that Hungary's government bypassed the country's ruling Communist party in making the decision to let the East Germans go.[17] Once the process to resolve the East German refugee crisis had already been set, Honecker made a final desperate appeal to Prime Minister Nemeth in a letter written from his hospital bed on September 4. He insisted that the Hungarians cooperate with East Berlin and prevent the East Germans from leaving Hungary.[18]

But Hungary's decision was announced, and an estimated 13,000 East Germans were permitted to leave Hungary for West Germany through Austria over the weekend of September 10. East German officials hoped that at least the crisis might then be defused. But waves of future refugees waited in the wings, their time still to come.

During these weeks the Soviet Union's support of Hungary's reformist regime coincided with a dramatic development in the bloc—Poland's formation of the first non-Communist government in Eastern Europe since World War II. Here too the Soviet reaction—and involvement—incensed authorities in East Berlin.

Poland's Solidarity had delivered Warsaw's Communists a humiliating defeat. They won 99 out of 100 freely contested seats in the Senate, and even many Communists who ran unopposed for seats in the lower house lost, as voters scratched out their names on the ballots. In its election commentary the Soviet government paper *Izvestiia* could make no excuses, calling the Solidarity victory an "unquestioned success."[19] But to make matters worse from East Berlin's perspective, as Solidarity was being frustrated by veiled threats from the Polish Communist party to block its admission to the government, Gorbachev intervened to the opposition's benefit. After a forty-minute telephone conversation between Gorbachev and the Polish Communist party's first secretary, Mieczyslaw Rakowski, the Polish Communists were persuaded to adopt a new position of "partnerlike cooperation" with Solidarity.[20] Thus events not only in Hungary but also in Poland were cornering East Germany into precarious isolation within the bloc.

During this same time, the coalescing leadership of East Germany's dissident movement had begun to mobilize its forces, exerting significant pressure on the regime. The chairman of East Germany's Federation of Evangelical Lutheran Churches, Bishop Werner Leich, in a sermon in Eisenach, explicitly called for the GDR leadership to begin far-reaching reforms.[21] Pressing their cause in the streets, an ever-increasing number of demonstrators showed themselves capable of challenging the authority of the Communist regime as seriously as the nationwide protests of 1953 had done. In agitated response, Communist chief executives from the districts of Erfurt, Schwerin, and Karl-Marx-Stadt declared that the GDR had entered a period "of the most severe class struggle."[22]

On September 10, the same day Hungary announced freedom of travel to East Germans within its borders, the GDR's first independent opposition group, New Forum, issued its founding document. Avoiding direct confrontation with Communist authorities, New Forum's leadership, dominated by Marxist intellectuals and former party members, called for dialogue to remedy the "disturbed relationship between state and society." New Forum was not, according to its founders, associated with "right-wing and anticommunist tendencies"[23] in the GDR and had no plans for the state's conversion to capitalism or reunification with the West.[24]

In its founding document, the group called upon GDR citizens to reject passivity and, according to Soviet form, begin "the restructuring of our society."[25] In the same spirit of power sharing taking place in Poland and Hungary, New Forum decided to file formal application to field its own candidates in eleven of fourteen electoral districts in parliamentary elections scheduled for May 1990.[26] Its petition coincided with an appeal by the Evangelical Church following a five-day national synod calling for introduction of a multiparty system in the GDR.[27]

East Germany's intransigent gerontocrats held their ground. On September 12, Yegor K. Ligachev, traveled to East Berlin, ostensibly to discuss agricultural matters, though in all likelihood to convince the Honecker regime that time was running out. If Gorbachev wished to have an emissary, Ligachev was perhaps one Soviet official Honecker might still listen to. The East German news service was pleased to report that Ligachev joined the regime in condemning West Germany's "defamation, enticement and lures" aimed at aggravating the refugee crisis.[28] Ligachev also lashed out at the Hungarians' behavior (while back in Moscow Gennadiy Gerasimov, the Foreign Ministry spokesman, merely referred to the "unusual" situation in Hungary).[29] In an interview with East German television, though, Ligachev offered his comrades in East Berlin—some of whom were still clinging to the hope they could outlast Gorbachev—what may have been interpreted as an implicit warning. Ligachev no longer doubted that the Gorbachev course was there to stay. The Kremlin official emphasized that the Soviet Union had no alternative to the policy of restructuring. "It is not a fad," said Ligachev, "but simply a necessity and a need."[30]

The Soviet Union was offering Honecker's regime, or so it appeared, a final opportunity for redemption: a last chance, as it were, to embrace the cause of *perestroika* before popular will and party reformers would sweep the country's old guard from power. Still, the Honecker regime, unmoved by mounting indications that it was losing the battle, continued to dig in. On September 15, citing the intention of West Germany's Social Democratic party to interfere in East German internal affairs, Horst Sindermann, president of the GDR Volkskammer, announced that the party delegation would be barred from a visit to East Berlin. The decision to withdraw the invitation to the West German Social Democrats underscored Honecker's obstinacy. It was, after all, the West German Socialists who had gone to lengths in recent years to legitimize the East German Communist regime. Even in the midst of the East German revolution, leading Social Democrats continued to reject unification, claiming instead that East German citizens would eventually exercise their right to self-determination by humanizing socialism in their country and retaining an independent state.

Meanwhile, GDR authorities moved to silence the voices of those considered by Communist reformers as constructive, even friendly oppositionists. On September 21, the East German Ministry of the Interior declared New Forum illegal, citing, despite some accommodating tones, the opposition group's hostility to the state and constitution. Bärbel Bohley, the painter, and Jutta Seidel, a dentist, both cofounders of New Forum, were later told by authorities that there was no "social need" for New Forum: a sufficient number of already existing organizations in the GDR could represent the social interests of the nation.[31] But former Communist party member Rolf Henrich, another cofounder of New Forum, remained convinced that a well-directed, proreform organization would eventually find political space in East Germany to work together with a reformed ruling Communist party.

For Henrich and other members of the New Forum leadership, it was a foregone conclusion that East Germany's reform would be rooted in socialism, not in capitalism.[32] Though she rejected attempts of the Communists to co-opt New Forum, Bärbel Bohley, a dedicated advocate of an independent GDR, later arrogantly criticized the government for breaching the Berlin Wall before East Germany had completed its internal political transformation.[33] For his part, Henrich argued that the Communist party would play a "decisive" role in the reform process and declared New Forum's readiness to "cooperate . . . in a friendly and constructive way."[34] Other members of the New Forum leadership saw themselves to the "right of the Socialist Unity Party . . . [though] ready for cooperation with the SED comrades."[35]

Of similar mind was the GDR's acting minister of culture and faithful follower of Gorbachev, Klaus Höpcke, who pushed for state tolerance of opposition groups like New Forum. Nor was Markus Wolf absent from the public scene at this critical time of transition. Wolf stepped up his public declarations in favor of reform and even attached himself to the New Forum movement, appearing on stage with the organization's members at public rallies.[36] New Forum never became a mere co-optation of the state, though this may well have been what Wolf and other Communist reformers had in mind. Nevertheless, New Forum was never able to establish itself as a viable political party. The widespread, virulent anticommunism that soon became evident in East Germany spoiled the hopes of a dominant wing of the New Forum leadership that reform socialism might be democratically implemented in the GDR. In fact in the March 18, 1990, elections New Forum, working in coalition with other Marxist-oriented reform groups, managed to attain only 2.9 percent of the electorate's support.[37]

On September 25, a wary, but recovering Honecker, who had not been seen in public since August 14, reappeared to receive credentials from new ambassadors from Zimbabwe and Turkey. His return to public life coincided with still further disruptions. The flow of refugees westward continued unabated—an estimated 100,000 by the end of

September. And large-scale demonstrations had now become commonplace in Honecker's once docile workers' and farmers' state. Perhaps most alarming for the authorities, discontent was not restricted to any particular segment of the society. In October Harry Tisch, head of the Communist party's labor union, conceded that increasing unrest among the country's 8.6 million workers could no longer be ignored.[38]

The founding of New Forum in mid-September 1989 had been followed by a stream of tiny, anti-Honecker opposition groups that formed throughout the autumn. Groups like United Left, Democracy Now, and Initiative for Peace and Human Rights rejected Honecker-style socialism but insisted on clinging to illusionary dreams of a reformed GDR (right-of-center Democratic Awakening was initially the only pro-unity opposition group).

These groups were not the only political organizations that offered East Germany's anti-Honecker forces a vehicle for operation. The old GDR bloc parties were now seeking to transform themselves from instruments of Communist party policy into independent democratic parties. The Christian Democratic Union jettisoned its leader Gerald Götting and replaced him with Lothar de Maizière, who later became the GDR's prime minister after the spring 1990 elections. The other parties followed suit in a scramble to stake out political territory, with the Liberal Democratic party of Germany, the National Democratic party of Germany, and the Democratic Farmers' party of Germany all severing ties to their former patron, the East German Communists.

Additional pressure mounted when some 5,000 GDR refugees camped on the grounds of West German Embassy facilities in Prague and Warsaw by the end of September. By month's end the number of those who had already safely reached West Germany had reached an estimated 110,000.[39] A meeting between West German Foreign Minister Genscher and Soviet Foreign Minister Shevardnadze (probably held on September 30) was reportedly instrumental in resolving this new stage of the refugee crisis.

Genscher is said to have pressed his concerns about the East Germans held up in the Czech and Polish embassies with his Soviet counterpart, who agreed that "something must happen." At this time Shevardnadze presumably consented to exert his influence.[40] Later the same day, East Berlin announced its willingness to allow the immediate departure to the West of what the GDR press still insisted on terming its country's "antisocial traitors and criminals."[41]

During the first days of October close to 14,000 East Germans boarded special trains destined for West Germany, though they were forced to travel first into the GDR, permitting Communist authorities the opportunity to expel their citizens formally. To prevent further disruption, East Germans, who hitherto had been free to travel to Czechoslovakia with only a personal identification card, were now blocked by authorities from visiting their neighbor to the south. In addition, according to reports in the West German press, Communist authorities were preparing to "fortify" the East German–Polish border, a new German wall now positioned in the East.[42] Ironically, the most potent threat to East Germany's Communist state was still to come, not, however, from those who fled or who wished to flee but from the angry, discontented millions who remained behind.

Gorbachev in East Berlin

In preparation for Gorbachev's visit to East Berlin for the celebration of the fortieth anniversary of the GDR, issuance of day visas for visitors from West Berlin came to a halt, and East German security organs went on special alert. Festivities planned for the weekend of October 6–8 would show the world that events of the past weeks were an aberration and that Honecker's ruling party was still in control. Honecker was determined to see that on this weekend nothing would mar recognition of the GDR's achievements. On October 4, under the watchful eyes of Stasi agents, representatives of New Forum, Democracy Now, Initiative for Peace and Human Rights, and other citizens' groups met in the Erlöser Church in East Berlin to discuss a common agenda for action. Specifically, they proposed in a joint communiqué that the GDR's next elections scheduled for the spring take place with the presence of a UN observers' team. The release of the proposal echoed widespread hope among the populace that Gorbachev's visit might finally bring about a change in East Germany's course.

Despite the lengthy and detailed security precautions taken by authorities, Gorbachev's visit unleashed evidence of increasingly virulent popular dissent. Officials made sure that Gorbachev himself was prevented from direct contact with demonstrators, but prodemocracy protests, whether in Dresden, Leipzig, Potsdam, or Jena, frequently invoking Gorbachev's name, demanded an immediate embrace of reform. Some 3,500 people nationwide were arrested or detained—over 1,000 in East Berlin alone.[43] In the capital itself, demonstrators gathered in front of the Palast der Republik, seat of the GDR parliament and a meeting place for Honecker and his guest Gorbachev, chanting prodemocracy slogans and urging the Soviet leader's intervention on their behalf.

When Gorbachev laid a wreath at the monument to the victims of fascism and militarism on the morning of October 6, he focused his attention on a group of anxious young East Germans whom he reportedly implored to be patient and not to panic.[44] While GDR citizens were carefully watching for signals from Gorbachev in East Berlin, Kremlin adviser Vadim Zagladin was asserting the inevitability of change at a press conference in Paris. Zagladin calmly predicted that "perestroika would reach each country in Eastern Europe sooner or later."[45]

As one of the Soviet Central Committee's chief West Europeanists, Zagladin had sided with the East German Communists in 1984 when the GDR was seeking to insulate its own détente with West Germany in spite of chills in superpower relations over the intermediate-range missile debate. Once again, Zagladin came down on the side of Soviet advocates of détente—this time, however, to the chagrin of East Berlin.[46] Nicolae Portugalov, the Soviet expert on Germany, was also among the Soviet delegates in Paris. He agreed with Zagladin that "perestroika [would] affect all the European socialist countries in one way or another and at different speeds." Although he was sure to insist that the Soviets had "decided not to interfere" in the GDR's affairs, Portugalov stressed that he meant "all" European Socialist countries, when he said no country would be immune from the impact of *perestroika*, including the GDR, Romania, and Bulgaria.[47]

Before Gorbachev's arrival in East Berlin, West Germany's tabloid *Bildzeitung* had reported that during his visit with the East German leadership the Soviet leader would propose a three-point plan for liberalization. The plan was said to include a call for greater independence of the four GDR bloc parties, relaxation of press censorship, and improved travel regulations.[48] According to other sources, Gorbachev actually told the GDR's Politburo during his October visit that he was aware that Honecker was trying to create a Berlin-Prague-Beijing axis but that plans for such an arrangement were thoroughly unacceptable[49] (at a dinner held in Gorbachev's honor, the East Germans placed the Soviet leader between Yasir Arafat and Nicolae Ceausescu).[50] In a report attributed to unnamed sources within the East German regime and filed with the West German daily *Die Welt*, the activities of the pro-Honecker wing of the party were already being severely crippled by cooperation between reform-minded officials from East Germany's districts (Bezirke), who enjoyed significant support from the GDR's Ministry of State Security and the Soviet intelligence service.[51]

Valentin Falin insisted that Moscow would not force anyone to accept its model of reform. The GDR remained, in Falin's words, "a sovereign state and [did] not need recommendations."[52] It is unclear whether Gorbachev made any direct attempt to push Honecker on the issue of reform when the two men met privately on the morning of October 7. When the entire Politburo convened later that same morning, Gorbachev refrained from criticizing the GDR. The founding of the GDR was "a turning point in Europe's history," he said, whose very "existence contributed to stability on the continent."[53] But when Gorbachev turned to comments on developments in the Soviet Union, by implication his message was clear:

> You comrades know we have great difficulties in the economic area, but we remain firmly committed to democracy, and we have of course learned from experience. One cannot overlook the signals of reality. Life itself punished those who react too late. We've learned this from our development.[54]

In reply to Gorbachev's statement, Honecker boasted of the GDR's manifold economic successes, avoiding even passing mention of the thousands of demonstrators now regularly protesting in favor of far-reaching reform. As Honecker concluded his remarks, Gorbachev sat silently, according to Politburo member Günter Schabowski, looking bewildered and almost amused, as if he wished to say, "Okay, comrades. Is there nothing further to discuss?"[55] Krenz observed that Gorbachev looked around the room to see just who had really understood his remarks. Honecker, though, clearly refused to witness the disintegration of his empire around him.

Although during his visit to East Berlin Gorbachev carefully avoided any direct public reference to East Germany's problems, his additional pleas for Honecker's regime to engage popular forces in dialogue and embark on reform were again unmistakable:

> We have no doubt that the Socialist Unity Party with all its intellectual potential, rich experience, and political authority is capable, in cooperation with all social forces, of finding answers to the questions which stand on the order of the day and concern its citizens.[56]

In the context of the country's spreading unrest, Gorbachev's demand that "the citizens themselves decide" whether to follow the Soviet course of reform could be understood only as an expression of empathy and encouragement for prodemocracy demonstrators and served as an implicit caution to East Berlin's orthodox regime.[57] More direct, according to Egon Krenz, was Gorbachev's parting remark, *"deistvuïte"* ("take action"), to a small group of "trusted East German comrades" at Schönefeld Airport in East Berlin.[58] Once in Moscow, the Soviet leader expressed with unfettered optimism his belief that events in the GDR would soon move in a direction of which he approved. Gorbachev claimed to have found in East Germany "many passionate supporters of perestroika."[59]

This same week the Hungarian Communist party moved ahead in its reform program, placing another crack in the East bloc's shell by announcing its intention to transform itself into a Socialist party that would bridge the gulf between traditional Marxism and European social democracy.[60] Honecker, still seemingly oblivious to the import of the developments around him and unmoved by the counsel of his Soviet benefactors, insisted that reform proposals that "lead to the weakening of socialism bear no fruit."[61] Soviet officials later told East German interlocutors that they were astonished at Honecker's failure to grasp the meaning of Gorbachev's visit to East Berlin.[62]

Confrontations with Protesters

On Monday, October 9, following Gorbachev's departure, Honecker met with a more ideologically sympathetic visitor, Chinese Vice Premier Yao Yilin, who could offer his own thoughts on how the GDR should meet the country's pressing problems. While East Germany's prodemocracy movement prepared for what had become a weekly event, a Monday demonstration in Leipzig, Honecker emerged from his meeting with Yao in East Berlin to compare the GDR's tense situation to the "counterrevolutionary" unrest in China the previous spring. Honecker ominously warned against any further "attempt[s] . . . to destabilize socialist construction or slander its achievements."[63]

Still reeling from the humiliation caused by the behavior of GDR citizens during Gorbachev's visit, Honecker reportedly authorized the use of force to suppress Monday night's demonstration in Leipzig. Many East Germans sensed that this Monday would be the long-awaited showdown with the regime that many had feared but anticipated. Although a number of pastors had warned their congregations to avoid the inner city on this day, by late afternoon crowds were assembling downtown, and parishioners spilled out of the doors and onto the steps of the Nicholas Church—an important gathering place for dissidents—awaiting a 6 p.m. service.

Armored cars, riot police, and "battle groups" of the Communist party's militia packed the side streets near the Karl Marx Square in front of Leipzig's university, while members of the Stasi mixed among the demonstrators. Doctors in the city informed local church officials that hospital rooms were being readied and extra staff made available to receive scores of injured.[64] According to other eyewitness accounts in the *Sunday Times* of London, "The great hall used for the biannual trade fair in Leipzig resembled the antechamber of a war: body bags, stocks of blood plasma and makeshift operating tables were prepared."[65] Honecker's solution to the GDR's problems was to bring Tiananmen Square to the heart of Central Europe.

At 5:30 p.m. an appeal was read over the loudspeakers that encircled Leipzig's inner-city square calling for peaceful dialogue between the state and its citizens. "We all need a free exchange of opinions about the continuation of socialism in our country," intoned the reader. "Therefore, we promise all citizens that we will use our full power and authority to ensure that this dialogue will occur, not only in the Leipzig area but with our national government."[66] The text was also read in St. Nicholas Church and several other churches and transmitted over the internal radios of police and security forces. Helmut Heckenber, acting Communist party chief of Leipzig's district, delivered the statement to local police officials.[67]

The appeal had been cowritten by the renowned conductor of Leipzig's Gewandhaus Orchestra, Kurt Masur; a theologian and oppositionist, Peter Zimmermann; a local cabaret artist, Bernd Lutz Langer; and three officials from the political leadership of Leipzig's district—Kurt Maier, Jochen Pommert, and Roland Wötzel. These were the individuals who, meeting late in the afternoon at Kurt Masur's house on the western edge of the city, together negotiated the countermand to Honecker's orders for a bloody crackdown. Their action charged with fresh confidence the 70,000 demonstrators who took to the streets of Leipzig that evening. East German police ordered correspondents of the Hungarian News Agency and reporters from two Hungarian dailies to leave Leipzig following the conclusion of the peaceful Monday night demonstration. This was no boding of ominous developments—if anything, it was a symbol of the final gasping attempt by GDR authorities to maintain some semblance of Socialist order and integrity.[68]

Although officials in Moscow have steadfastly denied any direct involvement in the developments of October 9,[69] Soviet influence governing the peaceful outcome of the Monday night demonstration is undeniable. The stage, of course, had been set with the Soviet repudiation of the Brezhnev Doctrine. During a three-day visit to France in July Gorbachev had most recently ruled out in unambiguous terms "the very possibility of the use of force or threat of force—alliance against alliance, inside the alliance, whatever." Given that East German power rested on the potential of Soviet force—as Timothy Garton Ash has observed, more "than anywhere else in Eastern Europe . . . [the GDR] was more strongly oriented toward—and ultimately dependent on—the Soviet Union than any other,"[70] this fact in itself was of immense importance.

But after October 9, the Soviet press alluded to reports that "high ranking army officers stationed in the GDR [may have been] directly or indirectly involved in the effort to avert a tragic outcome" at the Leipzig demonstration.[71] According to former West German chancellor Willy Brandt, top Soviet officers actually deserve the lion's share of credit for preventing a blood bath on October 9.[72] In Brandt's account, the Soviets had expressly urged the East German army against the use of arms against its citizens,[73] and the Soviet military leadership in East Germany had made it clear to East German authorities "that if they acted with military means against the people, the Russians would stay in their barracks."[74]

Former East German officials have reported that Gorbachev was in daily contact with the Soviet military command in East Germany at this time.[75] Moreover, Mikhail Moisseyev, chief of the USSR Armed Forces General Staff, later indirectly confirmed Brandt's account when he told the Soviet pioneer publication *Komsomalskaya* that the Soviet military in East Germany had been "instructed by the General Staff not to intervene in any matters pertaining to domestic [relations]." Soviet involvement may have in fact been more direct, if claims can be corroborated that in some instances Soviet tanks actually blocked the entrances of East German military compounds near Leipzig on October 9 to deny exit of members of the National People's Army.[76]

The fact that local party officials were able to countermand Honecker's orders for a crackdown in October was a sign that regional unilateralism had begun to pull at the fabric of Honecker's central authority. There had been challenges before to Communist leaders from within the ranks of the Politburo, but never had such a formidable challenge been posed from the provinces.

Another sign of regional confrontation with central authorities came on October 10 when Mayor Wolfgang Berghofer of Dresden, with approval of the district's party boss Hans Modrow, took the conciliatory step of meeting with local oppositionists. "My behavior and that of Wolfgang Berghofer," wrote Modrow later, "stood in conflict with the policies being promoted in Berlin. . . . We wanted dialogue, and sought consensus with the citizens' movement for a democratic transformation in the spirit of perestroika."[77] Berghofer's meeting with citizens' representatives was followed by the announcement that 500 detained demonstrators would be immediately released.

The GDR leadership met on October 10 and 11 in an emergency session of the Politburo to discuss the country's deepening crisis. Following their meetings, regime officials spoke for the first time of "necessary renewal."[78] This new reform-minded disposition included specifically the party's announced determination to engage in discussion with "well-intentioned interlocutors."[79] On October 12, *Neues Deutschland*, in a front page article retracted remarks Honecker had made earlier about the GDR's shedding no tears over those who chose to turn their back on their homeland and flee to the West. Now the party's central voice announced instead that socialism needed each individual. It has room and perspective for everyone. It is the future of the new generation. Exactly for this reason, we are not indifferent to the fact that people who worked and lived here have chosen to leave. . . . The causes for their decision may be varied. We must and will search for them, each in his way, everyone together.[80]

According to a report by the Berlin RIAS-television station, East Germany's Evangelical Bishop Gottfried Forck was entering into negotiations with the party leadership at that very time. The station further reported that the Free German Youth in East Berlin had proposed talks with local oppositionists. In Leipzig, twenty citizens' representatives proposed that Hans Modrow be directly involved in their next round of dialogue with local party officials.[81]

Gerasimov, spokesman for the Soviet Foreign Ministry, greeted the change of heart from the East Berlin Politburo. "We cannot make prescriptions for other countries," said Gerasimov, "but we've demonstrated in model fashion that problems should be solved through dialogue."[82] Whether seeking prescriptions or not, party ideologist Kurt Hager abruptly departed for Moscow to meet with Soviet officials. In an interview published in *Moscow News*, Hager, a close associate of Honecker's and the GDR's hitherto lead man on rejecting Soviet-style reform, was now heard to offer his fresh new thoughts on the prospects for East Germany's restructuring. Echoing Gorbachev's words in East Berlin, Hager conceded the regime was faced with the challenge of "opening a perspective for the future . . . for answers to the questions, which are important to our citizenry." The question of a free flow of information would now be eliminated from the list of East German taboos, according to Hager.[83] Even hawkish Margot Honecker, Erich Honecker's wife and head of the Ministry of Education, surprisingly added her voice to those now in favor of an "open climate."[84]

Though New Forum, the most visible of the opposition groups, continued to be treated by authorities as an organization hostile to the interests of socialism, restrictions on discussing reform in the press were lifted by GDR censors in the days after Hager's remarks. For the first time, party reformers seemed able to make themselves heard without fear of reprisal. In an interview with *Junge Welt*, the newspaper of the Communist party's youth arm, Klaus Höpcke urged retreat from centralism and embrace of "Socialist competition" in GDR society.[85] Dresden's mayor Wolfgang Berghofer boasted of his commitment to dialogue with the GDR citizenry, although even Berghofer evidently still found it necessary to deny he was involved in direct talks with the illegal New Forum. "My partners in the dialogue," said Berghofer, "do not consider themselves to be a delegation from the 'New Forum.'

[They] do not see themselves as an opposition . . . the questions raised by the citizens are directed, they themselves say, toward improvement of life within socialism in the GDR."[86]

Honecker's Ouster

In mid-October popular pressure for change increased. On October 18, while a record number of demonstrators (an estimated 120,000) marched in Leipzig demanding free elections and an end to Communist rule, the day that seemed inevitable finally came: the Central Committee announced the retirement of Erich Honecker after eighteen years at the GDR's helm. Markus Wolf later referred to "a medieval conspiracy" that overthrew Honecker in which "some members of the Central Committee . . . two of them . . . ministers" requested Wolf "to assume responsibility for the entire state security system," an offer he declined.[87]

Behind Honecker's ouster and the attempt to synchronize developments in the GDR with Soviet *perestroika* appear to have been, in addition to Honecker's portégé Egon Krenz, two other Politburo members, Günter Schabowski and Peter Lorenz and, later in the process, trade union boss Harry Tisch.[88] As Krenz, Schabowski, and Lorenz scurried to gain support for their plan, Tisch offered to travel to Moscow to inform Kremlin officials of the specifics of the conspirators' plans. "He welcomed the fact," Tisch later recalled of his conversation with Gorbachev, that finally "we had reached the point where we understood life had caught up with us."[89]

Schabowksi, who managed a list of Politburo members for the plotters, categorizing each individual as "winnable," "undecided," or "opponent or position unknown,"[90] was charged with informing the Soviet Ambassador in East Berlin of upcoming developments. Schabowski actually requested that the Soviet envoy use his influence to remove a complication that arose in the conspiracy when President Willi Stoph suggested that Honecker resign from his position as general secretary but be allowed to remain chairman of the state council.[91]

Though Krenz later described his motive in the anti-Honecker conspiracy as linked to his profound desire for reform, which first surfaced in the mid-1980s "when great changes were taking place in socialist societies, primarily in the Soviet Union,"[92] his actions may well have been related to his apparent demotion by Honecker the previous summer. When Honecker fell ill, it was Günter Mittag (the Politburo member responsible for the economy), not Krenz, who filled in for the East German leader.[93]

According to Schabowski's account of the conspiracy, he and Peter Lorenz had begun their collaboration with Krenz for Honecker's removal from power almost three weeks before the party boss actually resigned.[94] Ironically, Schabowksi, former editor in chief of *Neues Deutschland*, had been placed by Honecker himself in his position as East Berlin party chief in 1985 to replace Honecker's rival Konrad Naumann. The other conspirator, Lorenz, had previously called attention to himself as a potentially reform-minded party member in July 1988 when, in a local Communist publication, he had called for open dialogue and an end of "taboos when talking politics."[95]

"It wasn't possible to topple Honecker by a military putsch," said Schabowski. "It was only possible in the politburo. We wanted to make it appear that he resigned."[96] On October 17, the day deemed by the conspirators as "the point of no return," Egon Krenz arrived at his office at 8 a.m., two hours before the regular Tuesday Politburo meeting. A telephone conversation between Krenz and Schabowski firmed up details as well as nerve for the 10 a.m. session. As the twenty-five members assembled around the table (the twenty-sixth member, General Kessler, was in Nicaragua), President Willi Stoph began the meeting at Honecker's invitation by calmly calling for the general secretary's resignation and his replacement by Egon Krenz.

The Soviets and former East German officials involved in the plot adamantly deny that Moscow played any explicit role in Honecker's removal from power. A deputy spokesman of the Soviet Foreign Ministry said of Moscow's role: "It cannot be that our side would have expressed any (personal) wishes, that is no longer possible, no longer necessary, and I would say that it is no longer the norm today." Schabowski affirmed the Soviet claim: "The Soviet ambassador was not allowed to interfere as in former times. . . . When Walter Ulbricht was forced to resign, it was all discussed in Moscow. But now there was no Brezhnev doctrine."[97] Schabowski has conceded, however, that he and Krenz had told Falin and Gerasimov two weeks earlier—following the evident conflict of opinion between Honecker and Gorbachev at a private meeting of the leadership—that they "may be sure there will be a change."

On October 25, Shevardnadze issued a warning to other East bloc leaders who followed developments in East Germany with rapt, nervous attention. In a meeting with Polish President Wojciech Jaruzelski the Soviet envoy alluded to Moscow's policy of military noninterference, observing that "we don't set up order in other countries." Shevarnadze, of course, was not remiss in emphasizing the ever-vital "political" relationship between Socialist countries that seems to have encompassed the close consultation that took place between Moscow and East Berlin in the days before Honecker's ouster.[98]

The new East German leader who replaced Honecker belonged

to Gorbachev's generation. At fifty-two Krenz, who had been responsible for security affairs under Honecker, was the youngest member
of the GDR's Politburo. He also had, as Moscow well knew, the
reputation as a hard-liner and was thus an unlikely figure to step in
to placate the swelling popular unrest. In postrevolution memoirs,
Krenz predictably attempts to paint himself as having been a pro-
Gorbachev reformer-in-waiting all along.

According to his own account, Honecker's "crown prince," together
with Werner Felfe, was organizing a Politburo debate in the summer
of 1988 that was to center on the merits of *perestroika*. As Central
Committee secretary responsible for agriculture, Felfe had been coin-
cidently the only Politburo member to have met Gorbachev, when the
Soviet leader was in charge of the same portfolio in the Soviet Union.
"We were already convinced," writes Krenz, "that the politburo's
course, particularly in regard to developments in the Soviet Union,
was certain to fail."[99] But with Felfe's untimely death in September,
the balance of power appeared too uncertain for Krenz to push forward
with a "policy of renewal."[100]

If Krenz's account is to be believed, perhaps it was his memory
of the ill-fated attempt by Karl Schirdewan and Ernst Wollweber to
undermine Walter Ulbricht in 1957 that deterred him from taking
action against Honecker. Schirdewan and Wollweber had sought the
participation and support of Krenz (then a member of the Communist
party and a functionary in the Communist youth group), who at the
time lay in bed ill with the flu. But the party functionary and Central
Committee member hesitated to join the conspiracy, a choice that
saved his career while Schirdewan and Wollweber were ousted from
the party.[101]

Since 1983 Krenz had served as a full member of the Politburo
and, according to most observers, had by the mid-1980s become
Honecker's favored successor. For most East Germans, Krenz was just
another among the long list of Communists in the GDR (and elsewhere
in the bloc) who, seeing the writing on the wall, preferred to abandon
everything they had ever stood for rather than to abandon power in
the face of change. Wolf Biermann, the exiled East German song writer,
bluntly described the situation, cautioning his countrymen still in the
GDR. In an interview in West Germany, Biermann observed that the
"unbelievable speed with which the old bastards are transforming
themselves [could only make] one nervous."[102] Krenz's support of the
Beijing regime following the June crackdown at Tiananmen Square
earned him the nickname "Krenz Xiaoping," a name that became
prominently displayed on the banners and placards of demonstrators
during late October and November.

Though he confidently asserted that most East Germans were committed to staying the Socialist course, Krenz understood that time was short if he wished to stabilize his own position. "I was convinced," he writes, "that even many of those [citizens] who fled via West German embassies, across the border from Hungary to Austria, or later into the West by way of Czechoslovakia, were not leaving because of anti-socialist motives."[103] In fact, by Krenz's assessment, the "majority of the demonstrators [in the fall] were agitating for socialist renewal."[104]

In an hour-long nationally televised address following his accession to power, Krenz pledged a program of "continuity with renewal," adding that the door was now open for earnest "political dialogue."[105] But the suggestion of any measure of continuity with the past at this time was disquieting for tens of thousands of East Germans who were clearly growing tired of following their Socialist organizers and who themselves were more confident in pressing their cause in the streets.

The new reformer Krenz, who saw his own responsibility in placing the party once again in the "political offensive,"[106] insisted on uncompromising rejection of any return to capitalist conditions in East Germany. The issue of "socialism [was] not open to debate," and though party officials had begun to meet with members of citizens' groups, the Communists insisted on retaining their monopoly on power.[107] As Schabowski later reported, the idea of "'free elections' only surfaced, with trembling and hesitation, after a meeting of the *Volkskammer* in November."[108] In fact, direct and formal negotiations with oppositionists did not commence until the first round-table meeting on December 7, and elections were not announced until December 9. As Krenz recalled, there were two considerations guiding his plans for reform in the GDR. On the one hand, there was an

> unambiguous focus toward the goal of our struggle, namely to give socialism in the GDR a more human, democratic face, "to hold high socialist ideals and not to give up any of our commonly achieved achievements." On the other [hand] I affirmed the principle: "Our socialist, German republic is and will remain a sovereign country. We will solve our problems ourselves."[109]

On October 23, the number of participants at the Monday night demonstration in Leipzig had grown to an estimated 300,000. Oppositionists had no doubt been encouraged by the mid-week meeting between Schabowski and representatives of New Forum. This was the first official meeting of a member of the Politburo with leaders of the demonstrations. By the end of the month public meetings were being called by local Communist officials in cities throughout the GDR.

107

Despite pleas by the regime for a pause in popular pressure (accompanied by a declaration of amnesty on October 27 for those who had violated the travel laws), New Forum and other mobilizers of East Germany's protesters had pushed their regular demonstrations forward with undiminished intensity.

While Krenz traveled to Moscow to meet with Gorbachev on November 1, back in East Germany Markus Wolf was calling for public control of the security organs through elected representatives, an attempt to circumvent increasing hostility publicly directed toward the hated Stasi.[110] Before his departure to the Soviet Union, Krenz had sought assurance from Hans Modrow that the Dresden party chief would be prepared to assume new responsibility in the leadership.

Krenz wanted to be certain that Modrow "was prepared to participate," according to Modrow, not only because he "had become known as the GDR's 'hope' in the western media, [but also because] Krenz expected that Gorbachev would ask about [his] role."[111] Schabowski later remarked, that although he and Krenz had been principally responsible for Honecker's removal from power, "we were the wrong people," according to the faction led by Modrow and Wolf, "to put the GDR on the track of reform."[112]

Nonetheless, Krenz pushed fervently to remake his image. He interrupted his trip home from Moscow with a brief stop in Poland to make public note of the importance of the Polish model for East Germany's new reform course. Krenz was learning—"gaining pace," as Jens Reich, one of the founding members of New Forum, put it.[113] Once back in East Germany, Krenz, in a speech aired on television, appealed to the citizens of his country to remain at home and place "trust [in the regime's] policy of renewal."[114]

During the weekend of November 4 reports from Prague confirmed that East Germany had decided to let its citizens leave for the West from Czechoslovakia—a step toward a softer line. For the first time the GDR had consented to genuinely free travel for its citizens to the West. West Berlin's deputy mayor observed at the time that East Berlin's decision had rendered the Berlin Wall suddenly "superfluous."[115] Nevertheless, if the Communist regime thought that this move might take wind out of the sails of the country's surging prodemocracy movement, it had miscalculated yet again.

That same weekend the largest demonstration in the country's history took place in East Berlin. An estimated half-million marched through the broad boulevards of downtown East Berlin, carrying placards calling for free elections, free trade unions, freedom of travel, and the immediate dismantling of the security apparatus. Party reformers were mocked by the crowds as *Wendehälse*, a bird capable of twisting its head around—symbol of the hard-line Communists who overnight had discovered the virtues of democratization. Schabowski and Wolf, who attended the rally and tried to persuade an unreceptive audience of the genuine character of party reform, were driven by jeers and whistles from the stage.

The announcement by Interior Minister Friedrich Dickel that East Berlin would permit up to thirty days of travel abroad annually for East Germans (exceptions based on "national security" reasons remained) would have seemed a remarkable concession just weeks before. At this time, though, it was greeted with contempt by East German demonstrators whose confidence was growing by the day. Hans-Joachim Hoffmann, GDR minister of culture, called for the resignation of the ruling Politburo to give Egon Krenz a chance to win the public's confidence. On November 8, the entire Politburo stepped down (though several members were quickly reappointed), but Krenz's position remained tenuous. Hans Modrow was able to move a step closer to power at this time with his elevation to this highest of political bodies and his nomination as prime minister.

East Germany's Collapse

While pressure on the regime mounted inside the country, an equal danger from the tens of thousands of East Germans fleeing to the West showed little sign of subsiding. Moreover, Czechoslovakia, still directly affected by the unabating stream of GDR citizens into its territory, threatened during the first week of November to seal its border with East Germany. Thus, on November 7 a travel law was the central topic of discussion in East Berlin's Politburo meeting. Two days later on November 9, the party desperately flung open the twenty-eight-year-old Berlin Wall, a paradoxical strategy, in the words of Schabowski, to "open the border so they won't go."[116] "We had no idea at all," Schabowksi later reflected, "that the opening of the Wall would signal the beginning of the end of our republic."[117]

The precise process that led to the opening of the border on November 9 remains unclear. The most convincing account indicates that Schabowski, who announced on that Thursday evening that East German citizens would henceforth be permitted to travel to the West, was trying to proclaim a new travel decree permitting a gradual, orderly opening of the border commencing the following day (passports and personal identity papers would still be required). Schabowski noted in his press statement, for example, that authorities would retain the right to deny permission for travel to the West in "special exceptional cases."[118]

But as East Berliners received word of the announcement, thousands began spontaneously rushing to border crossing points. Bewildered border guards and members of the Volkspolizei, who had yet to receive explicit instructions, at first allowed East Germans to cross into West Berlin with stamps in their identity papers. But in a matter of a few short hours confusion led to pandemonium, as Berliners from both sides of the wall streamed together, leaving the GDR's border guards helpless, impotent bystanders to one of the most stunning chapters in postwar history. Returning to his hotel that evening, Hans Modrow was stopped by a young man who, having heard reports of the wall's opening, asked "where he could leave the GDR." Modrow, unaware of the eruption taking place, calmly responded that proper papers could be issued by state authorities at official locations the next day.[119]

In the wake of the breach of the Berlin Wall, parliamentarian Alfred Dregger spoke of "the great respect and wonderment" of his colleagues for the achievements of East German demonstrators who for weeks had assiduously pressed their cause for freedom in cities throughout the country. Indeed it was the pressure from the streets that had forced the opening of the wall. Moscow termed East Berlin's opening of the Berlin Wall a "correct decision," and Gerasimov was quick to report that the GDR had not asked Gorbachev "to give the green light" for the historic step. Foreign Minister Shevardnadze, too, wasted little time going on record with his great satisfaction with the East German decision, again emphasizing that the Soviet government did not try to influence East German officials on the matter.[120]

Hans Modrow asserts that the Soviets were first informed by the East German side about the wall's opening only when Krenz telephoned Soviet ambassador Kochemasov the morning of November 10.[121] A contrary view, however, was published in the *Sunday Times* of London, claiming that Krenz had telephoned Mikhail Gorbachev to discuss the crisis and that Gorbachev was directly involved in East Germany's decision to open the Berlin Wall. (It is nearly inconceivable that Krenz was not in close consultation with Soviet officials at the time.) Whether the Gorbachev-Krenz discussion on the matter of opening the wall actually took place, according to Valentin Falin the Soviets had encouraged the East Germans in this direction for some time. Falin claims that both Gorbachev and Yakovlev had repeatedly made the case with Honecker himself that the Soviet reformers by no means considered the Berlin Wall a particularly pleasing piece of furniture in the design of Europe's new common home.[122]

The opening of the borders on November 9 did not bring equilibrium to the country, nor did the Central Committee's announcement on the ensuing weekend of a program of radical changes, which included legalization of new political organizations and proposals for free elections. The purge of the government and party apparatus moved forward, having developed a momentum of its own. Forced to resign from a post he had held for thirteen years, Horst Sindermann, president of the Volkskammer, told the GDR parliament on November 13 that he "accept[ed] responsibility for all the failures of the former government."[123] Other former party officials, like the bewildered eighty-two-year-old former Stasi chief, Erich Mielke, were not capable of grasping the devastating blur of events. Mielke responded to angry outbursts from parliamentarians with his pathetic but memorable phrase: "But I love you all."[124]

The Communist party began to unravel at a staggering pace—membership was plummeting, officials throughout the country were resigning; several committed suicide. Krenz was forced to put everything on the table save the question of the GDR's sovereignty. "German reunification," he insisted, "is not on the agenda,"[125] a position Gorbachev himself affirmed.[126] Free elections were promised, but the regime rejected emulation of the West German economy in favor of what one East German official referred to as a "market-oriented planned economy."[127] East Germans were not interested in qualified democracy and market economies with adjectives, however. And the efforts of reformers now at the helm held little promise of steadying the country's course. In a poll taken in mid-November only 19 percent of East Germans said they had any trust in the Krenz regime.[128] During the first two weeks of November, demonstrators throughout the country pushed vociferously for Krenz's removal from office.

According to a top East German intelligence officer, the Soviets, increasingly anxious about the repercussions of instability inside East Germany, sent Valentin Falin to the East German capital. At a meeting said to have taken place in mid-November at the Soviet Embassy in East Berlin, Falin met alternately and jointly with Krenz and Modrow to negotiate details of a transition of power.[129] Gorbachev's faithful servant Markus Wolf was also reportedly present, who with his perfect mastery of Russian played the pivotal role of broker.[130]

On November 17, the Volkskammer formally elected Hans Modrow East Germany's prime minister. Two days after the Volkskammer struck Article One from the Constitution, which had guaranteed the Communist party's monopoly on power, Krenz stepped down as general secretary of the party. On December 6, Krenz surrendered his remaining posts as chairman of the Council of State and the National Defense Council, clearing the way for Hans Modrow—the man Honecker had once reproved for behaving like Dubcek[131]—to assume full responsibility for his country's reform. Though Markus Wolf was asked by Modrow to come out of retirement to revamp the security service, he declined, agreeing only to serve as "an unofficial consultant" to the GDR's new prime minister.[132]

Modrow immediately received glowing endorsements from the Soviet press as the quintessential reformer. *Pravda* described the GDR's new leader as "intelligent, sincere, open, [with a] principled attitude, genuine affinity with the working people, and popularity."[133] From the beginning of the upheaval in October, the rising star of East Germany's Communist reform movement had performed a bit of his own public relations, focusing attention on his authenticity as a "liberal." As he told an interviewer in late October, "Let's be open about it. . . . I am not in a situation where I have, as it were, to change my way of thinking. I am in a situation where I can carry on thinking in ways that I started thinking in some time ago . . . in Dresden."[134]

Soviet reformers thought that, with Modrow now in power, the worst in East Germany would be behind them. Although Gerasimov emphasized Moscow's intention to "refrain from assessing [developments]," the Soviet Union's open approval of the changes taking place was abundantly evident.[135] Shevardnadze told an association of journalists meeting in Moscow on November 19 that he considered developments inside East Germany "a completely normal process." "We have no doubts," he said, "that this is the only possible way."[136] The next day Gorbachev himself explicitly endorsed the changes taking place in the GDR and elsewhere. At a press conference in Moscow following a meeting with Canadian Prime Minister Brian Mulroney, Gorbachev pointed to the Eastern bloc's lag in technological progress as a key motive for new Communist politics, adding that the result of the changes would be "better societies, more open societies, and in international affairs societies more open to the world and ready for cooperation."[137]

Such warm tones of support for the changes in East Germany, at the very time upheaval was spreading to Czechoslovakia, could be viewed only as a direct assault on the authority of the bloc's remaining antireform forces in power in Prague, Bucharest, and Sofia. In the midst of this volatile period, the Soviets repeatedly warned the West not to interfere in the East bloc's process of transformation. Shevardnadze called discussion in the West of "exporting capitalism . . . a dangerous manifestation of old thinking," cautioning the leaders of democratic countries against proclaiming "victory in the Cold War" or gloating "about the disintegration of one or another social system."[138]

Roy Medvedev, a Soviet deputy and former dissident, shared the view of the Gorbachev regime that the events in Eastern Europe reflected socialism's renewal, not its collapse. He told an interviewer with an Italian newspaper in mid-November: "I do not believe that in the countries of Eastern Europe the communist idea will die. What is in crisis is communism of the state."[139] Similarly, Portugalov, speaking at a symposium sponsored by the conservative Hanns-Seidel Foundation at the end of the month in Munich, stressed that Communist parties would retain a decisive measure of influence in guiding their societies in the East bloc.[140]

East Germany's reform Communists were in complete agreement. Dresden's reform-minded mayor, Wolfgang Berghofer, told an interviewer from *Le Monde* that the party might no longer possess a "leadership role in the administrative sense" but that it was certain to retain its "vanguard position" as a result of "work accomplished." Moreover, in view of Solidarity's recent climb to power over Communists in Poland, Berghofer expressed his opinion that the Communist party in East Germany was "not obliged to make the same mistakes."[141] "For me," Hans Modrow later reflected, "this process of conducting dialogue, whether with representatives of New Forum or with steel workers in Edelstahlwerk Freital, . . . [was about] coming to the top of the movement, not to steer things back onto the old tracks, but rather to lead a reform of socialism."[142]

In this spirit, Modrow pressed on with the party's rhetoric about the essential dialogue between the state and its citizens. "The existence of a sovereign GDR state," observed Modrow, "was [our] departure point for questions of internal and external security."[143] In light of its new open border policy, however, East Germany confronted the urgent problem of reevaluating its relationship with the Federal Republic, which, with its powerful new leverage, was actively pressing its own agenda—economic support in exchange for further liberalization inside the GDR. Overnight the concept of a German confederation had suddenly emerged as a practical, salient topic in the political debate.

In principle the Soviets may have felt comfortable with Chancellor Helmut Kohl's proposal of November 28 for German confederation. Although they clearly rejected Kohl's view of confederation as a step-by-step process to unification, Gorbachev's experts on Germany had long become practiced in vaguely alluding to new arrangements, including confederation, for the development of inter-German cooperation. As recently as the summer, just before Gorbachev's trip to Bonn, Portugalov had told *Der Spiegel* that the reconstruction of "central Europe" could take into account the "concerns of the two German states—that is, of all Germans."[144]

In an interview in West Germany's *Frankfurter Allgemeine Zeitung* on November 17, Portugalov elaborated his thoughts on how the interests of the Germans could be accommodated in the common European home. In his view "federative structures in areas such as the economy, ecology, culture, and many other things" were quite conceivable. Portugalov stressed, however, that reunification remained "incompatible with the geopolitical and geostrategic requirements of stability" in Europe.[145] Egon Krenz had fallen into line at the time, telling the *Financial Times* of London on November 25 that he did not exclude the prospect of German confederation, though this would be conceivable only sometime in the distant future.[146] For Hans Modrow, a German confederation with provisions protecting GDR sovereignty seemed an appropriate "contribution to the construction of the European Home."[147]

Soviet insistence that East Germany pursue its own path of Socialist reform, albeit entertaining new forms of cooperation with the Federal Republic, found support in the GDR not only with Communist reformers but with oppositionists as well at this time. In fact, Krenz and Modrow were conveniently able to appropriate the motto, "For Our Country," which had originated in circles of dissident academics and intellectuals.

Church official Manfred Stolpe (today governor of the federal state of Brandenburg) stressed, for example, the search for common ground between Christians and Marxists and pleaded for discussions of reform to remain exclusively within the context of socialism. In a speech on November 14 at the Ernst-Moritz-Arndt University in Greifswald where he was awarded an honorary doctorate, Stolpe warned of increasing "resistance to renewal . . . and pan-German dreams [which] make us incapable of thinking and acting."[148]

The position maintained by Stolpe and other leading oppositionists echoed the sentiment of even West Berlin's Mayor Walter Momper. At the end of October Momper had dismissed out of hand "superfluous discussion about reunification, a discussion which leads to a dead end." In Momper's view, at the end of Eastern Europe's upheaval it was quite probable that there would be "a GDR, which like Poland and Hungary, stays in the Eastern alliance but is a democratic and pluralistic state."[149]

Gorbachev's reformers, watching with anxious fascination the unfolding of events in East Germany, undoubtedly still felt confident that a restructured GDR could be preserved. New confederative structures between the two German states would represent an important model for Soviet policy in Europe, according to Vladimir Markov, who had been chief correspondent for the Soviet news agency Novosti in Bonn between 1983 and 1987.

In this way, how the German question was resolved would measure the potential for two social systems to exist side by side in the new European common home.[150] Gorbachev affirmed his own recognition that the character of East-West German relations was undergoing fundamental change. In a meeting with the President of the West German Bundestag, Rita Süssmuth, and the president of the French National Assembly, Laurent Fabius, however, the Kremlin leader reiterated Soviet irritation over "patronizing and know-it-all attitudes" in the West, rejecting out of hand any notion that "reunification . . . [was] on the agenda."[151]

On December 8 an emergency congress of the East German Communists, meeting in East Berlin under the leadership of Mayor Berghofer, Markus Wolf, attorney (and leader party chief) Gregor Gysi, and Herbert Kroker (chairman of the Work Committee) pledged that the party would pursue a new path, a "third way" of democratic socialism. But as the reformers were busy charting their course the German Democratic Republic was slipping away at an astonishing pace.

Hans Modrow subsequently reported that when he first met with Gorbachev in December, Gorbachev remained confident that a reformed GDR would still survive as an independent, sovereign state. Modrow's own faith, though, had already begun to waver. Modrow describes his meeting with Gorbachev:

> On the initiative of Germany expert Valentin Falin a special conversation between Gorbachev and me took place. The purpose of the discussion was to come to an understanding about the character of the democratic changes in the GDR. It became apparent that Gorbachev still harbored illusions. I did not deter him in this regard because I, at least in part, still believed in this idea as well: democratization is a process that would strengthen socialism in the GDR. Indeed I had the fear—he had no idea—that [the process would lead] to a gradual disintegration of socialism in the GDR. Gorbachev thought, now the path is free for perestroika in the GDR.[152]

Schabowski, too, had been under the impression initially that Honecker's removal from power and the implementation of reforms would offer a window of several months' time to stabilize a new order in the GDR. Even the American president, mused Schabowski, is permitted to enjoy "a grace period of 100 days."[153] But as Krenz notes in his memoirs, Communist reformers very quickly "fell behind political developments in the GDR, [developments] whose own dynamic could no longer be influenced by us. The 'revolution' from below was already in gear. And it was faster."[154] The reign of reformer Hans Modrow lasted from November 1989 to March 1990. When Modrow left office, the successor to the Communist party, the Party of Democratic Socialism, was now the opposition, and formal unfication with the Federal Republic was but six months away.

Ironically, Honecker and his supporters had been right all along.[155] The simple thesis of his ideologist, Otto Rheinhold, had been correct, namely that East Germany was only imaginable as a Socialist alternative to West Germany. The GDR without (orthodox) socialism, Rheinhold had contended, would equal nothing less than unification on Western terms,[156] though few could have predicted the amazing pace of the disintegration of the East German state.

All that remained was the Soviet realization that the GDR had been lost, as Moscow scrambled to define the terms of its relationship with a new, uniting Germany.

6

Aftermath of an Inadvertent Revolution

Moscow never intended to cede what Charles Krauthammer rightly described as "the jewel of its East European empire."[1] It was the folly of Soviet reformers, who, believing that East Germany could be transformed into a legitimate and viable Socialist state, took steps that led to the dissolution of an empire. Their grand miscalculation, their conviction that the Communist system could be democratized, turned out to be a vital prerequisite to communism's collapse.

Historic Miscalculations

As Russian President Boris Yeltsin put it, Gorbachev simply sought the unattainable: to wed "communism and a market economy, public-property ownership and private-property ownership, the multiparty system and the Communist party with its monopoly on power."[2]

In East Germany the Kremlin had urged Honecker and his comrades to embrace *perestroika*. In a move of enormous consequence to East Berlin's rulers, Gorbachev made it known that Moscow was no longer prepared to intervene militarily to defend unpopular regimes in the bloc. Equally damaging, perhaps, the Gorbachev circle colluded with reform-minded Communists bent on undermining the authority of the Honecker regime. As early as the summer of 1987, Vladimir Kryuchkov, later Gorbachev's chairman of the KGB, traveled to Dresden, where he was apprised of the plans of East German reformers.[3]

As late as the summer of 1989, Soviet reformers remained steadfastly convinced that liberalization would pave the way for commu-

nism's renewal throughout Eastern Europe. Gorbachev's direct intervention, a telephone call to Polish Communist party leader Mieczyslaw
Rakowski, helped permit the formation in August 1989 of the first
non-Communist government in Eastern Europe since World War II.
Again it was the Kremlin that signaled approval to the Hungarians
that same summer to open their borders to East Germans fleeing to
the West. These steps did not ease tension in the bloc, however. Nor
did they strengthen, at least not for longer than a fleeting moment,
the hand of reform-minded Communists. These very measures, in fact,
served as a catalyst to revolutions, first in East Germany and then, as
the fire of upheaval spread, in Bulgaria, Czechoslovakia, and Romania.[4]

It may be true that the "collapse of communism," as a former
aide to Nikita Khrushchev asserts, has been "the result of a long
process of its own internal erosion . . . [an] erosion [that] started after
Stalin's death in 1953."[5] It was Gorbachev's policies of *perestroika* and
glasnost, however, that permitted, indeed promoted, the system's actual
dismantling.

It was not only Soviet reformers and their counterparts in East
Berlin (as elsewhere in the bloc) who had placed their faith, absurd
as it seems in retrospect, in the viability of reform communism. Because
some East German dissident intellectuals and clergy zealously extolled
the virtues of a humane socialism, Communist reformers were duped
into mistaking a tiny intelligentsia for popular grass-roots sentiment
in East Germany. Just two and a half weeks before Gorbachev himself
bowed to realities and accepted unification as inevitable, church official
and leading oppositionist Manfred Stolpe spoke, for instance, of a
"German affinity [that] will have to be lived and can be lived in two
states."[6] The very idea of reunification, in fact, according to Stolpe,
was "politically and historically incorrect, rouses emotions, and con-
fuses people."

Moreover, it is not difficult to understand how Gorbachev's circle
could have arrived at its disastrously faulty conclusions when important
segments of the Western intelligentsia had themselves capitulated to
dogma. While the background for revolution in East Germany and
Eastern Europe will command the attention of scholars and historians
for decades to come, so too will the failure of important currents of
intellectual and political circles in the West to anticipate communism's
unqualified rejection by the citizens of captive nations. In fact, this
body of opinion probably played an important role in communism's
collapse, as the near-uniform blindness of the German intelligentsia,
for instance, is certain to have reinforced the mistaken views of Soviet
reformers regarding the reformability of their system.

Prominent leaders of West Germany's Social Democratic party—a party that enjoyed close contact with Gorbachev's men—had also asserted that East Germans, once free to choose, would hear nothing of unification with a democratic capitalist West Germany. This point of view, vociferously articulated by West Berlin's Socialist mayor, Walter Momper, for example, won Momper the Soviet press's admiration and praise for his contribution to "realism."[7] When the Berlin Wall was opened on November 9, GDR-advocate Momper had tried arduously to explain that the momentous occasion was not a day of reunification but rather a day "of seeing each other again."[8]

The stage for such muddled thinking in West Germany had long been set. Before Willy Brandt had joined the pro-unity chorus in 1989, the former chancellor and honorary chairman of the Social Democratic party had insisted that German reunification was "the living lie of the second German Republic."[9] Brandt's long-time friend and ally, disarmament expert Egon Bahr, declared discussion of German unity "lies, hypocrisy" and "political environmental pollution."[10] And the Social Democrats' parliamentary spokesman, Horst Ehmke, insisted that Bonn focus attention on its own responsibility for Germany's division.[11] If one could be convinced of the manifold successes of East Germany's Communist society—even in its unreformed state—it was then easy to conclude that reunification would simply not be an option for the majority of East Germans.

In 1986 Germany's preeminent liberal columnist, Theo Sommer of *Die Zeit*, returned from the GDR to record his observations of a prospering German Socialist state. At the very time Gorbachev was beginning to withdraw support from East Berlin's orthodox regime, Sommer found a mood in East Germany, not filled with "resignation" but "movement." "Timidity has given way," he wrote, "to a confident composure, the greyness takes on everywhere friendlier colours, the depressing misery has disappeared. . . . Above all the country appears to be livelier, and the people have become happier."[12]

Three years before East Germany's revolution, Sommer was discovering a "relaxed" relationship "between the people and the rulers." "Reconstruction, modernisation, [and] restoration" were to be found everywhere, wrote Sommer. Moreover, a consumer state was flourishing, as "almost everything [could] be had in the GDR." And perhaps most important, East Germany's social system had been "developed . . . in many ways [that] put ours into the shadow." All this had led East Germans, Sommer concluded, to "offer [Honecker] something like a quiet reverence."[13] Günter Grass added to this climate of respect for East Germany after the breach of the wall: "There will be no reunification of the GDR and the *Bundesrepublik* under West German conditions," declared Grass. "The two fundamentally different

119

social systems can only exclude each other."[14]

Thus Soviet reformers were not alone in clinging to the fantasy of a democratic Communist East German state. Even across the Atlantic, some American journalists, perhaps most notably Carl Bernstein, joined in the gathering of pro-GDR forces in the West. Returning from East Berlin in January, Bernstein chronicled for *Time* magazine his own account of a people's "abiding love of East Germany." East Germans wanted to rebuild, yes, wrote Bernstein, but they wished to form

> a noncommunist socialist democracy, separate from the West but in some way affiliated. . . . I could hardly find any citizens who said they wanted a reunified, single Germany. . . . They love their country. The German Democratic Republic, not the Federal Republic of the West. They believe in socialism. Still.[15]

The socialism Bernstein insisted that East Germans still believed in was the mythic "third way," the centerpiece of East Germany's reformed Communist party. Gregor Gysi, chairman of the party, argued that

> the "third path" was necessary because the "first path," the Stalinist type of socialism, has been rejected, and the second, the path toward monopoly capitalism, is unacceptable because there are many problems it cannot resolve, such as employment and social protection.[16]

When the man in the street finally made himself heard, he rejected all forms of communism just as fervently and unambiguously as he embraced unification, leaving East Germany's pro-Gorbachev activists (and West Germany's as well) disillusioned and in disarray. New Forum, first prominent among opposition groups in the autumn of 1989, joined a ticket with other left-wing parties for the elections on March 18, 1990, and managed only 2.9 percent of the vote. This decisive repudiation of Marxism with "a human face" caused one of New Forum's leaders, Bärbel Bohley, to complain bitterly about the fruits of East Germany's infant democracy. East Germany's chance for re-newed socialism was being destroyed at the polls, she lamented, "with the voter behaving like a sheep again, yet fondly imagining he is taking part in his first free elections."[17]

Germany, Russia, and the Future of Europe

Once it became clear that East Germany had been lost, Moscow pressed, in many instances successfully, to forge exceedingly favorable links to the new Germany.

And throughout the unification process, a conservative-led government in Bonn, feeling indebted to the Soviet Union for its relinquishment of East Germany, went out of its way to protect Soviet interests and sensitivities. Foreign Minister Genscher's emphasis on the role of the Conference on Security and Cooperation in Europe—a structure with origins in Soviet proposals from the 1960s—sent the signal to Gorbachev that Germany wished to secure for Moscow a leading role in the new Europe.[18] Once Gorbachev yielded to Germany's demands for membership in NATO, Foreign Minister Genscher gave his assurance that NATO troops and nuclear weapons would not be shifted to eastern Germany. Bonn also sought to assuage Soviet security concerns by consenting to abide by post–World War II guidelines limiting the types of weapons Germany could develop and deploy and agreeing that the German Bundeswehr would not exceed 370,000 men—a number far lower than the 494,000-man West German army.

Germany pledged some DM 70 billion (approximately $40 billion), or nearly 3 percent of its GNP, to assist the Soviet Union. This was analogous to the amount the United States gave to Western Europe under the Marshall Plan. Moreover, the Federal Republic acted as advocate for Soviet membership in the new European Bank for Reconstruction and Development, the International Monetary Fund, and the World Bank. When the Americans and British expressed reluctance to invite Gorbachev to the July 1991 summit of the seven leading industrialized democracies, again it was the Germans who stepped forward to support Gorbachev's bid to be included. In fact, Chancellor Kohl went to Moscow before the summit to help Gorbachev prepare for the London meeting. In light of Germany's ever-expanding role as champion of Soviet causes, it came as no surprise that Soviet commentators were among the first to suggest that Germany become the sixth permanent member of the UN Security Council.[19]

Walter Laqueur observed a quarter of a century ago that "Russian-German relations have been one of the key issues in world affairs for the last hundred years."[20] In the new Europe, there is every reason to believe that this relationship between Berlin and Moscow will be no less important to the world than in the past. Although few in the United States or Europe seriously fear a new Rapallo agreement—Germany today would have no conceivable interest in exclusive collaboration with Russia as it did in 1922—Germany's relinkage to the East nevertheless gives cause for concern.

Europeans got a taste of Germany's conflicting impulses in the winter of 1990–1991, when Bonn hinted that it wished to pursue its own business-as-usual policy with the Kremlin, despite an agreement by EC foreign ministers to forfeit a scheduled $530 million of technical

121

assistance to Moscow because of its crackdown in the Baltics. In 1990 Germany signed a Treaty on Good-Neighborliness, Partnership, and Cooperation with the Soviet Union that further secured the favor of Kremlin leaders, but although they lodged no formal objections, some British, French, and American officials were left to wonder about the complete compatibility of the treaty with Germany's current NATO obligations. The treaty includes a provision that, in the improbable circumstance NATO felt compelled to engage the Soviet Union (or now the Commonwealth of Independent States) militarily, Germany would not take part in the campaign. As Charles H. Fairbanks, Jr., reminds us, led by anti-Western forces, Russia alone, with a population of 150 million, enormous resources, and a formidable nuclear arsenal, could pose a serious threat to Europe.[21]

During the Gulf War, Helmut Kohl argued that Germany was constitutionally prohibited—a point of dispute among Germany's own legal scholars—from sending troops to an out-of-area conflict, where multinational forces fought to thwart Saddam Hussein's aggression against Kuwait. Even when the prospect arose that NATO member Turkey might be attacked by Iraqi forces, however, Bonn erupted into an unseemly and confusing debate over the obligations of the German Bundeswehr. Some German officials have conceded that Germany was reluctant to commit troops to fight alongside its NATO allies at least in part because of Soviet objections.

Germany's energy will be absorbed over the next several years by the daunting task of making East Germany part of the Federal Republic.[22] Projected costs for unity now run in excess of $600 billion, and some German economists believe it will take at least until the end of the decade to raise the East German standard of living to that of West Germany. Couple this with the country's burgeoning immigration problem and it becomes clear that the Germans, preoccupied with troubles at home, are likely to lack focus in their policies abroad (since January 1989 West Germany has served as a magnet for more than 2.5 million immigrants).

That a majority of Germans can tell pollsters they view neutral Switzerland as a model for their country says as much as anything that Germany—with 79 million citizens, settled in the heart of the continent, managing Europe's largest economy—is far from grasping the international responsibility it assumes with unity. A fanciful desire to remain on the sidelines of conflict was reflected in German public opinion during the Gulf War. More than three-quarters of the German public voiced its support for the U.S.-led coalition to counter Iraq's aggression. Yet in near equal numbers they objected to the involvement of German troops in the conflict. Ironically, one concern over the new

Germany stems less from its potential militarism—the fear of a previous generation—than from its recognition that a responsible foreign policy must also include a military policy.

For these reasons, American policy makers should take Helmut Kohl at his word when he appeals that Germany's transition to a post–cold war era be guided by membership in a revamped NATO and a sustained American presence in Europe. An American presence reassures Europeans in East and West who feel uneasy about a Germany too independent, or too aggressive. Although Europeans see a united Europe as a restraining hand on Germany's shoulder, they also understand that the Germans will retain a dominant voice in EC institutions. An American presence also offers an anchor for Germany's Western orientation. Perhaps most important, though, an American presence provides the core, through both the means and the will, of any viable Western defense structure. No other country could have coordinated the immense international response against Iraq. And as the century draws to a close, no other country will be able to project power in the same way that U.S. forces can, even in an era witness to significant cuts in defense.

No longer do Germany and the other European democracies need to be U.S. protectorates. The inequality in resources that once existed during the cold war between the United States and Western Europe has been redressed (as the Germans have been apt to remind us). But "prosperity," as Dean Acheson observed a quarter of a century ago, "is not power; nor a guaranty of peace."[23] And it would be disastrously naive to think that, with NATO's primary mission fulfilled, threats to the Western democracies have altogether disappeared.

Notes

CHAPTER 1: THE GERMAN QUESTION

1. "Rheinhold Discounts 'Frivolous Experiments,'" *Foreign Broadcast Information Service, Eastern Europe (FBIS-EEU)*, September 27, 1989, p. 33.

2. Jim Hoagland, "Gorbachev's Nobel Lifeline," *Washington Post*, October 16, 1990.

3. Jim Hoagland, "Europe's Destiny," *Foreign Affairs*, Special Collection 1990, Grey Castle Press, vol. 69, p. 135.

4. Michael T. Kaufman, "Gorbachev Draws a Mixed Reaction from Soviet Bloc," *New York Times*, February 12, 1987.

5. Henry Kamm, "Prague Awaits the Glasnost Invasion," *New York Times*, November 17, 1987.

6. Robert Suro, "Dubcek Sees a Link with Gorbachev Effort," *New York Times*, January 10, 1988.

7. Quoted in "Rakowski Hails Gorbachev, Perestroika," *FBIS-EEU-88-130*, July 21, 1988, p. 31.

8. "Who's Afraid of Germany?" *Economist*, November 18, 1989, p. 54.

9. "Interview with Eduard Shevardnadze," *Izvestiia*, February 19, 1990.

10. "Gorbachev Answers Questions from L'Humanité," in *FBIS/USSR International Affairs*, February 10, 1986, p. CC 4.

11. *Pravda*, April 11, 1987; quoted in Gerhard Wettig, "Die UdSSR und der politische Wandel in Osteuropa" (The USSR and political change in Eastern Europe), in *Berichte des Bundesinstituts für ostwissenschaftliche und internationale Studien* (Reports of the Federal Institute for East-Scholarly and International Studies), no. 25, 1990, p. 8.

12. Quoted in Stephen Sestanovich "Inventing the Soviet National Interest" in *The National Interest*, no. 20 (Summer 1990), pp. 7–8.

13. Don Oberdorfer, *The Turn: From the Cold War to a New Era* (New York: Poseidon Press, 1991), p. 355.

14. Charles Gati, *The Bloc That Failed: Soviet-East European Relations in Transition* (Bloomington: Indiana University Press, 1990), p. 66.

15. Eduard Shevardnadze, *The Future Belongs to Freedom* (New York: Free Press, 1991), p. 137.

16. "Roy Medvedev Views Changes in East Europe," in *FBIS-SOV-89-220*, November 16, 1989, p. 33.

17. "Triumph der politischen Weisheit" (Triumph of political wisdom), *Der Morgen*, August 14, 1990.

18. "Shevardnadze Again Defends Security Policy," RFE/RL Report, no. 126, July 5, 1990, p. 7.

19. That Gorbachev and Brandt were soul mates seems evident. Brandt was

one of the first Western statesmen invited to a private meeting—a five-hour discussion in May 1985—with the new Kremlin leader. Interestingly, nearly four and a half years later, Brandt was again paying a visit to Gorbachev on October 17, 1989—one day before Erich Honecker's fall from power.

20. Mikhail Gorbachev, *Perestroika: New Thinking for Our Country and the World* (New York: Harper & Row, 1987), p. 201.

21. Norman M. Naimark, "Soviet–GDR Relations: An Historical Overview," in *Berichte des Bundesinstituts für ostwissenschaftliche und internationale Studien*, no. 51, 1989, p. 3.

22. Vyacheslav Dashichev, "Enormer Schaden für Moskau," *Der Spiegel*, February 5, 1990, p. 148.

23. Rheinhold Andert and Wolfgang Herzberg, *Der Sturz: Erich Honecker im Kreuzverhör* (The fall: Erich Honecker in cross-examination) (Berlin: Weimar, 1990), p. 21.

24. Ibid.

25. Ibid., pp. 19–21.

26. "Honecker Denies Guilt for Collapse of GDR," *FBIS-WEU-91-198*, October 11, 1991, p. 5.

27. Rolf Henrich, *Der Vormundschaftliche Staat* (The guardian state), (Hamburg: Rowohlt Taschenbuch Verlag, 1989).

28. "Parteiliches Handeln" (Party dealings), in *Der Spiegel*, July 3, 1989, p. 64.

CHAPTER 2: FROM A NEW WORLD VIEW

1. *The Gorbachev Challenge and European Security* (Baden-Baden: Nomos Verlagsgesellschaft, 1988), p. 11.

2. "Soviet President Chernenko Dies; Gorbachev Succeeds as Party General Secretary in Swift Transfer of Power," *Facts on File*, March 15, 1985, p. 177.

3. "Excerpts from Gorbachev's Speech to Communist Party Central Committee," *New York Times*, March 12, 1985.

4. *Kommunist*, no. 5, March 1985; translated in *Current Digest of the Soviet Press*, vol. 37, no. 16.

5. Roderic Lyne, "Making Waves: Mr Gorbachev's Public Diplomacy," *International Affairs*, vol. 63, no. 2 (Spring 1987), p. 207.

6. From the Program of the CPSU, adopted by the Twenty-Seventh Congress, March 1986, quoted in ibid., p. 209.

7. Serge Schmemann, "The Emergence of Gorbachev," *New York Times Magazine*, March 3, 1985.

8. "Gorbachev Report," *Foreign Broadcast Information Service, Soviet Union (FBIS-SOV)*, December 11, 1984, p. R 3.

9. Schmemann, "Emergence of Gorbachev."

10. Zdenek Mlynár, *Can Gorbachev Save the Soviet Union? The International Dimensions of Political Reform*, trans. Marian Sling and Ruth Tosek (Boulder, Colo.: Westview Press, 1990), p. 114.

11. Mikhail Gorbachev, "The Socialist Idea and Revolutionary Perestroika," *Pravda*, November 26, 1989.

12. Willy Brandt, *Erinnerungen* (Memoirs) (Frankfurt am Main: Proplyäen, 1989), p. 407.

13. In Lyne, "Making Waves," p. 209.

14. Ed A. Hewett, "Slow Change Ahead for Soviet Economy," *New York Times*, March 17, 1985.

15. "Soviet President Chernenko Dies," p. 178.

16. Leon Aron, "Gorbachev's Brest-Litovsk: The Kremlin's Grand Compromise in Eastern Europe," Backgrounder (Heritage Foundation, Washington, D.C.) August 15, 1989, p. 10.

17. See, for example, Michael J. Sodaro, *Moscow, Germany, and the West* (Ithaca, New York: Cornell University Press, 1990), p. 323.

18. Richard Halloran, "Export Ban Called Costly to Soviets," *New York Times*, May 14, 1985.

19. See Lyne, "Making Waves," p. 216.

20. Ibid.

21. Franz Josef Strauss, *Die Erinnerungen* (Memoirs) (Berlin: L. Siedler Verlag, 1989), p. 526.

22. Gorbachev replaced central committee secretaries with international responsibilities, Boris Ponomarev and Konstantin Rusakov, relieved Andrei Gromyko from his duties as foreign minister and replaced him with Eduard Shevardnadze, appointed four new deputy foreign ministers, and transferred nearly half the Soviet Union's ambassadors to Western and Eastern Europe. See Lyne, "Making Waves," p. 217. See also Dimitri Simes, "Gorbachev: A New Foreign Policy?" *Foreign Affairs*, vol. 65, no. 3 (1986), p. 477.

23. Quoted in Charles Gati, "Gorbachev and Eastern Europe," *Foreign Affairs*, vol. 5 (Summer 1987), p. 971.

24. "Soviet President Chernenko Dies," p. 177.

25. "Zagladin Calls for Closer European Ties," *FBIS-SOV*, August 2, 1985.

26. "Two Europes Decried, European Cooperation Urged" (from the "International Panorama" program presented by Fedor Mikhaylovich Burlatskiy) *FBIS-SU*, August 6, 1985, p. G 1.

27. "Editorial on Gorbachev's European Council Speech," *FBIS-EEU-89-132*, July 12, 1989, p. 1.

28. Quoted in Ilse Spittman, "Gorbachev besucht die SED" (Gorbachev visits the SED) in *Deutschland Archiv*, May 1986, p. 450.

29. Ibid.

30. "Tenth Congress of Polish United Workers Party: Speech by M.S. Gorbachev," *Pravda*, July 1, 1986, p. 1.

31. Jerry F. Hough, "Shifts in Soviet Foreign Policy, Maybe," *New York Times*, July 10, 1985.

32. Jerry F. Hough, "Gorbachev's Anti-Americanism," *New York Times*, November 4, 1988.

33. Esther B. Fein, "Pravda Revives Cry of 'U.S. Started the Cold War,'" *New York Times*, August 30, 1988.

34. On Valentin Falin, see ibid.; and "Soviets Promote Ex-Envoy Cool to U.S.," *New York Times*, October 21, 1988. On Aleksandr N. Yakovlev, see Bill Keller, "Riding Shotgun on Gorbachev's Glasnost Express: Aleksandr N.

Yakovlev," *New York Times,* October 28, 1988; and Jeane Kirkpatrick, "Moscow's Anti-American 'Reformer,'" *Washington Post,* October 17, 1988.

35. Norman M. Naimark, "Soviet-GDR Relations: An Historical Perspective," in *Berichte des Bundesinstituts für ostwissenschaftliche und internationale Studien* (Reports of the Federal Institute for East Scholarly and International Studies), no. 51, 1989, p. 10.

36. "Yakovlev Says Reunification up to Germans," *FBIS-SOV-89-219,* November 15, 1989, p. 24,

37. Gorbachev told an interviewer from *Time* magazine on August 28, 1985, that although desirable, Western cooperation was by no means essential to the success of Soviet *perestroika.*

38. "USSR Ambassador on Unification's Impact," *FBIS-WEU-90-153-U,* August 8, 1990, p. 12.

39. Philip Taubman, "Despite a Drive by Gorbachev, Economy Lags," *New York Times,* August 4, 1986.

40. Hannes Adomeit, "Gorbachev and German Unification: Revision of Thinking, Realignment of Power," *Problems of Communism* (July–August 1990), p. 8.

41. Quentin Peel, "Gorbachev Treats Europe's Leaders to a Few Home Thoughts," *Financial Times,* October 21, 1988.

42. Quoted in Lyne, "Making Waves," p. 211.

43. "Gorbachev Spurs 'Radical' Economic Decentralization," *Facts on File,* July 3, 1987, p. 475.

44. "Yugoslavia: Gorbachev Visits," *Facts on File,* vol. 48, no. 2470, March 25, 1988, p. 206.

45. Michael Farr, "New Soviet Credit Line Is Expected," *New York Times,* October 18, 1988.

46. Henry S. Rowen and Charles Wolf, Jr., *The Future of the Soviet Empire* (New York: St. Martin's Press, 1987), table 7–3. Quoted in Aron, "Gorbachev's Brest-Litovsk," p. 1.

47. Stanislav Kondrashev, "The Two Dimensions of Parity—Military-Strategic and Commonly Human," *Izvestiia,* February 4, 1989; quoted in Aron, "Gorbachev's Brest-Litovsk," p. 6.

48. "East-West Relations and Eastern Europe (A Soviet-American Dialogue)," *Problems of Communism* (May–August 1988), p. 60.

49. R. G. Bogdanov, *Vestnik Ministerstva inostrannykh del SSSR,* no. 15, August 15, 1988; in Eugene B. Rumer, "The German Question in Moscow's 'Common European Home': A Background to the Revolutions of 1989," *A Rand Note* (Santa Monica, Calif.: Rand Corporation, 1991), p. 5.

50. "Comecon Moscow Summit Held, " *Facts on File,* December 12, 1986, p. 918.

51. "Gorbachev, Kadar Confer," *Facts on File,* June 27, 1986, p. 471.

52. Robin Knight, Jeff Trimble, and Christopher Bobinski, "Gorbachev to East Europe: Shape Up," *U.S. News & World Report,* July 25, 1988, p. 40.

53. Tass, May 26, 1987. In April 1989, during a trip to Cuba, Gorbachev sought to convince Fidel Castro's regime to consider domestic changes that would ease Moscow's subsidy relationship with the tiny island nation. By U.S. estimates, the

Soviet Union was spending at the time $6–8 billion annually in military aid and economic support. See Bill Keller, "Gorbachev-Castro Face-Off: A Clash of Style and Policies," *New York Times,* April 2, 1989.

54. In Mlynár, *Can Gorbachev Save the Soviet Union?,* p. 124.

55. "Gorbachev Endorses Bloc's Transformation," *Washington Post,* November 22, 1989.

56. In Gerhard Wettig, "Die UdSSR und der politische Wandel in Osteuropa" (The USSR and political change in Eastern Europe), in *Berichte des Bundesinstituts für ostwissenschaftliche und internationale Studien* no. 25, 1990, p. 9.

57. Gorbachev, "Socialist Idea and Revolutionary Perestroika."

58. Mlynár, *Can Gorbachev Change the Soviet Union?* p. 144.

59. Interview with Eduard A. Shevardnadze, *Ogoněk,* November 1990, p. 4; quoted in Wettig, "Die UdSSR und der politische Wandel in Osteuropa," p. 9.

60. Otto Pick, "Problems of Adjustment: The Gorbachev Effect in Eastern Europe," *SAIS Review,* vol. 8, no. 1 (Winter-Spring 1988), p. 63.

61. Vasil Bilak, *Radio Hvezda,* February 10, 1987.

62. "Rock Fans, Police Clash," *Facts on File,* June 12, 1987, p. 435.

63. "Official Disputes 'Distorted' Reports on Rock Fans," *FBIS-EEU,* June 11, 1987, p. G 3.

64. Quoted in Philip Taubman, "The Kremlin Worries That Too Many Know Too Much," *New York Times,* January 26, 1986.

65. Hungary, which had first implemented economic reform in 1968, won Soviet Prime Minister Nikolai Ryzhkov's praise in April 1988 for its role as "the path-blazer of non-standard solutions." *Pravda,* April 19, 1988; quoted in Aron, "Gorbachev's Brest-Litovsk," p. 9.

66. Charles Gati, "Gorbachev and Eastern Europe," *Foreign Affairs,* vol. 65, no. 5 (Summer 1987), p. 972.

67. "Envoy to Moscow on Relations with USSR," *FBIS-EEU-90-039,* February 27, 1990, p. 31.

68. "Gerasimov in Italy: Discusses Brezhnev Doctrine," *FBIS-SOV-89-173,* September 8, 1989, p. 24.

69. Mlynár, *Can Gorbachev Save the Soviet Union?* p. 126.

70. Gorbachev, "The Socialist Idea and Revolutionary Perestroika."

71. "19th All-Union Conference of the CPSU: Foreign Politics and Diplomacy," *Pravda,* July 26, 1988.

72. Mikhail Gorbachev, "For a 'Common European Home,' for a New Way of Thinking," Moscow: Novosti, April 10, 1987, p. 10.

73. Mikhail Gorbachev, *Perestroika: New Thinking for our Country and the World* (New York: Harper & Row, Publishers, 1987), pp. 148, 165.

74. Quoted in Milan Svec, "East European Divides," *Foreign Policy,* no. 77 (Winter 1989–1990), p. 49.

75. Ibid., p. 50.

76. "Economist Bogomolov Discusses East Bloc Diversity," *FBIS-SOV-88-146,* July 29, 1988, p. 4.

77. "Bogomolov Discusses Economic Reform," *FBIS-SOV-88-174,* September 8, 1988, p. 71.

78. Jacques Renard et al., "Comment le Plan Secret de Gorbachev a échoué"

(How Gorbachev's secret plan failed), *L'Express,* July 6, 1990.

79. "Hungary: Gorbachev Vows Noninterference," *Facts on File,* April 7, 1989, pp. 243–44.

80. The stunning findings of a central committee panel studying post-World War II history signaled another vital step toward autonomy for the East bloc states. The panel's report, made public on February 16, 1989, acknowledged that communism had been forced on Eastern Europe by "political and military means" by Stalin's Soviet Union.

81. "Shishlin Interviewed on Polish Crisis," *FBIS-SOV-88-174,* September 8, 1988, p. 31.

82. Adomeit, "Gorbachev and German Unification," p. 3.

83. Angela Stent, "Doctrinal Discord," *New Republic,* January 8 and 15, 1990, p. 17.

84. David Remnick, "A Soviet Conservative Looks Back in Despair: Ligachev Cites Nation's 'Deplorable State,'" *Washington Post,* October 15, 1990.

85. "Gorbachev Hails European Change in Visit to France," *Facts on File,* July 7, 1989, p. 489.

86. Gorbachev, "The Socialist Idea and Revolutionary Perestroika."

87. "Yugoslavia: Gorbachev Visits," *Facts on File,* March 25, 1988, p. 206.

88. "More Chats with Public," *FBIS-SOV-89-206,* October 26, 1989, p. 32. See also "Gorbachev Continues Official Visit to Finland," *FBIS-SOV-89-206,* October 26, 1989, p. 30.

89. "Yakovlev on Relations with Finland, Perestroika," *FBIS-SOV-89-207,* October 27, 1989, p. 43.

90. "Akhromeyev Addresses Finnish Forum on Defense," *FBIS-SOV-89-176,* September 13, 1989, p. 28.

91. "Article Welcomes 'Finlandization' of East Europe," *FBIS-SOV-89-181,* September 20, 1989, p. 21.

92. Remnick, "A Soviet Conservative Looks Back in Despair."

CHAPTER 3: THE DILEMMA OF LEGITIMACY

1. "Basic Law," in Peter H. Merkl, *The Origin of the West German Republic* (New York: Oxford University Press, 1963), p. 213.

2. Ibid., p. 248.

3. Bonn was also a convenient choice for Konrad Adenauer. The home of the former mayor of Cologne and West Germany's first chancellor was nearby Rhondorf.

4. A notable exception to the Hallstein Doctrine was Bonn's establishment of diplomatic relations with the Soviet Union in September 1955, the same year the Soviets established diplomatic ties with East Berlin. Martin McCauley, *The German Democratic Republic since 1945* (New York: St. Martin's Press, 1983), p. 39.

5. Gerhard Schröder had first initiated these steps in 1961–1962 with Adenauer's approval. Schröder served as minister of the interior (1953–1961), foreign minister (1961–1966), and minister of defense (1966–1969). See William E. Griffith, *The Ostpolitik of the Federal Republic of Germany* (Cambridge, Mass.:

MIT Press, 1978), pp. 120–30.

6. David Marsh, *The Germans: Rich, Bothered and Divided* (London: Century, 1989), p. 55.

7. Jeffrey Herf, *War by Other Means: Soviet Power, West German Resistance, and the Battle of the Euromissiles* (New York: Free Press, 1991), p. 107.

8. Egon Bahr, "Vortrag in der evangelischen Akademie in Tutzing am 15. 7. 1963," (Lecture at the Protestant Academy in Tutzing on July 15, 1963) in Peter Brandt and Herbert Ammon, *Die Linke und die national Frage* (Hamburg: Rowohlt, 1981), p. 235.

9. Michael Balfour, *West Germany: A Contemporary History* (New York: St. Martin's Press, 1982), p. 250.

10. Willy Brandt, *People and Politics: The Years 1960–1975* (London: Collins, 1978), p. 397.

11. Willy Brandt, *Erinnerungen* (Memoirs) (Frankfurt am Main: Propyläen, 1989), p. 234.

12. Serge Schmemann, "The Border Is Open; Joyous East Germans Pour through the Wall; Party Pledges Freedoms, and City Exults," *New York Times,* November 11, 1989.

13. Eduard Neumaier, "Der Gast, der aus der Kälte kommt" (The guest who comes in from the cold), in *Zurück zu Deutschland: Umsturz und demokratischer Aufbruch in der DDR* (Back to Germany: collapse and democratic transformation in the GDR) (Bonn: Bouvier Verlag, 1990), p. 23.

14. Flora Lewis, "The Germans Aren't Tempted," *New York Times,* July 24, 1987.

15. Karin L. Johnston, "A Break with the Past? The Changing Nature of East German Foreign Policy," in Gale A. Mattox and John Vaughn, Jr., *Germany through American Eyes* (Boulder, Colo.: Westview Press, 1989), pp. 31–34.

16. See A. James McAdams, "Inter-German Detente: A New Balance," *Foreign Affairs* (Fall 1986), p. 151.

17. Marsh, *The Germans,* pp. 143–44. See also "Trostreiche Tüttelchen," *Der Spiegel,* January 23, 1989.

18. From Article 6 of the GDR's 1974 amended constitution.

19. Erich Honecker, *The German Democratic Republic: Pillar of Peace and Socialism* (New York: International Publishers, 1979), p. 97.

20. See Michael Sodaro, "The GDR and the Third World: Supplicant and Surrogate," in Michael Radu, ed., *Eastern Europe and the Third World: East vs. South* (New York: Praeger, 1981), pp. 106–41; and Woodrow J. Kuhns, "The German Democratic Republic in the Soviet Foreign Policy Scheme," *Soviet Union/Union Sovietique,* vol. 12, no. 1 (1985), pp. 91–96.

21. Erich Honecker, *Reden und Aufsätze* (Speeches and essays), vol. 1 (East Berlin, 1975), p. 241.

22. Timothy Garton Ash, "The German Revolution," *New York Review of Books,* December 21, 1989.

23. Henry Krisch, *The German Democratic Republic: The Search for Identity* (Boulder, Colo.: Westview Press, 1985), p. 7.

24. David Childs, *The GDR: Moscow's German Ally* (London: Unwin Hyman, 1988), p. 12; and Balfour, *West Germany.*

25. Walther Rathenau, who became Germany's foreign minister in 1922, signed the Treaty of Rapallo with the Soviet Union, a pact guided by Germany's desire for friendly political, military, and economic relations with the Soviet Union.

26. Ann L. Phillips, *Soviet Policy toward East Germany Reconsidered: The Postwar Decade* (New York: Greenwood Press, 1986), pp. 32–35. Semenov, who served as Moscow's ambassador to Bonn from 1978 to 1986, never lost, it seems, his fascination for the potential that West Germany's capitalist economy could offer the Soviet Union. Helmut Schmidt recalls in his memoirs, *Men and Powers*, a 1966 meeting with Semenov, at the time assistant foreign minister, in which his Soviet interlocutor was still dwelling on the idea of close economic collaboration with West Germany. See Helmut Schmidt, *Men and Powers: A Political Perspective*, trans. Ruth Hein (New York: Random House, 1989), p. 7.

27. Dennis L. Bark and David R. Gress, *A History of West Germany: From Shadow to Substance* (Oxford: Basil Blackwell, 1989), p. 114.

28. Ibid., p. 5. The Albanians were excluded as well. See also Childs, *The GDR*, p. 20.

29. The trip was first reported by East German authorities in 1978. See Hermann Weber, *Geschichte der DDR* (History of the GDR) (Munich: Deutscher Taschenbuchverlag, 1985), p. 36.

30. The dominant opinion of Germans living in the western zones that a united government would not be restored unless Soviet control were accepted led to the provisional establishment of the Federal Republic. See Bark and Gress, *History of West Germany*, p. 59.

31. Childs, *The GDR*, p. 25.

32. *Neues Deutschland,* October 14, 1949; quoted in Weber, *Geschichte der DDR*, p. 29.

33. Norman M. Naimark, "Soviet-GDR Relations: An Historical Overview," p. 6. For a description of Soviet overtures to resolve the German question, see Childs, *The GDR*, pp. 42–46.

34. See *Zur Geschichte der DDR: Von Ulbricht zu Honecker* (On the history of the GDR: from Ulbricht to Honecker) (Bonn: Friedrich Ebert Foundation, 1986), p. 19.

35. Weber, *Geschichte der DDR*, p. 234.

36. Naimark, "Soviet-GDR Relations," p. 9.

37. Martin McCauley, "The German Democratic Republic and the Soviet Union," in David Childs, ed., *Honecker's Germany* (London: Allen & Unwin, 1985), p. 152.

38. Childs, *The GDR*, p. 29.

39. From a hitherto secret Soviet document, excerpted in *Thuringer Allgemeine*, no. 126, June 16, 1990, quoted in "Moskau wollte radikale Wende," in *Pressespiegel*, Berlin: Gesamtdeutsches Institut, no. 12, July 5, 1990, p. 16.

40. Childs, *The GDR*, p. 31.

41. Ibid., p. 33.

42. *Zur Geschichte der DDR*, p. 244.

43. Quoted in ibid., p. 27.

44. Childs, *The GDR*, p. 59.

45. Balfour, *West Germany*, p. 201.

46. Helmut M. Muller et al., *Schlaglichter der Deutschen Geschichte* (Key events in German history) (Mannheim: Meyers Lexikonverlag, 1986), p. 363.

47. Norman M. Naimark, "Is It True What They're Saying about East Germany?" *Orbis* (Fall 1979), p. 571.

48. *Neues Deutschland*, June 16, 1961.

49. Woodrow J. Kuhns, "The German Democratic Republic in the Soviet Foreign Policy Scheme," *Soviet Union/Union Sovietique*, vol. 12, no. 1 (1985), p. 80.

50. *Zur Geschichte der DDR*, p. 34.

51. Ibid., pp. 34–35.

52. Childs, *The GDR*, p. 73.

53. Ibid., p. 80.

54. Melvin Croan, "East Germany: The Soviet Connection," in the Washington Papers series, vol. 4, no. 36 (Washington, D.C.: Center for Strategic and International Studies [CSIS], 1976), p. 26.

55. A. James McAdams, "The New Logic in Soviet-GDR Relations," *Problems of Communism* (September–October, 1988), pp. 48–49. See also A. James McAdams, *East Germany and Detente: Building Authority after the Wall* (Cambridge: Cambridge University Press, 1985), pp. 110–15.

56. *Neues Deutschland*, April 1, 1971.

57. Ilse Spittmann, "Warum Ulbricht stürzte" (Why Ulbricht fell from power), *Deutschland Archiv*, June 1971; quoted in Melvin Croan, "East Germany: The Soviet Connection," p. 28.

58. McAdams, "The New Logic," p. 51.

59. Childs, *The GDR*, p.85.

60. Honecker Letter to Chancellor Kohl, *Neues Deutschland*, October 10, 1983.

61. When Bonn announced its guaranteed credit of DM 950 million to East Berlin on July 25, 1984, West German officials also stated that the GDR had consented to eleven measures aimed at improving inter-German travel. In addition, East Berlin had reportedly given assurances that "several thousand" of its citizens would be allowed to emigrate to the West that year. (By the end of the year over 30,000 East Germans had been allowed to emigrate to West Germany.) Hannes Adomeit, "The German Factor in Soviet *Westpolitik*," *Annals of the American Academy of Political and Social Science*, special volume, *Soviet Foreign Policy in an Uncertain World*, ed. John J. Stremlau (September 1985), p. 27.

62. "East of Eden: A Survey of Eastern Europe: 'Who, Whom, Then?'" *The Economist*, August 12, 1989, p. 18.

63. Quoted in Wolfgang Seiffert, "Die Deutschlandpolitik der SED im Spannungsfeld der sowjetischen Interessenlage" (The German policy of the SED in scope of Soviet interests), *Deutschland Archiv*, March 1987, p. 280.

64. "The Neues Deutschland Hails Gorbachev Report," *Foreign Broadcast Information Service, Eastern Europe (FBIS-EEU)*, March 11, 1986, pp. E 1, E 2, E 3.

65. Quoted in Ilse Spittmann, "Gorbatschow besucht die SED" (Gorbachev visits the SED), *Deutschland Archiv*, May 1986, p. 450.

66. "Shevardnadze Reply Toast," *FBIS-EEU*, February 4, 1987, p. E 10.

67. Quoted in Dettmar Cramer, "Der Bundespräsident in der Sowjetunion" (The federal president in the Soviet Union), *Deutschland Archiv*, August 1987, p. 793.

68. Ibid., p. 792.

69. Gerhard von Glinski, "Angenehme Stimmen ihres Herrn" (Pleasant voices of the boss), *Rheinischer Merkur*, July 17, 1987, p. 2.

70. Schmidt, *Men and Powers*, pp. 104–5.

71. Interview with Eduard Shevardnadze in *Argumenty i Fakty*, 2/1990, p. 2; quoted in Gerhard Wettig, "Die UdSSR und der politische Wandel in Osteuropa" (The USSR and political change in Eastern Europe), *Berichte des Bundesinstituts für ostwissenschaftliche und international Studien*, no. 25, 1990, p. 38.

72. "Lerne beim Deutschen" (Learn from the Germans), *Der Spiegel*, vol. 38 (1990), p. 180.

73. Jochen Thies, *Deutschland von Innen: Beobachtungen aus Wechselnder Perspektive* (Germany from within: observations from changing perspectives) (Bonn: Aktuell, 1990), p. 227.

74. Schmidt, *Men and Powers*, p. 96.

75. Ibid., p. 106.

76. For a study of the West German–Soviet trade relationship during the first three decades after the war, see Angela Stent, *From Embargo to Ostpolitik: The Political Economy of West-German Soviet Relations, 1955–1980* (Cambridge: Cambridge University Press, 1981).

77. Wolfgang Hoffmann, "Träumen vom Milliardengeschäft" (Dreams of billions in business), *Die Zeit*, April 24, 1987.

78. Genscher's speech in Potsdam from November 6, 1988; quoted in Marsh, *The Germans*, p. 49.

79. "FRG's Strauss Visits Moscow, Meets with Officials," *FBIS-SOV-87-249*, December 29, 1987, p. 51.

80. "Further on Visit of FRG's Strauss to Moscow," *FBIS-SOV-87-251*, December 31, 1987, p. 26.

81. Sten Martenson, "Moskau ist an wirtschaftlicher Zusammenarbeit interessiert" (Moscow is interested in economic cooperation), *Stuttgarter Zeitung*, February 2, 1987.

82. Thomas F. O'Boyle, "Russians Are Coming to Bonn, and Germans Are Positively Aglow," *Wall Street Journal*, June 3, 1988.

83. Mikhail Gorbachev, *Perestroika: Die zweite russische Revolution* (Perestroika: the second Russian revolution) (Munich, 1987), p. 261.

84. Franz Josef Strauss, *Die Erinnerungen* (Memoirs) (Berlin: Siedler Verlag, 1989), p. 133.

85. "Mehrheit der westdeutschen vereint Gefahr aus dem Osten" (Majority of West Germans say no danger from the east), *Frankfurter Allgemeine Zeitung*, December 5, 1988, p. 4.

86. A poll by ZDF television from November 6, 1989; quoted in Marsh, *The Germans*, p. 47.

87. "W Germans and Moscow Sign DM3bn Line of Credit," *Financial Times* (London), October 26, 1988.

88. David Marsh, "Kohl Encounters Cool Breezes in Moscow," *Financial Times* (London), October 26, 1988.

89. Quoted in Günther Wagenlehner, "Gorbatschow und die deutsche Frage" (Gorbachev and the German question), *Deutschland Archiv*, September 1989, p. 1005.

90. Egon Krenz with Hartmut König and Günter Rittner, *Wenn Wauern Fallen: Die Friedliche Revolution: Vorgeschichte-Ablauf-Auswirkungen* (When walls fall: the peaceful revolution: history-process-consequences) (Vienna: Paul Neff Verlag, 1990), p. 119.

91. Nicolae Portugalov, "FRG after Elections: Notes by an Observer," *Moscow News*, no. 9, 1987, p. 77.

92. In *Zur Geschichte der DDR*, p. 90.

93. The government declaration by Otto Grotewohl, *Neues Deutschland*, October 13, 1949; quoted in Hermann Weber, *Geschichte der DDR*, p. 27.

94. Ibid., *Zur Geschichte der DDR*, p. 93.

95. Quoted in Croan, "East Germany: The Soviet Connection," p. 96.

96. See Angela Stent, "Intra-German Relations: The View From Bonn," in Robert Gerald Livingston, ed., *The Federal Republic of Germany in the 1980s: Foreign Policies and Domestic Changes* (New York: German Information Center, 1983), pp. 23-26.

97. Stephen R. Burant, ed., *East Germany: A Country Study* (Washington, D.C.: U.S. Government Printing Office, 1988), p. 167.

98. *U.S. Joint Publications Research Service*, no. 71618, August 3, 1978, p. 8.

99. Eberhard Schulz, "Sowjetische Deutschland-Politik: Noch immer unentschlossen?" (Soviet German policy: still undecided?), *Deutschland Archiv*, September 1987, p. 942.

100. "Jedes Land Wählt seine Lösung" (Each country chooses its own solution), Interview with Kurt Hager in *Stern*, April 7, 1987, p. 143.

101. Leonid Potshchivalov, "We and the Germans," *Literaturnaya Gazeta*, July 20, 1988.

102. "CSU Chairman Strauss Comments on USSR Visit," *FBIS-WEU-87-001*, January 4, 1988, p. 3. See also "Strauss Speaks of Gorbachev Talk, Germany Policy," in *FBIS-WEU-87-002*, January 5, 1987, p. 5.

103. "Portugalov Interviewed on FRG-GDR Ties," in *FBIS-SOV-88-033*, February 19, 1988, p. 37.

104. Boris Meissner, "Das 'neue Denken' Gorbatschows und die Wende in der sowjetischen Deutschlandpolitik" (The "new thinking" of Gorbachev and the shift in Soviet policy on Germany), in *Die Deutschen und die Architektur des europäischen Hauses* (The Germans and the architecture of the European home), Werner Weidenfeld, ed. (Köln: Verlag Wissenschaft und Politik, 1990), p. 72.

105. "Gorbachev Interview with *Der Spiegel*," *FBIS-SOV-88-206*, October 25, 1988, p. 33.

106. Karl-Eduard von Schnitzler, "Wider besseres Wissen" (Against better judgment), *Neues Deutschland*, December 3–4, 1988; reprinted in *Pressespiegel*, no. 20, December 15, 1988, pp. 1–2.

107. Hannes Adomeit, "Gorbachev and German Unification: Revision of Thinking, Realignment of Power," *Problems of Communism* (July–August 1990), p. 5.

108. See Fred Oldenburg, "'Neues Denken' in der sowjetischen Deutschlandpolitik" (New thinking in Soviet policy on Germany), *Deutschland Archiv*, November 11, 1987, pp. 1154–60. See also F. Stephen Larrabee, "The View from Moscow," in F. Stephen Larrabee, ed., *The Two German States and European Security* (New York: St. Martin's Press, 1989), p. 201.

109. "Former Envoy Falin Assesses 'Offer' by FRG's Kohl," *FBIS-SOV*, March 20, 1987, p. G 6.

110. Oldenburg, "'Neues Denken,'" p. 1157.

111. "Berlin—'Nicht das letzte Wort" (Berlin—not the last word), *Der Spiegel*, October 5, 1987, p. 14.

112. "Wir sagen ja zum europäischen Haus" (We say yes to the European house), interview with Valentin Falin, *Vorwärts*, no. 42, October 17, 1987.

113. "Call for Change on W. Berlin Policy Questioned," *FBIS-SOV-88-170*, September 1, 1988, p. 24.

114. "Berlin—'Nicht das letzte Wort.'"

115. "Further on Gerasimov Berlin Wall Statement," *FBIS-SOV-87-200*, October 16, 1987, p. 18.

116. "Gerasimov Discusses West Berlin, Shikany," *FBIS-SOV-87-199*, October 15, 1987, p. 16. "Falin Views on 4-Power Agreement Examined," *FBIS-SOV-87-194*, p. 35.

117. "Further on Gerasimov Berlin Wall Statement."

118. "Wir sagen ja zum europäischen Haus."

119. "The New World Disorder?" interview with Valentin Falin and others, *New Perspectives Quarterly*, vol. 7, no. 2 (Spring 1990), p. 23.

120. Quoted in Wolfgang Leonhard, "Die Sowjet-Reformen und die DDR" (The Soviet reforms and the GDR), *Deutschland Archiv*, July 1989, p. 760.

121. "So stand der Wagen vor dem Pferd," interview with Vyacheslav Dashichev, *Der Spiegel*, vol. 27, 1988, p. 127.

122. *Neues Deutschland*, June 10, 1988, p. 2.

123. See the interview with Vyacheslav Dashichev, "Ohne freie Marktwirtshaft scheitert die Perestroika . . ." (Without a free market perestroika will fail), *Osteuropa*, no. 6, June 1990, pp. 495–502.

124. Vyacheslav Dashichev, "Econonomer Schaden für Moskau," *Der Spiegel*, February 1990, p. 148.

125. Ibid.

126. Ibid.

127. Ibid., p. 150.

128. *Die Welt*, June 9, 1988; and *Frankfurter Allgemeine Zeitung*, June 8, 1988; quoted in Wolfgang Seiffert, *Die Deutschen und Gorbatschow: Chancen für einen Interessenausgleich* (The Germans and Gorbachev: chances for a balance of interests) (Erlangen: Straube, 1989), p. 54.

129. Dashichev, "Enormer Schaden für Moskau,"p. 148.

130. Ibid., p. 152.

131. Ibid., p. 154.

132. *Moscow News*, no. 25, 1989, p. 6; quoted in Naimark, "Soviet-GDR Relations," p. 14.

133. "*Pravda* Profiles FRG's Helmut Kohl," *FBIS-SOV-89-084*, May 3, 1989, p. 35.

134. Michael J. Sodaro, *Moscow, Germany, and the West: From Khrushchev to Gorbachev* (Ithaca: Cornell University Press, 1990), p. 359.

135. "Yakovlev, Biryukova, Silayev Meet FRG Banker," *FBIS-SOV-89-106*, June 5, 1989, p. 34.

136. "Gorbachev's Turn," *The Economist*, June 10, 1989, p. 47.

137. "He Came, They Saw, He Conquered," *The Economist*, June 17, 1989, p. 54.

138. "Text of Soviet-FRG Joint Statement," *FBIS-WEU-89-112*, June 13, 1989, p. 9.

139. "Portugalov Views Soviet-German Relations," *FBIS-SOV-89-109*, June 8, 1989, p. 15.

140. "Gorbachev Reportedly to Visit GDR 7 Oct.," *FBIS-EEU-89-119*, June 22, 1989, p. 25.

141. Hamburg DPA, "Gorbachev: German 'Reunification Not on Agenda,'" *FBIS-SOV-89-222*, November 20, 1989, p. 34.

142. "Portugalov Says Wall Had 'Lost Main Function,'" *FBIS-SOV-89-219*, November 15, 1989, p. 2.

143. "Germany Policy Adviser at the CPSU Central Committee," by Novosti correspondent Vladimir Markov: "Two Systems, One Nation," *Frankfurter Allgemeine Zeitung*, November 17, 1989, p. 2; in *FBIS-SOV-89-222*, November 20, 1989, pp. 33–34.

144. Nicolae Portugalov, "The Soviet View: Two Germanys, in Confederation," *New York Times*, December 15, 1989.

CHAPTER 4: PRELUDE TO UPHEAVAL

1. Vladimir Tismaneanu, "Nascent Civil Society in the German Democratic Republic," *Problems of Communism* (March–June 1989), p. 92.

2. Hannes Adomeit, "Gorbachev and German Unification: Revision of Thinking, Realignment of Power," *Problems of Communism* (July–August 1990), p. 6.

3. Quoted in "What Gorbachev Did Not Say," *Newsweek*, April 28, 1986, p. 46.

4. Wolfgang Seiffert, "Ist die DDR ein Modell?" (Is the GDR a model?), *Deutschland Archiv*, May 1987, pp. 470–74. See also Seiffert, "Die Deutschland-politik der SED im Spannungsfeld der sowjetischen Interessenlage" (The Germany policy of the SED in the scope of Soviet interests), *Deutschland Archiv*, March 1987, p. 282.

5. "Wenn das Kombinat Herr im Haus ist: Generaldirektor Boris Iwano-witsch Fomin berichtet über Erfahrungen von einer Studienreise" (When the combine is head of the house: general director Boris Ivanovich Famin reports on experiences from a study trip), *Neues Deutschland*, February 1, 1987.

6. See Robert J. McCartney, "West German Aid Helps East Germany Avoid Crisis," *Washington Post*, August 8, 1989.

7. Günter Schabowski, *Das Politbüro*, Frank Sieren and Ludwig Koehne, eds. (Hamburg: Rohwohlt Taschenbuch Verlag, 1990), p. 34.

8. Ibid., pp. 36–37.

9. Egon Krenz, with Hartmut König and Günter Rittner, *Wenn Wauern Fallen: Die Friedliche Revolution: Vorgeschichte-Ablauf-Auswirkungen* (When walls fall: the peaceful revolution: history-process-consequences) (Vienna: Paul Neff Verlag, 1990), p. 23.

10. Ibid., p. 24.

11. Doris Cornelsen, in Gert-Joachim Glaessner, ed., *Die DDR in der Ära Honecker* (The DDR in the Honecker era) (West Berlin: Westdeutscher Verlag, 1988), p. 370.

12. "Honecker kritisiert Lieferkürzungen der Sowjetunion" (Honecker criticizes cutbacks in deliveries from the Soviet Union), *Frankfurter Allgemeine Zeitung,* December 5, 1988.

13. "Unsere Unzureichende Effektivität: DDR-Arbeiter beschweren sich beim Staatsrat über Mangel im System" (Our insufficient effectiveness: GDR workers complain about shortcomings in their system), *Der Spiegel,* December 19, 1988.

14. "Delivery Backlogs, Supply Problems," *Foreign Broadcast Information Service, Eastern Europe (FBIS-EEU)-88-126,* June 30, 1988, p. 26.

15. Quoted in "Honecker kritisiert Lieferkürzungen," December 5, 1988.

16. Interview with Kurt Hager, *Stern,* April 9, 1987. Reprinted in "German Unification," *World Affairs,* guest editor Jeffrey Gedmin, vol. 152, no. 4 (Spring 1990), p. 199.

17. Norman M. Naimark, "Soviet-GDR Relation: An Historical Overview," *Berichte des Bundesinstituts für ostwissenschaftliche und internationale Studien* (Reports of the Federal Institute for East-Scholarly and International Studies), no. 51, 1989, p. 19. Fred Oldenburg, "The Impact of Gorbachev's Reform on the GDR," *Berichte des BIOst,* no. 25, 1988, pp. 9–11.

18. "Bild: Honecker Wants to Resign Next Spring," *FBIS-EEU,* June 2, 1987, p. G 1.

19. *Bild,* June 15, 1987, p. 1; in "Bild Reports Mielke's Nephew Wants to Leave Nation," *FBIS-EEU,* June 15, 1987, p. G 3.

20. Interview with Erich Honecker, "Jyllands Posten," *Deutschland Archiv,* May 1988, pp. 569–70.

21. "Pacifists Praise 'Great Echo' of Gorbachev's Reforms," *FBIS-EEU,* June 1, 1987, p. G1.

22. Thomas F. O'Boyle, "Winds of Change Coming from Moscow Stir Hopes for Liberty in East Germany," *Wall Street Journal,* February 19, 1988.

23. "Commentary Denounces 'Glasnost,'" *FBIS-EEU-88-022,* February 3, 1988, p. 10.

24. "SED Attempts to Calm Quarrel with Church," *FBIS-EEU-87-235,* December 8, 1987, p. 15.

25. *Neues Deutschland,* February 17, 1988; reprinted in *Deutschland Archiv,* April 1988, pp. 453–54.

26. Interview with Manfred Stolpe, *Der Spiegel,* February 15, 1988; in Tismaneanu, "Nascent Civil Society in the German Democratic Republic," p. 98.

27. *Der Tagesspiegel,* West Berlin, September 22, 1988; quoted in Matthias Hartmann, "'Hier Ändert sich Nichts'; Zur Synodaltagung des Kirchenbundes" (Nothing is changing here: on the council meeting of the church federation), *Deutschland Archiv,* October 1988, p. 1027.

28. John Tagliabue, "In East Bloc, an Expanding Network of Dissenters," *New York Times,* March 22, 1988.

29. "FRG Paper on Honecker's 'Snubbing' of USSR," *FBIS-EEU-88-174,*

September 8, 1988, p. 16.

30. *Der Spiegel,* July 11, 1988; *FBIS-EEU-88-133,* July 12, 1988.

31. "Press Plays Down Extent of Change in Hungary," *FBIS-EEU-88-101,* May 25, 1988, p. 16.

32. "ND Deletes Genscher Comments on Rights, Wall," *FBIS-EEU-88-115,* June 15, 1988, p. 19.

33. "Die DDR und der 'Sputnik,'" *Neues Deutschland,* November 24, 1988.

34. Gedmin, "German Unification."

35. *Neues Deutschland,* June 10, 1988; in Barbara Donovan, "Signs of Cultural Liberalization in the GDR?" *Radio Free Europe* (RAD Background Report/111), June 21, 1988, p. 1. Donovan notes that while GDR officials rejected any reappraisal of the past, a number of GDR intellectuals had begun to broach such controversial subjects in literary journals, testing the limits of party tolerance.

36. "SED-Presse mit neuer Führung" (SED press with new leadership), *Die Welt,* November 17, 1989.

37. "Where Sputnik Can't Land," *The Economist,* November 26, 1988, p. 52.

38. Ibid., p. 52.

39. "'Prawda'-Schmuggel in die 'DDR'" (Pravda smuggled into the GDR), *Die Welt,* December 20, 1988.

40. "Sowjetische Filme in der DDR wieder freigegeben" (Soviet films released again in the GDR), *Süddeutsche Zeitung,* February 22, 1989.

41. See Barbara Donovan, "Criticism in the GDR of the Soviet Film *Repentance*," *RFE/RAD* Background Report/215, November 9, 1987.

42. "Shevardnadze Interviewed on Perestroika Changes," *FBIS-SOV-89-209,* October 31, 1989, p. 23–24.

43. "Ein Orden rettet DDR-Zeitschrift" (An award saves GDR magazine), *Frankfurter Allgemeine Zeitung,* December 23, 1988.

44. "Hager: Kein Nachholbedarf an Demokratie" (Hager: No need to catch up on democracy), *Frankfurter Allgemeine Zeitung,* January 16, 1988.

45. Barry Newman, "East Berlin Leaders Recoil from Glasnost," *Wall Street Journal,* January 31, 1989.

46. Ibid.

47. "Czech, East German Protests Crushed," *Facts on File,* January 20, 1989, p. 26.

48. Henry Kamm, "East German Theorist Rejects Soviet-Style Change," *New York Times,* February 28, 1989.

49. *Frankfurter Rundschau,* March 14, 1989.

50. "Kein Herz für Gorbatschow: DDR-Behörden verhindern Ausstellung in Sowjetischer Kaserne" (No heart for Gorbachev: GDR authorities prevent exhibition in Soviet compound), *Die Welt,* April 1, 1989. ADN emphatically denied these reports. See "DDR: Meldungen über Ausstellungsverbot erlogen" (GDR: False reports on prohibition of exhibit), *Frankfurter Rundschau,* April 3, 1989.

51. "Personnel Changes in Moscow Embassy Reported," *FBIS-EEU-89-119,* June 22, 1989, p. 26.

52. "SED beginnt mit Parteibuch-Umtausch" (SED begins with change in membership books), *Frankfurter Allgemeine Zeitung,* August 21, 1989.

53. *Neues Deutschland*, May 1, 1989.

54. Günter Schabowski, *Der Absturz* (The fall) (Berlin: Rowohlt, 1991), p. 165.

55. "Unnamed GDR Opposition Member Interviewed," *FBIS-EEU-89-141*, July 25, 1989, p. 30.

56. "ZDF Prevented from Filming," *FBIS-EEU-89-130*, July 10, 1989, p. 22.

57. "In SED-Kadern herrscht Frustration" (In SED cadres frustration reigns), *Die Welt*, June 26, 1989.

58. Ibid.

59. "Shevardnadze Meets GDR's Honecker," *FBIS-SOV-89-111*, June 12, 1989, p. 16.

60. "GDR Foreign Minister Interviewed," *FBIS-SOV-89-111*, June 12, 1989, p. 18.

61. "Gorbachev Reportedly to Visit GDR 7 Oct," *FBIS-EEU-89-119*, June 22, 1989, p. 25.

62. "Reunification 'A Matter for the German People,'" *FBIS-SOV-89-132*, July 12, 1989, p. 47.

63. "Moskauer gegen die Mauer" (Moscovites against the wall), *Die Welt*, November 20, 1989.

64. *Neues Deutschland*, July 3, 1989; "Daily on Honecker's Soviet Trip, USSR Ties," *FBIS-EEU-89-130*, p. 2.

65. "Honecker's Speech at Rally in Maynitogorsk," *FBIS-EEU-89-129*, July 7, 1989, p. 39.

66. Leon Aron, "Gorbachev's Brest-Litovsk: The Kremlin's Grand Compromise in Eastern Europe," Backgrounder (Washington, D.C.: Heritage Foundation), August 15, 1989, p. 9.

67. "Radio Stations Cause GDR 'Concern, Surprise,'" *FBIS-EEU-89-135*, July 17, 1989, p. 19.

68. "Unity Strained at Warsaw Pact Summit," *Facts on File*, July 14, 1989, p. 520.

69. Krenz, *Wenn Mauern Fallen*, p. 27.

70. "SED Official Hints at Ideological Split in Bloc," *FBIS-EEU-89-132*, July 12, 1989, p. 12.

71. Ibid.

72. "Ungarische Reformpolitik in der SED-Press; interview von 'Neues Deutschland' mit Parteichef Grosz" (Hungarian reform policies in the SED press: 'Neues Deutschland' interviews Party Chief Grosz), *Neue Züricher Zeitung*, August 1, 1989.

73. "Hager Comments on Development of Socialism," *FBIS-EEU-89-137*, July 19, 1989, pp. 23–26.

74. "DDR verbittet sich Ratschläge zu Reformen" (GDR forbids proposals for reform), *Frankfurter Allgemeine Zeitung*, August 4, 1989.

75. "East Bloc Differs on Invasion," *Facts on File*, 1989, p. 624.

76. "Mazowiecki Vows More Capitalism," *Facts on File*, 1989, p. 614.

77. "'Sputnik': Breschnew war mehrmals klinisch tot: Magazin spricht von 'Marionette'/Vergleich mit Stalin" (Sputnik: Brezhnev was more than once clinically dead: Magazine tells of "Marionettes"/comparison with Stalin), *Die Welt*, February 7, 1989.

78. "Gorbachev Hails European Change in Visit to France," *Facts on File*, July 7, 1989, p. 490.

79. Steven Emerson, "Where Have All the Spies Gone," *New York Times Magazine*, August 12, 1990, p. 19.

80. In 1989 the Stasi had a budget estimated at $1 billion. "Destasifying Germany: The Undergrowth of Evil," *The Economist*, December 1, 1990, p. 19.

81. Ibid., p. 20.

82. Ibid.

83. Ibid.

84. "Honecker befahl Stasi-Einsatz in Polen: Spitzel hörten Kirchenführer und Walesa ab" (Honecker ordered Stasi work in Poland: informers eavesdropped on church leaders and Walesa), interview with a former high-ranking Stasi official, *Die Welt*, May 30, 1990.

85. Henry Krisch, *The German Democratic Republic: The Search for Identity* (Boulder, Colo.: Westview Press, 1985), p. 122.

86. Quoted in Matthias Hartmann, "Signale vom Evangelischen Kirchentag" (Signals from the Evangelical church meeting), *Deutschland Archiv*, August 1987, p. 842.

87. Quoted in Barbara Donovan, "Ten Years of Church-State Rapprochement in the GDR," RAD Background Report/38, Radio Free Europe/Radio Liberty, Munich, p. 2.

88. In Tismaneanu, "Nascent Civil Society," p. 95.

89. Quoted in Ronald D. Asmus, "Is There a Peace Movement in the GDR?" *Orbis* (Summer 1983), p. 324.

90. Robert F. Goeckel, "Church and Society," in Marilyn Rueschemeyer and Christiane Lemke, eds., *The Quality of Life in the German Democratic Republic: Changes and Developments in a State Socialist Society* (New York: M.E. Sharpe, Inc., 1989), p. 222.

91. Letter from Bishop Werner Leich to Erich Honecker, published in "Dialog zwischen Kirche und Staat" (Dialogue between church and state), *Deutschland Archiv*, April 1988, p. 457.

92. Ibid., p. 456.

93. Tismaneanu, "Nascent Civil Society," p. 90.

94. "Church Urges SED to Change Domestic Policy," *FBIS-EEU-88-127*, July 1, 1988, pp. 28–29.

95. For details of church newspaper censorship during this period, see Frithjof Heller, "Unbotmässiges von 'Grenzfall' bis 'Wendezeit'" (Unruliness from "Grenzfall" to "Wendezeit"), *Deutschland Archiv*, November 1988, pp. 1188–96.

96. Quoted in Ernst Elitz, *Sie waren dabei: Ost-deutsche Profile von Bärbel Bohley zu Lothar de Maizière* (They were there: East German profiles from Bärbel Bohley to Lothar de Maizaière) (Stuttgart: Deutsche Verlags Anstalt, 1991), p. 133.

97. "Evangelische Kirche in der DDR" (The Evangelical church in the GDR), *Deutschland Archiv*, September 1987, p. 993–94.

98. "Stolpe Speaks on Domestic, Foreign Issues," in *FBIS-EEU-89-117*, June 20, 1989, p. 37.

99. "Church Conference Calls for Reform, Free Press," *FBIS-EEU-88-123*,

June 27, 1988, p. 16.

100. "Stolpe Speaks on Domestic, Foreign Issues," *FBIS-EEU-89-117*, June 20, 1989, p. 40.

101. "Evangelical Church Official Interviewed on Reform," *FBIS-EEU-89-159*, August 18, 1989, p. 21.

102. "Stolpe Says Krenz 'Gorbachev's Candidate,'" *FBIS-EEU-89-205*, October 25, 1989, p. 26.

103. Gedmin, "The Citizen Must Feel He Is Trusted," in *German Unification*, p. 209.

104. Ibid.

105. *Der Spiegel*, September 25, 1989; in "Church Official Blames Governments," *FBIS-EEU-89-185*, p. 24.

106. "Krenz, Leich Meeting Produces Positive Message," *FBIS-EEU-89-205*, October 25, 1989, p. 26. See also "Bishop Leich Warns against 'National Euphoria,'" *FBIS-EEU-90-006*, January 9, 1990, p. 46.

107. June 17 was the West German national holiday commemorating the East German workers' uprising of June 17, 1953. Robert Leicht, "Gratwanderung ohne Absturz; Redner am 17. Juni: Manfred Stolpe, Mittler zwischen Staat und Kirche" (Balancing act without a fall: Manfred Stolpe, mediator between state and church), *Die Zeit*, June 22, 1990.

108. "Member Seeks to 'Root Out' Fear," *FBIS-EEU-195*, October 11, 1989, p. 20.

109. Quoted in Tismaneanu, "Nascent Civil Society," p. 93.

110. Quoted in Karl Wilhelm Fricke, *Opposition und Widerstand in der DDR: Ein Politischer Report* (Opposition and resistance in the GDR: a political report) (Cologne: Verlag Wissenschaft und Politik, 1984), p. 177.

111. Ibid.

112. Quoted in Asmus, "Is There a Peace Movement in the GDR?" p. 311.

113. Fricke, *Opposition und Widerstand in der DDR*, p. 181.

114. Tismaneanu, "Nascent Civil Society," p. 105.

115. "Zum 17. Januar und den Folgen," (On January 17 and its consequences), *Deutschland Archiv*, April 1988, p. 431.

116. "Action Extended against Peace Groups," *FBIS-EEU-87-234*, December 7, 1987, p. 22.

117. "East Germany vs. 'Glasnost,'" *Die Zeit*, reprinted in *World Press Review*, April 1988, p. 34.

118. "Wir brauchen vor allem Glasnost; Der DDR-Schriftsteller Stephan Hermlin über die Reformfähigkeit des SED-Staats" (We need glasnost above all: the GDR author Stephan Hermlin on the ability of the GDR state to reform); (interview with Stephan Hermlin), *Der Spiegel*, February 6, 1989.

119. David Childs, *The GDR: Moscow's German Ally* (London: Unwin Hyman, 1988), p. 213.

120. "Wir brauchen vor allem Glasnost," p. 70.

121. Ilse Spittmann, "SED setzt auf Zeitgewinn" (The SED counts on winning time), *Deutschland Archiv*, June 1988, p. 689.

122. "Wir brauchen vor allem Glasnost."

123. Elizabeth Pond, "East Germany's Unique Peace Movement Faces Harder

Times," *Christian Science Monitor,* January 5, 1984.

124. "'New Forum' Continues as 'Citizens' Initiative,'" *FBIS-EEU-89-195,* October 11, 1989, p. 19.

125. Quoted in Elitz, *Sie waren dabei,* p. 28.

126. "Writers Ask 'Democratic Dialogue at All Levels,'" *FBIS-EEU-89-184,* September 25, 1989, p. 23.

127. Karl-Heinz Arnold, *Die ersten hundert Tage des Hans Modrow* (The first hundred days of Hans Modrow) (Berlin: Dietz Verlag, 1990), pp. 9–10.

128. "Pastor on Problem of Citizens Leaving Country," *FBIS-EEU-89-160,* August 21, 1989, p. 5.

129. "Priest Interviewed on Resolution with FDP," *FBIS-EEU-89-159,* August 18, 1989, p. 22.

130. See "East German CDU Chairman Resigns," RFE/RL Daily Report, No. 155, August 16, 1990, p. 1–2.

131. Quoted in *40 Jahre Sozialistische Einheitspartei Deutschlands* (Forty years, Socialist Unity party of Germany) (Bonn: Friedrich Ebert Stiftung, 1985), p. 26.

132. Fricke, *Opposition und Widerstand in der DDR,* p. 111.

133. Ibid., p. 106.

134. Weber, *Geschichte der DDR,* p. 287.

135. Ibid., p. 289.

136. Ibid.

137. Ibid., p. 288. See also Wolfgang Harich, "East Germany: Revolt of a Communist," *New Republic,* May 4, 1957, pp. 388–90.

138. Harich, "East Germany: Revolt of a Communist," pp. 389–90.

139. Fricke, *Opposition und Widerstand in der DDR,* p. 116.

140. Weber, *Geschichte der DDR,* p. 294.

141. Fricke, *Opposition und Widerstand in der DDR,* p. 185.

142. Schabowski, *Das Politbüro,* p. 27.

143. A. James McAdams, "The New Logic in Soviet-GDR Relations," *Problems of Communism* (September–October, 1988), p. 56.

144. "Austritte aus der SED nach 'Sputnik' Verbot" (Resignations from the SED after the "Sputnik" ban), *Süddeutsche Zeitung,* January 10, 1989.

145. "Hidden Opposition of the GDR," *East European Reporter,* vol. 3., no. 3. (Autumn 1988), p. 65.

146. "Church Expects Changes in SED Leadership," *FBIS-EEU-88-199,* October 14, 1988, p. 19.

147. Henry Krisch, *The German Democratic Republic: The Search for Identity* (Boulder, Colo.: Westview Press, 1985), p. 85.

148. Ehrhart Neubert, "Metaphysik des Sozialismus?" (Metaphysics of socialism), *Deutschland Archiv,* September 1989, p. 1040.

149. Krenz, *Wenn Mauern Fallen,* p. 125.

150. "SED beginnt mit Parteibuch-Umtausch," *Frankfurter Allgemeine Zeitung.*

151. "Erich Honecker beförderte und ernannte Generale" (Erich Honecker promotes and names generals), *Neues Deutschland,* February 6, 1987.

152. According to one report, Mielke himself attempted to straddle the fence between Honecker's Politburo and the Gorbachev leadership during this period. Interview with an unidentified high-ranking official of the State Security Ministry

by Manfred Schell and Werner Kalinka, "Honecker erpresst Mielke: 'Wo liegt deine Pensionsgrenze?'" (Honecker blackmails Mielke: "where is your retirement age?"), *Die Welt*, June 8, 1990.

153. Interview with an unidentified high-ranking officer of the State Security Ministry by Manfred Schell, "Wie Krenz zum Verlierer wurde. Wolf und Falin zogen die Fäden" (How Wolf became the loser: Wolf and Falin pulled the strings), *Die Welt*, May 25, 1990, p. 6.

154. Werner Stille, *Im Zentrum der Spionage: Mit einem Nachwort von Karl Wilhelm Fricke* (In the center of espionage: with an afterword by Karl Wilhelm Fricke) (Mainz, 1986), p. 117; in Fricke, "Mitteilungen und Mutmassungen," p. 231.

155. "Wolf on Stasi, RAF Terrorists, Criminal Charges," *FBIS-EEU-90-129*, July 5, 1990, p. 45.

156. William Drozdiak, "East Germany's Wolf: The Spy Who Came into the Fold," *Washington Post*, November 19, 1989.

157. Schabowski, *Das Politbüro*, pp. 24–25.

158. Wolfgang Seiffert, "Eine Strategie mit langem Atem?" (A long-term strategy?), *Der Spiegel*, no. 15, April 10, 1989. Wolf rejected the authenticity of Seiffert's account in an interview with *Süddeutsche Zeitung* ("Jeder einzelne wird gebraucht und gefordert" [Every individual is needed and will be called upon]), September 23–24, 1989.

159. Interview with Markus Wolf in *Stern*, "Every Strike Is Perilous," December 21, 1989.

160. Leslie Colitt, "East Germany's Ex-Spy Chief Speaks Up for Perestroika," *Financial Times*, March 15, 1989.

161. See also Franz Loeser's essay-review of *Troika*, "Die Dreharbeiten sind in vollem Gange!; Gedanken zu Markus Wolf's Troika" (The film plans are already in the works; thoughts on Markus Wolf's Troika), *Deutschland Archiv*, June 1989, pp. 639–42.

162. Markus Wolf, *Troika*, 5th ed. (Dusseldorf: Classen, 1990), p. 19.

163. Ibid., p. 86.

164. Ibid., p. 104.

165. Ibid., p. 109.

166. Serge Schmemann, "Old Master Spy in East Berlin Tells Why He Backs Changes," *New York Times*, November 21, 1989.

167. "Vienna Paper Analyzes Markus Wolf's Retirement," *FBIS-EEU*, February 13, 1987, p. E 1.

168. Quoted in Seiffert, "Eine Strategie mit langem Atem?" p. 60.

169. Interview with Markus Wolf in *Stern*, December 21, 1989. See also Schmemann, "Old Master Spy in East Berlin Tells Why He Backs Changes."

170. "Former Stasi Chief Wolf on Spies in FRG," *FBIS-EEU-90-114*, June 13, 1990, p. 30.

171. Interview by Schell and Kalinka, "'Wo liegt deine Pensionsgrenze'?"

172. "Wolf on Stasi, RAF Terrorists, Criminal Charges," *FBIS-EEU-90-129*, July 5, 1990, p. 46.

173. Schabowski, *Der Absturz*, p. 285.

174. Quoted in Elitz, *Sie waren dabei*, p. 72.

175. Hans Modrow, "Abschied von der zweiten Heimat" (Taking leave from the second homeland), *Die Zeit*, April 27, 1990.

176. Ibid.

177. Ibid, p. 4.

178. "Parteiliches Handeln" (Party dealings), *Der Spiegel*, July 3, 1989.

179. Ibid., p. 64. See also "Vierter Mann" (The fourth man), *Der Spiegel*, September 17, 1988. Modrow denies he had met Gorbachev before December 1989, though speculation abounded that the two men had first met during their student days in Moscow in the early 1950s. Gorbachev studied at the Lomonosov University; Modrow, at the Komsomol University.

180. Schabowski, *Der Absturz*, p. 286.

181. Thomas Ammer, "Spuren des 'neuen Denkens' in der SED" (Traces of "new thinking" in the SED), *Deutschland Archiv*, September 1988, p. 917. One wonders, though, what Modrow contributed to his talks with Chinese officials in Beijing in early July 1989, when he was briefed by Wu Xueqian (Politburo member and vice premier of the State Council) on "the latest antisocialist riots in the PRC." See *Neues Deutschland*, July 3, 1989; in "Dresden's Modrow, SED Delegation Visit Beijing," *FBIS-EEU-89-128*, July 6, 1989, p. 33.

182. Interview with Markus Wolf, "Ich würde gern nach Stuttgart fahren" (I'd like to travel to Stuttgart), *Der Spiegel*, January 2, 1989.

183. Wolf would not confirm that the Stasi had spied on Modrow but told an interviewer, "I even suspect that that is what happened." "Cites Stasi Surveillance Policy," *FBIS-EEU-90-117*, June 18, 1990, p. 36.

184. Interview by Schell and Kalinka, "Wie Krenz zum Verlierer wurde: Wolf und Falin zogen die Fäden."

185. "Markus Wolf Views Causes of Changes," *FBIS-EEU-89-223*, November 21, 1989, p. 43.

186. "Former Stasi Chief Wolf on Spies in FRG," *FBIS-EEU-114*, June 13, 1990, p. 30.

CHAPTER 5: REVOLUTION

1. Quoted in Micha Wimmer et al., eds., *Wir sind das Volk: Die DDR im Aufbruch* (We are the people: the GDR in upheaval) (München: Wilhelm Heyne Verlag, 1990), p. 18.

2. Quoted in "Die Mauer wird nicht niedergelegt" (The wall will not be taken down), *Frankfurter Allgemeine Zeitung*, August 14, 1989.

3. "Falin Interviewed on Iron Curtain, Other Issues," *Foreign Broadcast Information Service, Soviet Union (FBIS-SOV)-89-091*, May 12, 1989, p. 30.

4. Judy Dempsey, "Hungary Pulls Back Iron Curtain: East Germans are Flowing West via Budapest," *Financial Times*, August 8, 1989.

5. Henry Kamm, "East Germans Put Hungary in a Bind," *New York Times*, September 2, 1989.

6. Ibid.

7. "Die 'Prawda' unterstützt die DDR" (Pravda supports the GDR), *Frankfurter Allgemeine Zeitung*, August 15, 1989.

8. "Portugalov: Reformen in der DDR nicht erzwingen" (Portugalov: Not demanding reforms in the GDR), *Süddeutsche Zeitung,* September 6, 1989.

9. "Falin on Possible 'Mass Demonstrations,'" *Die Welt,* September 18, 1989.

10. "Former Honecker Advisor on Economic Problems," *FBIS-EEU-89-166,* August 29, 1989, p. 19.

11. Günter Schabowski, *Das Politbüro,* Frank Sieren and Ludwig Koehne, eds. (Hamburg: Rohwohlt Taschenbuch Verlag, 1990), p. 97.

12. Jim Hoagland, "Hungary Had Soviet Approval: U.S. Also Reportedly Informed of Plans for East Germans," *Washington Post,* September 17, 1989.

13. Judy Dempsey, "The Man Who Let the East Germans Go," *Financial Times,* September 18, 1989.

14. Hoagland, "Hungary Had Soviet Approval."

15. Leigh Bruce, "Hungarian Tells of Meeting with Kohl on Opening Border," *International Herald Tribune,* September 24, 1990.

16. Dempsey, "The Man Who Let the East Germans Go."

17. Bruce, "Hungarian Tells of Meeting with Kohl."

18. Ibid.

19. "Solidarity Enjoys 'Unquestioned Success,'" *FBIS-SOV-89-109,* June 8, 1989, p. 13.

20. "Gorbachev Persuades Communists," *Facts on File,* August 25, 1989, p. 13. Charles Gati, *The Bloc That Failed: Soviet-East European Relations in Transition* (Bloomington: Indiana University Press, 1990), p. 168.

21. John M. Goshko, "E. Berlin Seen Unlikely to Bar Trips to Hungary," *Washington Post,* September 17, 1989.

22. "Bundesregierung weist Kritik der DDR mit Schärfe zurück" (Federal Republic adamantly rejects criticism from the GDR), *Die Welt,* September 8, 1989.

23. "'New Forum' Urges Moderation, Dialogue," *FBIS-EEU-89-192,* October 5, 1989, p. 22.

24. Serge Schmemann, "East German Movement Overtaken by Followers," *New York Times,* October 16, 1989.

25. "German Unification," *World Affairs,* ed. Jeffrey Gedmin, vol. 152, no. 4 (Spring 1990), pp. 210–11.

26. Serge Schmemann, "Opposition Forms in East Germany: Group Applies to Run in May against the Communists for Seats in Parliament," *Washington Post,* September 20, 1989.

27. Ibid.

28. "Kravlikowski, Ligachev Condemn FRG Actions," *FBIS-EEU-89-176,* September 13, 1989, p. 19.

29. "Goodbye to Berlin," *The Economist,* September 16, 1989, p. 49.

30. "Ligachev Interviewed on GDR TV," *FBIS-SOV-89-178,* September 15, 1989, pp. 19–20.

31. "Ministry Refuses to Register 'New Forum,'" *FBIS-EEU-89-185,* September 26, 1989, p. 27.

32. "Henrich Says Socialism 'Asiatic Despotism,'" *FBIS-EEU-89-203,* October 23, 1989, p. 25.

33. Elizabeth Pond, *After the Wall: American Policy toward Germany* (New York: Priority Press Publications, 1990), p. 19.

34. "'New Forum' Spokesman Sees Need for New 'Identity,'" *FBIS-EEU-89-193*, October 6, 1989, p. 40.

35. "Seeks New Road," *FBIS-EEU-89-192*, October 5, 1989, p. 23.

36. Wimmer et al., eds., *Wir sind das Volk*, p. 43.

37. Alliance 90 did gain seats in the Bundestag in the December 2, 1990, all-German elections thanks to a special electoral provision that allowed a party which received 5 percent of the vote in either West or East Germany to receive representation in the parliament.

38. Girard C. Steichen, "Leipzig March Draws 120,000," *Washington Times*, October 17, 1989.

39. "Stacheldraht an der Grenze zu Polen?" *Die Welt*, October 7/8, 1989.

40. Bernt Conrad, "Genscher ist Sieger, die Flüchtlinge die Gewinner" (Genscher is the victor: the refugees are the winners), *Die Welt*, October 2, 1989. A contradictory view was expressed by Social Democratic deputy Bahr, who said the exit of East Germans over the weekend of September 30–October 1 did not come about because of Soviet influence. In "Falin Expects 'Follow-up Solution' on GDR Refugees," *FBIS-SOV-89-192*, p. 30.

41. "Exodus Prompts Travel Curbs," *Facts on File*, October 6, 1989, p. 747.

42. "Stacheldraht an der Grenze zu Polen?"

43. Pond, *After the Wall*, p. 11. "'Chinesische Lösung,'" in *Der Spiegel*, 51/89.

44. Gisela Helwig, "Wir wollen raus—Wir bleiben hier" (We want out—we're staying here), *Deutschland Archiv*, October, 1989, p. 1075.

45. "Gorbatschow: Macht keine Panik. Ost-Berlin sperrt Grenzübergänge" (Gorbachev: don't panic, East Berlin closes border crossings), *Die Welt*, October 7, 1989.

46. A. James McAdams, "The New Logic in Soviet-GDR Relations," *Problems of Communism* (September–October 1988), p. 55.

47. "Portugalov's 'Bitter Feelings' on GDR Crisis," *FBIS-SOV-89-195*, October 11, 1989, p. 22.

48. "Paper Says Gorbachev to Propose Changes," *FBIS-EEU-89-193*, October 6, 1989, p. 33.

49. "Envoy to Moscow on Relations with USSR," *FBIS-SOV-90-039*, February 27, 1990, p. 20.

50. Schabowski, *Das Politbüro*, p. 77.

51. "Unnamed SED Leader Outlines Need for 'Action,'" *FBIS-EEU-89-195*, October 11, 1989, p. 22.

52. "Falin Expects 'Follow-up Solution' on GDR Refugees," *FBIS-SOV-192*, October 5, 1989, p. 30.

53. Egon Krenz with Hartmut König and Günter Rittner, *Wenn Mauern Fallen: Die Friedliche Revolution: Vorgeschichte-Ablauf-Auswirkungen* (When walls fall: the peaceful revolution: history-process-consequences) (Vienna: Paul Neff Verlag, 1990), p. 86.

54. Schabowksi, *Das Politbüro*, p. 74.

55. Ibid., pp. 74–75.

56. Wimmer et al., eds., *Wir sind das Volk*, p. 62.

57. "Citizens Should 'Decide' on Reform," *FBIS-SOV-89-194*, October 10, 1989, p. 26.

58. Krenz, *Wenn Mauern Fallen,* p. 96.

59. "Gorbatschow kritisiert Honecker: Stasi knüppelt Verzweifelte nieder" (Gorbachev criticizes Honecker: Stasi beats up on desperate citizens), *Die Welt,* October 9, 1989.

60. Henry Kamm, "Communist Party in Hungary Votes for Radical Shift," *New York Times,* October 8, 1989.

61. Wimmer et al., eds., *Wir sind das Volk,* p. 64.

62. Lally Weymouth, "Germany's Urge to Merge," *Washington Post,* March 4, 1990.

63. Gedmin, "German Unification," p. 196.

64. John P. Burgess, "Church in East Germany Helped Create *die Wende,*" *Christian Century Foundation,* December 6, 1989, p. 1141.

65. "London Paper Views Gorbachev's Influence," *Sunday Times* (London), November 19, 1989.

66. Jackson Diehl, "Leipzig's Leaders Prevent a Bloodbath," *Washington Post,* January 14, 1990.

67. Ibid.

68. "MTI Reports Hungarian Reporters Booted Out," *FBIS-EEU-89-194,* October 10, 1989, p. 15.

69. "Gremitskikh: No Comment on Soviets' Leipzig Role," *FBIS-SOV-89-239,* December 14, 1989, p. 20.

70. Timothy Garton Ash, "The German Revolution," *New York Review,* December 21, 1989, p. 14.

71. "'Newspeak' Attitude to Ceausescu Commented On," *FBIS-SOV-90-012,* January 18, 1990, p. 38.

72. "Soviets May Have Prevented Leipzig 'Bloodbath,'" *FBIS-SOV-89-240,* December 15, 1989, p. 22.

73. Diehl, "Leipzig's Leaders Prevent Bloodbath."

74. Weymouth, "Germany's Urge to Merge."

75. Craig R. Whitney, "Soviet Forces Were Ordered to Stay in Barracks, East Germans Say," *Washington Post,* December 3, 1989.

76. Weymouth, "Germany's Urge to Merge."

77. Hans Modrow, *Aufbruch und Ende* (Upheaval and the end) (Hamburg: Konkret Literatur Verlag, 1991), p. 17.

78. Wimmer et al., eds., *Wir sind das Volk,* p. 73.

79. "SED-Chefideologe nach Moskau" (SED chief ideologist goes to Moscow), *Die Welt,* October 13, 1989.

80. "Erklärung des Politbüros des Zentralkomitees der Sozialistischen Einheitspartei Deutschlands" (Declaration of the Politburo of the Central Committee of the Socialist Unity Party of Germany), *Neues Deutschland,* October 12, 1989.

81. "Margot Honecker Calls for 'Open Climate,'" *FBIS-EEU-89-197,* October 13, 1989, p. 35.

82. "SED-Chefideologe nach Moskau," *Die Welt,* October 13, 1989.

83. Wimmer et al., eds., *Wir sind das Volk,* pp.75–76.

84. "Margot Honecker Calls for 'Open Climate,'" *FBIS-EEU-89-197.*

85. ADN, "Deputy Minister Urges Socialist 'Boldness,'" *FBIS-EEU-89-202,*

October 20, 1989, p. 33.

86. Ibid., October 18; "Dresden Mayor Denies Talks with 'New Forum,'" *FBIS-EEU-89-200,* October 18, 1989, p. 21.

87. *FBIS-EEU-90-120,* July 5, 1990, p. 2.

88. Krenz also reportedly enjoyed the support of, at least initially, Alexander Schalck-Golodkowski, Honecker's minister in charge of foreign currency procurement. See *Die Schalck-Papiere: DDR-Mafia zwischen Ost und West* (The Schalck papers: GDR-Mafia between East and West) (Vienna: Zsolnay, 1991), p. 410.

89. "Gorbachev Saw Fall as Internal Affair," *FBIS-WEU-91-102,* May 28, 1991, p. 12.

90. Günter Schabowksi, *Der Absturz* (The fall) (Berlin: Rowohlt, 1991), p. 249.

91. Schabowski, *Das Politbüro,* p. 99. See also ibid., p. 263.

92. "He Stopped the Shooting," interview with Egon Krenz by James O. Jackson and Frederick Ungeheuer, *Time,* December 11, 1989, p. 46.

93. "After the Party," *The Economist,* October 14, 1989, p. 54.

94. Serge Schmemann, "A Wistful Glance Back at When the Wall Fell," *New York Times,* July 10, 1990.

95. "Politburo's Lorenz Calls for 'Open Dialogue,'" *FBIS-EEU-88-143,* July 26, 1988, p. 33.

96. Schmemann, "A Wistful Glance Back."

97. Ibid.

98. "Warsaw Pact Envoys Meet in Poland," *Facts on File,* November 3, 1989, p. 821.

99. Krenz, *Wenn Mauern Fallen,* p. 24.

100. Ibid., p. 25.

101. Ernst Elitz, *Sie waren dabei: Ost-deutsche Profile von Bärbel Bohley zu Lothar de Maizière* (They were there: East German profiles from Bärbel Bohley to Lothar de Maizière) (Stuttgart: Deutsche Verlags-Anstalt, 1991), p. 47.

102. *Wir sind das Volk,* p. 90.

103. Krenz, *Wenn Mauern Fallen,* p. 30.

104. Ibid., p. 31.

105. Serge Schmemann, "East Germany Removes Honecker and His Protege Takes His Place," *New York Times,* October 19, 1989.

106. Krenz, *Wenn Mauern Fallen,* p. 32.

107. *Wir sind das Volk,* pp. 85–86.

108. Schabowski, *Das Politbüro,* p. 110.

109. Krenz, *Wenn Mauern Fallen,* p. 21.

110. *Wir sind das Volk,* p. 100.

111. Modrow, *Aufbruch und Ende,* p. 21.

112. Schabowski, *Der Absturz,* p. 285.

113. Serge Schmemann, "500,000 in East Berlin Rally for Change; Emigres Are Given Passage to West," *New York Times,* November 5, 1989.

114. *Wir sind das Volk,* p. 103.

115. Schmemann, "500,000 in East Berlin Rally."

116. Schmemann, "A Wistful Glance Back."

117. Schabowski, *Das Politbüro,* p. 139.

118. *Wir sind das Volk,* p. 121.

119. Modrow, *Aufbruch und Ende*, p. 26.

120. "Shevardnadze Satisfied with GDR Exit Policy," *FBIS-SOV-89-217*, November 13, 1989, p. 37.

121. Modrow, *Aufbruch und Ende*, p. 25.

122. "The New World Disorder?" Interview with Valentin Falin and others, *New Perspective Quarterly*, vol. 7, no. 2 (Spring 1990), p. 23.

123. Craig R. Whitney, "A Contrite Government: Contrite Deputies Say Party Failed the East Germans," *New York Times*, November 14, 1989.

124. Quoted in *After the Wall*, p. 17.

125. Serge Schmemann, "The Open Frontier; East Germans Flood the West, Most to Rejoice, Then Go Home," *New York Times*, November 12, 1989.

126. "Gorbachev: German 'Reunification Not on the Agenda,'" *FBIS-SOV-89-222*, p. 34.

127. Whitney, "A Contrite Government."

128. Schmemann, "The Open Frontier."

129. Elizabeth Pond interviewed Heinz Arnold, Hans Modrow's private secretary, who claimed that Falin was in Berlin, not to articulate Gorbachev's wishes, but on a fact-finding mission for the Soviet leadership. See "A Wall Destroyed: The Dynamics of German Unification in the GDR," *International Security*, vol. 15, no. 2, p. 44.

130. "Wie Krenz zum Verlierer wurde: Wolf und Falin zogen die Fäden" (How Krenz became the loser: Wolf and Falin pulled the strings), *Die Welt*, May 25, 1990. See also Lally Weymouth, "East Germany's Dirty Secret," *Washington Post*, October 14, 1990.

131. Karl-Heinz Arnold, *Die ersten hundert Tage des Hans Modrow* (The first hundred days of Hans Modrow) (Berlin: Dietz Verlag, 1990), p. 25.

132. William Drozdiak, "East Germany's Wolf: The Spy Who Came into the Fold," *Washington Post*, November 19, 1989.

133. "Modrow Profiled as 'Popular Political Figure,'" *Pravda*; in *FBIS-SOV-89-224*, November 22, 1989, p. 35.

134. "Modrow Emphasizes 'Constructive Dialogue,'" *FBIS-EEU-89-204*, October 24, 1989, p. 48.

135. "Czech TV Cites Soviet Spokesmen on E. Europe," *FBIS-EEU-89-224*, November 22, 1989, p. 24.

136. "Shevardnadze Cited on Regional Changes," *FBIS-EEU-89-222*, November 20, 1989, p. 50.

137. "Gorbachev Endorses Bloc's Transformation," *Washington Post*, November 22, 1989.

138. "Gorbachev Warns West of Taking Advantage of Eastern Europe Turbulence," *Facts on File*, November 17, 1989, p. 853.

139. "Roy Medvedev Views Changes in Eastern Europe," *FBIS-SOV-89-220*, November 16, 1989, p. 32.

140. "Soviet Union will von Föderalismus lernen" (The Soviet Union wants to learn from federalism), *Die Welt*, November 21, 1989.

141. "Dresden Mayor Berghofer Supports Reforms," *FBIS-EEU-89-219*, November 15, 1989, p. 51.

142. Modrow, *Aufbruch und Ende*, p. 18.

143. Ibid., p. 34.

144. "Portugalov Views Soviet-German Relations," *FBIS-SOV-89-109*, June 8, 1989, p. 15.

145. "Portugalov on Intra-German Relations," *FBIS-SOV-89-222*, November 20, 1989, p. 34.

146. Cited in Pond, *After the Wall*, p. 18.

147. Modrow, *Aufbruch und Ende*, p. 47.

148. "Stolpe on Dialogue between Church, State," *FBIS-EEU-89-226*, November 27, 1989, p. 57. See also "Church Official Wishes Success for Reform," *FBIS-EEU-89-223*, November 21, 1989, p. 42.

149. "Momper Urges Reconsideration of German Policy," *FBIS-WEU-89-208*, October 30, 1989, p. 17.

150. "DDR Testfall für Perestroika in der UdSSR?" (GDR test case for perestroika in the USSR?), *Die Welt*, November 24, 1989. See also "Sowjetunion will vom Föderalismus lernen, *Die Welt*, November 21, 1989.

151. "Gorbachev: German 'Reunification Not on the Agenda,'" *FBIS-SOV-89-222*, November 20, 1989, p. 34.

152. Hans Modrow, "Abschied von der zweiten Heimat" (Taking leave of the second homeland), *Die Zeit*, April 27, 1990.

153. Schabowski, *Das Politbüro*, p. 141.

154. Krenz, *Wenn Mauern Fallen*, p. 88.

155. Schabowski, *Das Politbüro*, p. 111.

156. "Rheinhold Discounts 'Frivolous Experiments,'" *FBIS-EEU-89-186*, September 27, 1989, p. 35.

CHAPTER 6: AFTERMATH

1. Charles Krauthammer, "Bless Our Pax Americana," *Washington Post*, March 22, 1991.

2. "We Are Taking Over," interview with Boris Yeltsin, *Newsweek*, December 30, 1991, p. 21.

3. Fred Oldenburg, "Sowjetische Deutschland-Politik nach der Oktober Revolution in der DDR" (Soviet policy toward Germany after the October revolution in the GDR), *Deutschland Archiv*, January, 1990, p. 69.

4. See Walter Süss, "Revolution und Öffentlichkeit in der DDR" (Revolution and the public in the GDR), *Deutschland Archiv*, June 1990, pp. 907–19.

5. Michael Dobbs, "Soviet System Was Eroded from Within," *Washington Post*, December 29, 1991.

6. "Evangelical Church Official on Travel Regulations," *Foreign Broadcast Information Service, Eastern Europe (FBIS-EEU)-89-007*, January 11, 1989, p. 28.

7. "USSR-GDR Sociologists' Group Meets in Moscow," *FBIS-SOV-89-223*, November 21, 1989, p. 21.

8. Amity Shlaes, "Socialist Meets Socialist at the Wall," *Wall Street Journal*, November 13, 1989.

9. Jens Hacker, "Social Democrats Bury the German Question," *German Comments*, July 1989, p. 43.

10. Ibid.

11. Ibid., p. 52.

12. Melvin J. Lasky, "Voices in a Revolution," preprint of an article for *Encounter,* June 1991, p. 18.

13. Ibid.

14. Ibid.

15. Carl Bernstein, "Voices of East Berlin," *Time,* January 22, 1990, p. 44.

16. "GDR Contacts with FRG, Unification Calls Noted," *FBIS-SOV-89-237,* December 12, 1991, p. 31.

17. Elizabeth Pond, *After the Wall: American Policy toward Germany* (New York: Priority Press, 1990), p. 61.

18. Robert Gerald Livingston, "Relinquishment of East Germany," in Richard F. Staar, ed., *East-Central Europe and the USSR* (New York: St. Martin's Press, 1991), p. 96.

19. Marc Fisher, "Germans Are of Two Minds about Security Council Role," *Washington Post,* September 19, 1990.

20. Walter Laqueur, *Russia and Germany: A Century of Conflict* (London: Weidenfeld and Nicolson, 1965), p. 10.

21. Charles Fairbanks, Jr., "Russian Roulette: The Dangers of a Collapsing Empire," *Policy Review* (Summer 1991), p. 5.

22. Stephen F. Szabo, "The New Germany," *Journal of Democracy* (January 1992), pp. 97–107.

23. Dean Acheson, "Europe: Decision or Drift," *Foreign Affairs,* January 1966, p. 200.

List of Names and Foreign Terms

Brandt, Willy. President of the West German Federal Council, 1957–1958; minister of foreign affairs and federal vice chancellor, 1966–1969; chancellor of West Germany, 1969–1974.

Brezhnev, Leonid. First (subsequently general) secretary of the CPSU, 1964–1982; president, 1977–1987; succeeded by Yuri Adropov.

Brezhnev Doctrine. Implicit in Soviet policy long before it acquired this name, the Brezhnev Doctrine maintained that the Soviet Union had a right and responsibility to intervene, militarily if necessary, in the affairs of other Communist states to prevent any perceived weakening of the Socialist bloc.

CDU. Christian Democratic Union, a conservative West German political party.

Ceausescu, Nicolae. Secretary general, Romanian Communist party, 1969–1989. Ceausescu and his wife were executed in December 1989 in the aftermath of the country's anti-Communist revolution.

CPSU. Communist party of the Soviet Union.

CSCE. (Conference on Security and Cooperation in Europe). Accords signed by thirty-five nations in Helsinki in 1975. East European dissidents often used the human rights obligations of the so-called Helsinki accords as leverage against Communist regimes. (Signatories pledged to ease the flow of people or information through family reunification, educational exchanges, and circulation of foreign publications, for example.)

CSU. Christian Social Union, a conservative West German political party; the Bavarian sister party of the CDU.

Dubcek, Alexander. Key figure in the 1968 movement for reform in

153

Czechoslovakia known as the Prague Spring. At the time of the Prague Spring, Dubcek was first secretary of the Communist party of Czechoslovakia.

Falin, Valentin. Adviser to Mikhail Gorbachev; ambassador to West Germany, 1971–1978; deputy director, International Information Department, Central Committee of the CPSU, 1978–1983; political commentator for *Izvestiia,* 1983–1986; appointed chief of Novosti, 1986.

FDP. Free Democratic party, a centrist-liberal West German political party.

Freie Deutsche Jugend (Free German Youth). East Germany's Communist youth organization.

FRG. Federal Republic of Germany (West Germany).

GDR. German Democratic Republic (East Germany).

Genscher, Hans-Dietrich. Member of the FDP (Free Democratic party) of West Germany; minister of the interior, 1969–1974; minister of foreign affairs, 1974–present.

Gerasimov, Gennadiy. Head of the Department of Information, USSR Ministry of Foreign Affairs, 1986–1990.

Glasnost. A policy of "openness" or greater freedom of expression introduced by Mikhail Gorbachev in the Soviet Union in 1986; Gorbachev's campaign of *glasnost* was aimed at relaxing state control over cultural, intellectual, religious, and other activities and rendering the activities of state officials and organizations accountable to greater public scrutiny.

Gorbachev, Mikhail. General secretary, CPSU, 1985–1991.

Grosz, Karoly. Prime minister of Hungary, 1987–1988; general secretary, Hungarian Socialist party, April–October 1989.

Hager, Kurt. Ideologist for the East German Communist party; member of the Politburo, 1963–1989.

Helsinki Accords. See *CSCE.*

Henrich, Rolf. East German Communist party reformer; attorney secretary, Collegium of State Attorneys for the District of Frankfurt/Oder.

Honecker, Erich. East German head of state, 1971–1989; earlier was chairman, East German Communist youth organization (Freie Deutsche Jugend), 1946–1955; became full member of the Politburo, 1958.

Höpcke, Klaus. East German Communist party reformer; deputy minister of culture.

Horn, Gyula. State secretary, Hungarian Ministry of Foreign Affairs, 1985–1989; minister of foreign affairs, 1989–1990.

Husak, Gustav. General secretary, Communist party of Czechoslovakia, 1971–1987.

Izvestiia. Official newspaper of the Soviet government.

Jaruzelski, Wojciech. Polish army officer and politician; minister of defense, 1968–1983; Polish head of state, 1985–1989; ordered the 1981 crackdown on Solidarity.

Kádár, János. General secretary, Hungarian Communist Workers' party, 1985–1989.

Khrushchev, Nikita. Became first secretary of the Central Committee of the CPSU in 1953 following Stalin's death; emerged as premier of the Soviet Union in 1958; undertook certain reforms and risked a program of "de-Stalinization," in which he sought to tear down Stalin's cult of personality; ousted from power in 1964.

Kohl, Helmut. Chancellor, Federal Republic of Germany, 1982–present; governor of Rhineland-Palatinate, 1969–1976; leader of the opposition in the Bundestag, 1976–1982.

Krenz, Egon. Replaced Erich Honecker in October 1989 as general secretary of East Germany's Communist party.

Kryuchkov, Vladimir A. Chairman of the KGB, 1988–1991; staff member, Communist party Central Committee, 1959–1967; deputy chairman of the KGB, 1978–1988.

Medvedev, Roy. Soviet historian, sociologist, and dissident; elected to the Congress of People's Deputies of the USSR and to the Supreme Soviet of the USSR, 1989.

Medvedev, Vadim. Deputy head of the Propaganda Department of the Central Committee CPSU, 1970–1978; secretary of the CPSU Central Committee, 1986; in 1988 named secretary in charge of ideology and propaganda; granted full membership to the CPSU's Central Committee and the Politburo, 1988.

Mielke, Erich. East German Politburo member, 1976–1989; minister of state security, 1957–1989.

Modrow, Hans. East German Communist reformer; member, Central Committee of the East German Communist party; first secretary, Communist party for the district of Dresden; prime minister of East Germany, 1989.

Moscow News. Soviet periodical, which became a forum for Communist reformers.

Neues Deutschland. East Germany's Communist daily newspaper.

New Forum. East German opposition group founded in September 1989; one of the most prominent dissident groups during the autumn revolution.

Ostpolitik. A West German policy toward the Soviet Union, Eastern Europe, and East Germany adopted by Willy Brandt after he became chancellor in 1969; advocates of *Ostpolitik* rejected a confrontational approach toward the East in favor of détente, with the conviction that change could be fostered in the behavior of Soviet bloc states (especially East Germany) through rapprochement with ruling Communist regimes.

Perestroika. Economic program of "restructuring" introduced by Gorbachev in 1987, in which he sought to invigorate the centrally controlled stagnant Soviet economy.

Portugalov, Nicolae. Representative of Soviet news agency Novosti in Bonn, 1972–1979; Soviet Central Committee expert on Germany.

Pravda. Daily newspaper of the CPSU.

Rheinhold, Otto. East German Communist party theorist; member of the Communist party's Central Committee, 1967–1989.

Schabowski, Günter. East German Politburo member, 1984–1989; Communist party chief executive for the district of East Berlin, 1985–1989.

SED (Socialist Unity party of Germany). East German Communist party.

Shevardnadze, Eduard A. Soviet minister of foreign affairs, 1985–1991.

Solidarity. Began as an unofficial strike committee in 1980 among shipyard workers of Gdansk, who demanded higher wages and the right to form free trade unions and strike; self-governing unions were formed under the guidance of Solidarity, whose estimated 10 million members during the 1980s represented a movement of grass-roots opposition to Communist rule; Solidarity was outlawed after the imposition of martial law in December 1981 but regained its legal status in April 1989 and was permitted to compete in Poland's partially free elections held in June of that year.

SPD. Social Democratic party of Germany, a liberal West German political party.

Stasi. Colloquial expression for East Germany's secret police.

Stolpe, Manfred. Formerly in charge of organizational work of the Protestant church in East Germany; active in dissident movement; joined Social Democratic party (SPD) in 1990; governor of Brandenburg, October 1990–present.

Strauss, Franz Josef. West German politician; Christian Social Union governor of Bavaria, from 1978 until his death in 1988.

Ulbricht, Walter. East German head of state, 1950–1971.

Wolf, Markus. Head of East German foreign intelligence operations, 1958–1987.

Yakovlev, Aleksandr. Adviser to Mikhail Gorbachev; held various positions in the Central Committee of the CPSU, including deputy head of the Department of Science and Culture (1953–1956) and instructor with the Department of Propaganda and Agitation, 1962–1964; became head of the Central Committee CPSU Propaganda Department, 1985; became member of the Politburo, 1987.

Zhivkov, Todor. Prime minister of Bulgaria, 1962–1971; head of state, 1971–1989.

Index

About the Author

Jeffrey Gedmin is a research associate at the American Enterprise Institute. His articles on foreign affairs have appeared in the *American Spectator*, the *Christian Science Monitor*, the *Wall Street Journal*, *World Affairs*, and elsewhere.

Mr. Gedmin taught at Gonzaga College High School, a Jesuit preparatory school in Washington, D.C., from 1981 to 1988. He received his Ph.D. from Georgetown University, where he has taught German language and international relations since 1985.

A NOTE ON THE BOOK

This book was edited by Dana Lane of the
publications staff of the American Enterprise Institute.
The index was prepared by Patricia Ruggiero.
The text was set in Palatino, a typeface designed by
the twentieth-century Swiss designer Hermann Zapf.
Publication Technology Corporation, of Fairfax, Virginia,
set the type, and Edwards Brothers Incorporated,
of Ann Arbor, Michigan, printed and bound the book,
using permanent acid-free paper.

The AEI PRESS is the publisher for the American Enterprise Institute for Public Policy Research, 1150 17th Street, N.W., Washington, D.C. 20036; *Christopher C. DeMuth*, publisher; *Edward Styles*, director; *Dana Lane*, assistant director; *Ann Petty*, editor; *Cheryl Weissman*, editor; *Susan Moran*, editorial assistant (rights and permissions). Books published by the AEI PRESS are distributed by arrangement with the University Press of America, 4720 Boston Way, Lanham, Md. 20706.